Michigan's Best Campgrounds

A Guide to the Best
150 Public Campgrounds
in the Great Lakes State

Other books by Jim DuFresne:

Isle Royale National Park: Foot Trails & Water Routes

Porcupine Mountain Wilderness State Park

Michigan State Parks

Michigan's Best Hikes For Children

50 Hikes In Lower Michigan

Michigan: Off The Beaten Path

Hiking In Alaska

Alaska

Tramping In New Zealand

Michigan's Best Campgrounds

A Guide to the Best
150 Public Campgrounds
in the Great Lakes State

Jim DuFresne

PEGG LEGG
PUBLICATIONS

Michigan's Best Campgrounds
Published by Thunder Bay Press
Production and maps by Pegg Legg Publications

© 2005 by Jim DuFresne
First Edition 1992
Second Edition 2000
Third edition 2005

Printed in the United States of America

04 03 02 01 00 5 4 3 2 1

ISBN 1-882376-73-0
All information in this book is accurate to the best of the author's knowledge at
press time, but is subject to change at any time. Author and publisher assume no
liability for inaccuracies.

2325 Jarco Drive
Holt, Michigan 48842 USA

Contents

CENTRAL UPPER PENINSULA

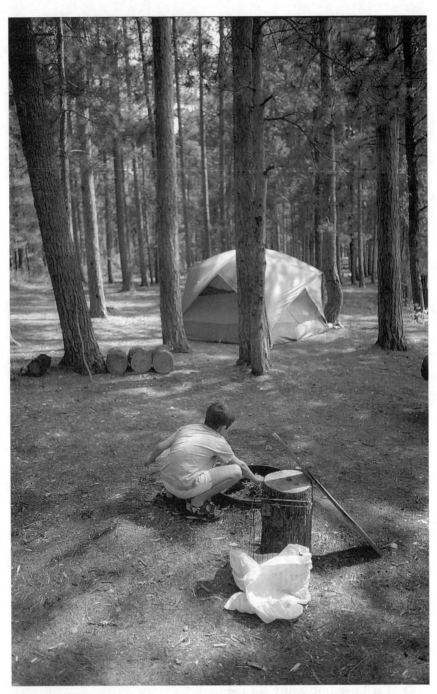

A young camper builds a fire at a site in the Pigeon River Country State Forest east of Vanderbilt. The state forest has a half dozen rustic campgrounds where families can usually find an open site in one of them, even on the weekends.

Why Camp?

Why camp? Why not?

It's affordable and nearby. It's lodging on the lake, great scenery from your front door, a nine-inch bluegill at the end of your line. It's fresh air, towering pines, a crackling fire on a starry night. It's an air mattress in a two-person tent or a waterbed in a recreational vehicle complete with a microwave oven, television and an ice-maker in the freezer.

Camping is anything you want it to be. The purpose of this guide is not to tell you how to camp—there are many other books that will do that—but where to go. And in Michigan there are many places to go. Across the state there are approximately 1,280 campgrounds with 92,803 designated sites on public and private land. Within the Michigan State Park System alone there are 14,500 sites, the third highest of any state park system in the country. Add another 1,680 sites in the three national forests, 3,200 sites in the state forests and countless more in country parks and private campgrounds and you can see the need for a guide.

To narrow it down, this guidebook covers only public campgrounds and has chosen the best 150 facilities throughout the state. It's been my experience that the very nature of public land allows those campsites to be located more often along lakes, rivers or the Great Lakes and have the acreage to provide opportunities for hiking, swimming, boating and other traditional activities of the summer camping season.

For the purpose of easy reference the state has been divided into eight regions; Southeast, Heartland, Lake Michigan, Lake Huron, Northwest and The Straits (covering both the tip of the Lower Peninsula and the east end of the U.P.), Central Upper Peninsula. and Western Upper Peninsula. The book has also been divided into two types of campsites:

Modern: Although modern campgrounds vary widely, all of these have at least electrical hookups at each site and a modern restroom with showers. When the facility also provides on-site spigots, sanitation stations for trailers or other amenities it has been clearly noted. Keep in mind that the high cost of equipping sites with electricity forces most parks to keep them relatively close together. For the want of an outlet, you sacrifice solitude.

Rustic: These campgrounds lack hookups and for the most part modern restrooms and showers unless noted. Vault toilets (also known as pit toilets, outhouses and the shack) are a way of life in rustic campgrounds. Also noted in each one is the terrain, forest and ground

RESERVATIONS ON THE INTERNET

It's hard to pass up site number 38 at Tawas Point State Park. The large, shady site is along one of the finest beaches on Lake Huron where you can pitch a tent or park a trailer in full view of Tawas Bay.

At site number 38 you can enjoy the sunrise with your morning coffee or cool off with an afternoon swim...if you can ensure it's still available when you arrive Friday evening. Now you can.

Site-specific reservations, choosing a site as opposed to being assigned one by a ranger, is available at almost all parks that maintain campgrounds. Campers can now book their favorite sites online at *www.michigan.gov/dnr*. You can also make site-specific reservations through the Michigan Central Reservation Service at ☎ (800) 44-PARKS.

By clicking on a "Search Sites" button a list of all the sites in a campground appears along with a 20- to 40-word description for each one. Once you have chosen a site and confirmed its availability, you use a credit card to finish the transaction and received an immediate confirmation.

The advantages of site-specific reservations are that with advance planning you can finally snag that beachfront site at your favorite park. The disadvantages of site-specific reservations are that everybody else can to.

cover. A rustic campground whose sites are well spread out in a thick forest with good underbrush is going to provide privacy between campers and a feeling that you're actually spending a night in the woods. Occasionally semi-modern campgrounds are listed. These sites also do not have hookups but do provide either showers or restrooms with flush toilets.

RESERVATIONS

Information on fees, reservations, amenities, and season of operation is given as well as a description of the campground and the area. Reservations allow you to secure a site in advance so no matter how late you arrive you're guaranteed a spot for your trailer. Most modern campgrounds and a handful of rustic facilities offer this service.

Free-spirited campers and those who despise booking anything in advance need not despair. The 150 state forest campgrounds as well as sites in the Manistee-Huron National Forests and the Pictured Rocks National Lakeshore are still filled on a first-come, first-served basis. But if you need to be assured that come Friday evening you'll be sitting in the middle of a campground roasting marshmallows over a crackling fire, here's where you can reserve a site:

State Parks: You can reserve a site in 73 different state park campgrounds and many campers do. The Central Reservation System for Michigan State Parks handles 170,000 reservations a year, the overwhelming majority for a campsite in July and August.

Sites are reserved in advance on a six-month rolling window and a MasterCard or Visa credit card is needed to instantly book and confirm a site over the phone. Sites are booked by calling the Central Reservation System at ☎ (800) 44-PARKS from 8 A.M. to 8 P.M. Monday through Friday or 9 A.M. to 5 P.M. Saturday and Sunday. You cannot reserve a site through the individual park headquarters but can online at *www.michigan.gov/dnr*. Each reservation costs $2 plus the nightly charge of the site.

National Parks: In 1998 the National Park Service unveiled a new central reservations system for its most popular campgrounds at many national parks, including Platte River Campground in Sleeping Bear Dunes National Lake Shore. To book a site call the National Park Reservation Service at ☎ (800) 365-2267 from 10 A.M. to 10 P.M. daily or go online to at *http://reservations.nps.gov*.

National Forests: Sites can also be reserved in selected campgrounds in the Upper Peninsula national forests. In Manistee, you can book sites at Sand Lake and Bowman Bridge. In Hiawatha, sites can be reserved at Camp Seven Lake, Colwell Lake, Flowing Well and Little Bay de Noc and at Ottawa at Black River Harbor north of Bessemer. To book a reservation call the National Recreational Reservation Service at ☎ (877) 444-6777. You can also make reservations online through its web site at *www.reserveusa.com*. Each reservation costs $9 plus the nightly charge of the site.

County Parks: You can reserve a site at many county park campgrounds by calling the park office in advance. Phone numbers and reservation fees are provided later in this guidebook with the descriptions of the campgrounds.

SEASONS & FEES

Seasons of operation are also listed with each campground description. Some campgrounds are literally locked during the off-season, others simply lack a host to collect fees. State forest campgrounds are technically open year-round though during the winter the roads may not be plowed and the handles may be removed from water pumps.

One last thing; in these deficit budget times, keep in mind that public facilities, policies and fees can change quickly. Some are small such as a $1 increase in a camping fee, some are quite significant such as the state's decision to close a number of state forest campgrounds. It's best to always call the information number provided to double check. One thing that will never change, however; a scenic little campground on a lake in the middle of the woods will always be a scenic little campground on a lake in the middle of the woods.

And that's the main reason why this guidebook should be in every camper's glovebox.

Southeast Michigan

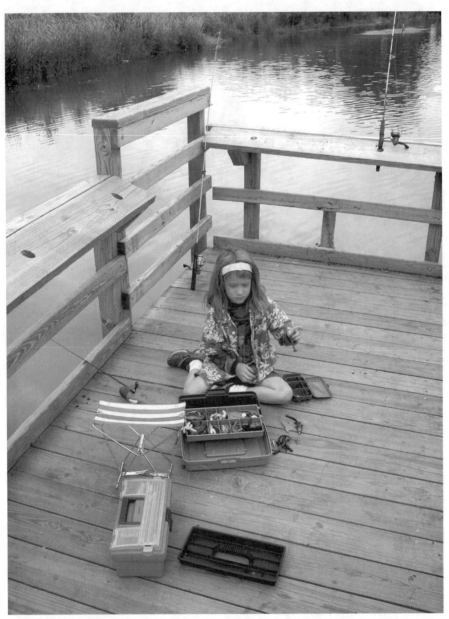

A young camper sorts through her tackle box at Sterling State Park looking for just the right fishing lure. The state park offers many opportunities for shore anglers to catch a variety of fish including walleye.

1

Sterling
State Park

Campground: Modern
County: Monroe   **Nearest Community:** Monroe
Sites: 256   **Reservations:** Yes
Fee: $22-$29 plus vehicle entry permit
Information: State park office ☎ (734) 289-2715

After closing in 2002 for renovation, this 1,000-acre park on the west end of Lake Erie reopened a year later to rave reviews by those who mattered the most: campers and visitors.

The $17 million project was the most the DNR has ever spent to revitalize a state park but officials felt it was necessary because of Sterling's role as a gateway park. Like Warren Dunes near the Indiana border and Porcupine Mountains just east of Wisconsin, Sterling is often the first state park out-of-state visitors will stop at when entering Michigan.

Directions: Sterling State Park is 15 miles north of the Ohio border and reached from I-75 by departing at exit 15 and heading east on Dixie Highway for a mile.

Campground: The park's original campground was in a coastal wetland overlooking Sandy Creek Lagoon in the northwest corner of park. Campers were literally flooded out from time to time due to strong easterly winds that shifted shallow Lake Erie to the west.

The heart of the renovation and its single biggest cost was rebuilding the campground on higher ground at the south end of the park. The new campground has 256 sites in an open setting and overlooks the widest and nicest section of beach in the park.

Only two sites, numbers 25 and 26, are directly on the beach but the rest have a good view of the lake and all of them have electrical service, paved pads and a fire ring. There are also 39 pull-through sites for large recreation vehicles along with 77 sites with full hookups—water, sewer and 50-amp electrical service.

Day-Use Facilities: Sterling features more than a mile of beachfront along Lake Erie with a shallow swimming area. Bordering the beach is an open grassy picnic with tables and grills. The park renovation also included raising and repaving the park road along its causeway, consolidating the day-use parking lots into a single lot for 1,500 cars and adding new picnic shelters, bathrooms and a unique children's playground.

Fishing: Other improvements include rebuilding Sterling's boat launch by increasing parking to 250 vehicles, upgrading the restrooms and adding a fish cleaning station.

Lake Erie is renown for its walleye fishing and from April through mid-July, the prime season to catch a walleye, the boat launch is often filled. Anglers also fish the Great Lake

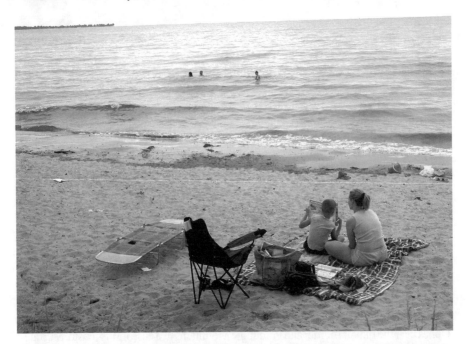

A family enjoys the beach at Sterling State Park, the only Michigan state park that is on Lake Erie.

for many other species including perch. There are bait and tackle shops along Dixie Highway for minnows and last-minute lures.

For boatless anglers, Sterling offers shore fishing opportunities on its two lagoons in the middle of the park. Most of the species caught are panfish, crappies and bass but occasionally a walleye will be hooked in the lagoons. Extending east from the park's pedestrian bridge is a paved trail that winds pass three new fishing piers and then into the campground.

Hiking: One of the most popular additions to the park is the pedestrian bridge that now provides direct access from the campground and the day-use area on the east side of a lagoon to *Marsh View Nature Trail* on the west side. Marsh View is a 2.8-mile loop around the main lagoon is equipped with 11 interpretive stations and a nature shelter with two spotting scopes. The birding is excellent in the spring and fall at Sterling.

The trail is also paved and is part of an extensive bike path system throughout the park, prompting campers to pack along their bicycles.

Season: Being the only state park on Lake Erie, Sterling is often filled throughout the summer season, particularly on the weekends. For reservations call ☎(800) 447-2757 or go online at *www.michigan.gov/dnr*.

2

Portage Lake
Waterloo Recreation Area

Campground: Modern
County: Jackson   **Nearest Community:** Jackson
Sites: 194   **Reservations:** Yes
Fee: $22 to $28 plus vehicle entry permit
Information: State park office ☎ (734) 475-8307

At 20,367-acres Waterloo Recreation Area is the largest state park unit in southern Michigan and offers a wide range of activities in a rolling, lake-studded setting. That includes camping at five campgrounds, including two modern units bordering its largest lakes.

Of the park's campgrounds, Portage Lake is the most scenic facility. On a colorful October weekend, after the summer rush is long gone, there's no better place to set up camp in Southeast Michigan.

Directions: From I-94, six miles east of Jackson, depart at exit 147 and head north on Race Road and then east on Seymour Road. The campground entrance is off Seymour Road.

Campground: Portage Lake Campground is on a rolling, semi-open bluff above Big Portage Lake and is part of a developed area on the west side of the park that also includes a swimming beach, boat launch and foot trails. The 194 modern sites offer a bit of shade but little privacy when the campground is full and none are directly on the water. Several overlook the lake while hardwoods and hills surround the area so it's easy to escape into the woods even on a busy weekend.

Campground amenities include several restroom buildings with showers, electric hookups, a sanitation station for recreational vehicles and firewood sales during the summer.

Day-Use Facilities: A short walk from the campground is a designated swimming area with a sandy beach on Big Portage Lake, a bathhouse and extensive picnic grounds. Nearby, families will find playground equipment and a baseball field.

Fishing: Waterloo provides access to 17 lakes with most of them featuring bass and panfish fisheries. There is a developed boat ramp and a fishing pier on Big Portage Lake, the largest in the park at 360 acres. Most anglers work the lake for largemouth bass with fish in the one to three pound range common and occasionally one tips the scales at four pounds or more. In the winter, it is a favorite spot for ice anglers in pursuit of panfish.

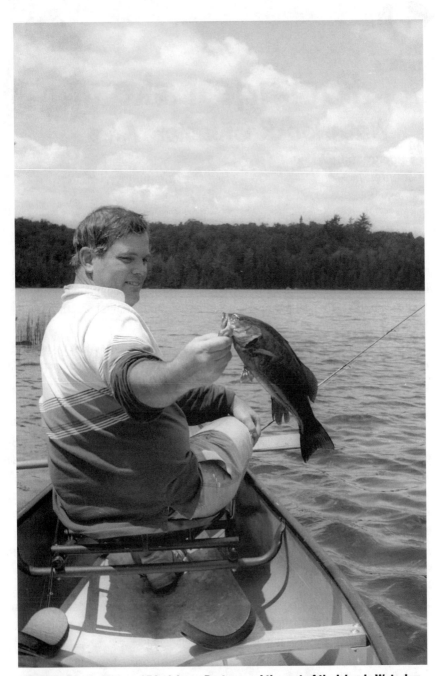

A happy angler holds up a 15-inch bass. Portage and the rest of the lakes in Waterloo Recreation Area support a productive fishery. Catches include largemouth bass that occasionally tip the scales at four pounds or more. There is an improved boat launch for campers at Portage Lake.

**PORTAGE LAKE
CAMPGROUND**

Hiking: The half-mile long *Dry Marsh Trail*, an interpretive path that takes a close look at bogs and marshes, begins near the campground. Interpretive brochures are available at the contact station. In the day-use area is the trailhead for the *Waterloo Pinckney Trail*. This backpacking route is a 35-mile, three-day trek that ends at Silver Lake Day-Use Area in Pinckney Recreation. Don't have three days to spare? Then the trek from Big Portage Lake to the scenic overlook and cross on top of Sackrider Hill makes for a one-way hike of 5.5 miles or a round trip of 11 miles.

Interpretive Center: Within Waterloo Recreation Area is the Gerald Eddy Geology Center. The interpretive facility contains exhibits, displays and video and slide programs that examine rocks, minerals and oil resources in Michigan as well as its glacial and geologic history. The center (☎(734) 475-3170) is open year-round from 10 A.M. to 5 P.M. Tuesday through Saturday with extended hours in the summer. From I-94, depart at exit 157 and head north on Pierce Road and then west on Bush Road where the entrance is posted.

Season: From July through mid-August, the campground is full on most weekends and holidays and 50 to 90 percent filled Sunday through Thursday. You can reserve a site in advance by calling the state parks Central Reservation System at ☎ (800) 447-2757 or online at *www.michigan.gov/dnr.*.

3 Crooked Lake

Pinckney Recreation Area

Campground: Rustic
County: Washtenaw   **Nearest Community:** Pinckney
Sites: 25   **Reservations:** No
Fee: $10 plus vehicle entry permit
Information: Park headquarters ☎ (734) 426-4913

This may be southeast Michigan but the drive to this campground is surprisingly scenic. It begins with North Territorial Road and even though houses are popping up like mushrooms in the spring it's still a winding avenue past rolling farms and woodlots. Once in the park you follow a narrow dirt road through the hills of this rugged area north of Ann Arbor, reach a high point of 1,008 feet and then descend to the lakeshore campground.

Crooked Lake not only combines a sense of being in the woods with a scenic site, but being in Pinckney Recreation Area, a 10,021-acre state park unit, it offers a variety of opportunities for hiking, mountain biking, fishing and paddling in a chain of lakes.

Directions: From I-94 depart at exit 159 and head north on M-52 for six miles to North Territorial Road and then east. From US-23 north of Ann Arbor depart at exit 49 and turn west onto North Territorial Road for 12 miles. The campground is reached by turning north onto Dexter-Townhall Road from North Territorial and then left on Silver Creek Road to enter the park and drive past its headquarters. The dirt road ends at Crooked Lake.

Campground: This pleasant campground is situated on a hillside overlooking Crooked Lake. The sites are spread out in a semi-open area partially shaded by pines and large oaks. Only one site, number 7, is directly on the shoreline but most of them have at least a partial view of the water. The sites are well spread out and a few, number 13 in particular, are even off by themselves. Sites have fire rings and tables; vault toilets and a hand pump for water are located in the loop.

Day-Use Facilities: There is no swimming or beach on Crooked Lake. But just down the road is the day-use beach on Silver Lake featuring an open grassy area, marked swimming area, tables, pedestal grills, a store and a boat rental concession.

Fishing: Within the campground is an unimproved dirt boat launch while next to it is a handicapped access fishing pier. Children will enjoy the dock but small panfish is all you can expect to catch in water this shallow. Crooked Lake has only a few homes along the shore opposite of the campground while its south end features a group of small islands. You

A site with a view of the water at Crooked Lake Campground in Pinckney Recreation Area, a state park north of Ann Arbor. Crooked Lake is one of the few rustic campgrounds in Southeast Michigan.

---

can follow a channel into Pickerel Lake where at its east end flat bottom boats and canoes can even enter another small lake. Along with panfish, Crooked features bass, northern pike and crappie. Pickerel, which has a fishing pier at its west end, is stocked every spring with rainbow trout.

Hiking: Crossing Silver Lake Road just uphill from the campground is *Crooked Lake Trail,* a four-mile loop that begins in the Silver Lake Day-Use Area. To avoid problems with mountain bikers, hikers are urged to follow the trail in a counterclockwise direction and in three miles will cross a foot bridge over the channel between Crooked and Pickerel Lakes.

Biking: The trail is also a popular route for mountain bikers who must follow it in a clockwise position. Traveling in this direction, bikers will reach Silver Lake Day-Use area in a mile.

Season: The rustic campground is serviced May though October. Crooked Lake tends to fill up on the weekends from late June through early August but usually there are open sites in midweek. You can reserve a site in advance by calling ☎(800) 447-2757 or online at *www.michigan.gov/dnr.*

4 Proud Lake
State Park

Campground: Modern
County: Oakland   **Nearest Community:** Wixom
Sites: 130   **Reservations:** Yes
Fee: $20 plus vehicle entry fee
Information: State park office ☎ (248) 685-2433

Wixom and the I-96 corridor in southwest Oakland County is a growing overload of shopping centers, strip malls, apartment complexes and other signs of a metropolitan Detroit area bursting at the seams. You pass through all this and just before reaching Proud Lake skirt an incredibly large trailer park.

Not the kind of setting most people envision for a camping trip but be patient. Once in the park it's like entering a different world. Proud Lake is a 4,700-acre recreation area whose rolling forested hills, wetlands and undeveloped stretch of the Huron River is the fortress against the uncontrolled growth of Oakland County. Next to Addison Oaks County Park (see page 26), Proud Lake is probably the most pleasant modern campground in Southeast Michigan.

Directions: The state recreation area is just east of Milford or 12 miles southwest of Pontiac. From I-96, depart at exit 159 and head north on Wixom Road. The road passes through the town of Wixom and then makes a 90-degree turn left. You head right onto Glengary Road and the campground entrance is less than a mile to the east.

Campground: The campground is in the east half of the park and totally separated from the day-use beach and canoe livery. It's a large loop of 130 modern sites in an open, grassy area on a bluff that overlooks a chain of lakes formed by the Huron River. These are scenic lakes as the opposite bank is an undeveloped shoreline of cattails and marshes.

Sites are open and close together as is typical of most state park modern campgrounds but most have a good view of the water below. Tables, fire rings and hookups are provided in each site while along the loop are two restroom buildings with showers, vault toilets and a sanitation station. The only drawback at Proud Lake is the major power line that runs across the west end of the lake and skirts the campground.

Day-Use Facilities: A staircase leads from the campground to an open grassy area along Proud Lake. No beach here but the swimming area is shallow with a bottom of soft sand. Nearby is limited playground equipment. The main swimming area for Proud Lake is Powers Beach, located off Wixom Road in the west half of the park. The small sandy beach and pond was made by impounding the Huron River. Nearby are two picnic areas.

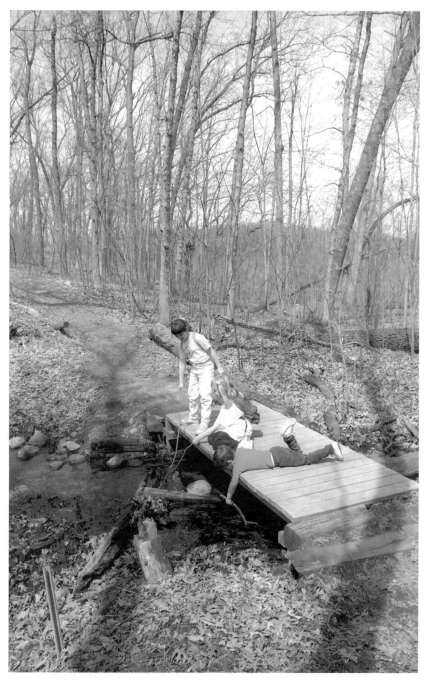

Proud Lake State Park has an 11-mile network of hiking trails that wind around lakes, across streams and along a segment of the Huron River. A spur from the campground provides campers access to the rest of the system.

Fishing: An improved boat launch with a cement slab is located next to the swimming area but parking is back in the campground. Both Proud Lake and the Huron River are fished for panfish and smallmouth bass. The river within the park, from Moss Lake to Wixom Road, also has a special flies-only, catch-and-release trout season during April.

Hiking: A foot trail leads from the west end of the campground loop and connects with *Marsh Trail* and the rest of the park's 11-mile trail system. Marsh Trail is a 1.25-mile loop around a wetland area. Across the park road from this loop is the winter ski center and the *Main Ski Loop,* a two-mile trail that winds through a red pine plantation and hardwoods before heading back to the parking area.

Canoeing: A popular activity during the summer is paddling the Huron River and within the park is a canoe rental concession located off Garden Road on the opposite side of the river from Powers Beach. The Heavner Canoe Center (☎(248)685-2379) is open 11 A.M. to 8 P.M. weekdays and from 9 A.M. to 9 P.M. weekends and holidays. You can either paddle up the river and then turn around or make arrangements with the concessionaire to be picked up down river.

Season: Proud Lake is open year-round with vault toilets during the winter. Because it's so close to metropolitan Detroit, the campground is heavily used on weekends from early May through mid-September.

5 Addison Oaks
Oakland County Park

Campground: Modern
County: Oakland   **Nearest Community:** Lake
Sites: 174   **Reservations:** No
Fee: $24 to $28
Information: Park office ☎ (248) 693-2432

A trip to Addison Oaks County Park is a drive through the country; passing apple orchards, strawberry farms and fields where horse and cattle still graze. It's not the Northwoods but this 794-acre park offers a remarkable escape from the urban sprawl of this region of the state as well as some of the best campsites to be found anywhere in Southeast Michigan.

You won't find that deep-in-the-woods serenity that many state forest campgrounds up north provide, but you will discover wooded sites, some even with electricity, and much to do here. Activities range from fishing and swimming to volleyball, renting a pedal boat and even playing a round of disc golf.

Directions: From M-59 depart north on M-150 (Rochester Road) and follow it through downtown Rochester. The park is nine miles north of Rochester and reached by turning west (left) on Romeo Road.

Campground: In 2003 Addison Oaks was upgraded with a $2.6 million renovation that included expanding the campground with 82 new modern sites along with new restroom buildings. On the north side of Buhl Lake, but not on the water itself, is the modern campground and another labeled "primitive." There are now 132 modern sites in both an open grassy area and an area bordered by woods. The sites include tables, fire rings with grills, cement slabs and hookups for water and electricity. There's a large restroom with showers while nearby is a new children's playscape and a sanitation station.

The primitive campground is a loop with 42 sites that are well separated from each other on a wooded hillside of towering white and red pine and hardwoods. Add a thick undergrowth and you have some of the most secluded sites in southern Michigan. Sites 51-73 have electric outlets and are considered semi-modern, the rest are rustic. The loop is serviced by a pair of handicapped-access vault toilets and spigots for water. Modern sites are $28 a night, semi-modern $26 and primitive $24 for non-Oakland residents.

Day-Use Facilities: Along the south side of Buhl Lake, less than half mile from the campgrounds, is a large open day-use area that includes tables, pedestal grills, several shelters, horseshoe pits, volleyball courts, play equipment and an 18-hole disc course that is played with Frisbees.

Along Adams Lake, a spring-fed pond, is the park's swimming area. The facilities include a large sandy beach surrounded by a grassy slope, lifeguards, bathhouse and a concession building.

Boating: There is a unimproved launch on Buhl Lake next to the boat rental along with additional parking for vehicles and rigs. Boats are rented daily during the summer from 7 A.M. to sundown and include pedal boats and row boats.

Fishing: Buhl is heavily fished during the summer but attracts little attention after October. Prime species are bluegill, pumpkinseed sunfish and black crappie. Anglers also catch an occasional largemouth bass and every year a few three- to four-pound northern pikes are landed. The boat rental shop also sells live bait.

Hiking: On its east side, the park maintains almost four miles of foot trails but most of them simply wind through the open day-use area or follow park roads back to the campground.

Mountain Biking: On the west side of park is a five-mile network of trails designated for mountain bikers. *Buck Run Loop* winds through a hilly, wooded area and the rest pass through open fields where come fall you often see deer. Mountain bikes can be rented at the park.

Season: Camping is from mid-May to mid-October with the exact dates depended on the weather. This is a popular campground and fills daily June through Labor Day. You cannot reserve a site except for group sites.

6

Metamora-Hadley
Recreation Area

Campground: Modern
County: Lapeer   **Nearest Community:** Hadley
Sites: 214   **Reservations:** Yes
Fee: $19 plus a vehicle entry permit
Information: State park office ☎ (810) 797-4439

This would be a nice campground anywhere in the Lower Peninsula; for Southeast Michigan it's exceptional. Located in the southern half of Lapeer County, less than a half hour drive from Pontiac, Metamora-Hadley surrounds man-made Lake Minnawanna. The 683-acre state park unit features not only the lake and fishing opportunities but a nice beach, wooded trails and even shoreline sites. Yet the park draws only 220,000 visitors a year, most of them day users.

This campground can accommodate you even if your family doesn't want to sleep in a tent. Metamora-Hadley was one of the first state parks to offer mini-cabins. The small cabins are located within the campground and sleep four but otherwise it's just like camping, where you would spend most of your day outside.

Directions: From I-75 depart at exit 81 and head north on M-24 through Lake Orion and Oxford. At Pratt Road, 20 miles north of the interstate, turn west (left) for two miles and then south (left) on Hurd Road to the park entrance.

Campground: Metamora-Hadley has 214 sites on two loops along the west side of the lake. The first loop reached has sites 128-214 in an open, grassy area shaded by a handful of towering pines and hardwoods. Twenty of them are right on the water, directly across from the park's day-use area. The second loop is far more scenic with sites 1-127 situated in a hilly area lightly forested in oaks and maples. Nine sites are on the edge of a shoreline bluff with a scenic view of the entire lake. Posted trailheads and the two mini-cabins are located here and both loops have sanitation stations, shower and restrooms, tables and fire rings at every site and limited playground equipment.

Day-Use Facilities: At the north end of the lake is a wide beach and open, grassy picnic grounds. Facilities include a bathhouse, tables, pedestal grills and a concession operator who rents rowboats, canoes and pedalboats. Along the east side of the lake in a pleasant wooded setting is another picnic area with a shelter.

The most popular time to camp at Metamora-Hadley Recreation Area and many other state parks is during their Harvest Festivals when campers participate in organized Halloween activities throughout the weekend.

Fishing: Lake Minnawanna, a 60-acre impoundment of the South Branch of Farmers Creek, features several species of fish but is best known by bass anglers. Anglers concentrate in the southern half of the lake and around a small island on the east side using standard bass baits and lures. Other species caught include bluegill, perch and an occasional northern pike.

There is an unimproved boat launch and dock at the north end of the lake with additional parking for a handful of vehicles. There are also three fishing piers along the west shore of the lake; at the boat launch and one at each campground loop.

Hiking: The park has a six-mile network of trails that basically forms a loop from the campgrounds around the lake to the beach area on the east side. On the west side you wander from a marsh area to woods to open fields. On the east the path winds through a wooded area and an especially nice walk is to begin near the mini-cabins, cross the South Branch of Farmers Creek and then follow the loop around the picnic area, a round-trip hike of almost two miles.

Season: The campground is open April through October. Despite being so close to metropolitan Detroit, Metamora-Hadley receives only moderate use on weekdays during the summer and sites are often available on non-holiday weekends. You can make reservations by calling ☎(800) 447-2757 or online at *www.michigan.gov/dnr*.

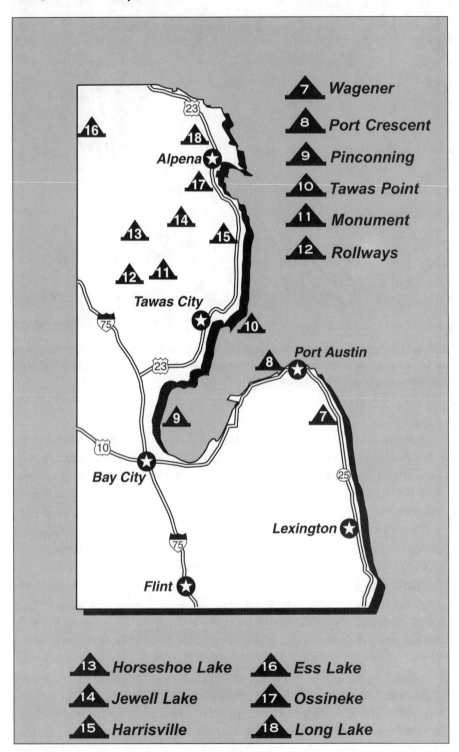

7 Wagener
8 Port Crescent
9 Pinconning
10 Tawas Point
11 Monument
12 Rollways

16 Alpena
18
17
14
13
15
12 11
Tawas City
10
75
23
Port Austin
8
9
7
10
25
Bay City
75
Lexington
Flint

13 Horseshoe Lake
14 Jewell Lake
15 Harrisville
16 Ess Lake
17 Ossineke
18 Long Lake

Lake Huron

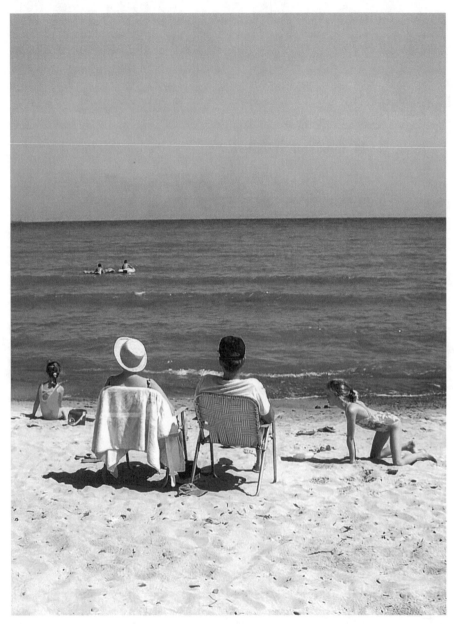

A family enjoys the Lake Huron surf at Wagener County Park. Wagener's beach is one of the best in Michigan's Thumb, a region that is only a two-hour drive from most of Metro Detroit.

7 Wagener
Huron County Park

Campground: Modern
County: Huron   **Nearest Community:** Harbor Beach
Sites: 96   **Reservations:** Yes
Fee: $12 to $15
Information: Park office ☎ (989) 479-9131

At 132 acres, Wagener County Park is the largest unit in the Huron County Park system and includes a 96-site modern campground, rental cabins, a Lake Huron beach and more than two miles of hiking trails. Its best feature however, might be its location in the Thumb. Michigan's most distinct appendage is only a two-hour drive from the northern Detroit suburbs and less from Flint and Saginaw, yet is a world away from the cities.

Convention and visitor's bureaus promote the Lake Huron region as the *Sunrise Side* of the state but many people think of Michigan's Thumb as the *Slowside*. Not overrun by the tourist industry—or tourists—it's an area that can be refreshingly relaxing even on a holiday weekend. Wagener Park is an ideal place to pitch the tent or park the trailer while exploring the small towns and rural charm of this quiet corner of the Lower Peninsula.

Directions: Wagener County Park is on M-25, five miles south of Harbor Beach.

Campground: The 96 modern sites at Wagener are well spread out and divided into three different camping areas. Sites 1 through 38 are closest to the water in a semi-open grassy area and within view of Lake Huron. This area includes the Lakeview sites that are close to the shoreline and an additional $5 per night. Sites 39 through 68 are in a more wooded setting and sites 101 through 128 are in a grassy field near the entrance of the park. Restrooms at the park include coin-operated showers.

The park also has eight camper cabins for rent. Located just inside the woods, the single-room structures sleep six in a pair of bunk beds and a double bed and include a table, electric lights and outlets and a fire ring outside.

The daily rate for a site with a full hookup is $18, for electric only $15 and for tent camping with no utilities $12. Camper cabins are $40 Monday through Thursday and $50 on the weekends and have a two-night minimum requirement.

Day-Use Facilities: Wagener has one of the nicest beaches on the east side of the Thumb. The wide strip of sand borders a designated swimming area while nearby is a bathhouse and play equipment. The adjoining picnic area has grills, tables and two pavilions that can be reserved and rented in advance.

Camper cabins

WAGENER
COUNTY PARK

Lake Huron

Hiking: Wagener has two miles of foot trails that basically form a mile-long loop with a handful of crossover spurs. The hiking is easy and begins by skirting Lake Huron for a quarter mile before heading into the wooded heart of the park. Keep an eye out for old-growth trees near the trail, including a giant white pine that somehow survived devastating forest fires in 1871 and 1881.

Fishing: The park maintains an improved boat launch with additional trailer parking for anglers who troll Lake Huron for salmon and lake trout. There is no shore fishing in Wagener but fishing is popular along the breakwalls at the small boat harbor in Harbor Beach.

Season: The campground is open from May 1 to Oct. 15. The facility is busy on most weekends from mid-July to early August but is rarely filled. A two-night minimum and a $7 reservation fee is required to reserve a site in advance. Call the park office (☎ (989) 479-9131) for reservations. For more information on Huron County parks call the Huron County Road Commission at ☎ (517) 269-6404 or check its web site at *www.huroncountyparks.com.*

8 Port Crescent
State Park

Campground: Modern
County: Huron   **Nearest Community:** Port Austin
Sites: 137   **Reservations:** Yes
Fee: $23 plus a vehicle entry permit
Information: State park office ☎ (989) 738-8663

In the mid-1800s Port Crescent was a booming lumbering town of almost 700 residents, known for its salt wells, fine sand and good docks. Today it's one of the most scenic state parks along Lake Huron and known for having the only "true dunes" on the east side of the state. The windblown, open dunes are located west of the park's day-use area and drop down to the shoreline. They are nowhere near the size of those along Lake Michigan but still form an interesting area to wander through. And to small children, sand dunes are sand dunes regardless of their size.

The 565-acre unit also includes three miles of almost pure white beach along Saginaw Bay, a wooded interior of jack pine and oak, a scenic network of hiking trails and a campground overlooking the bay that includes 25 beachfront sites.

Directions: The park is five miles southwest of Port Austin along M-25.

Campground: Port Crescent's campground is located in the eastern half of the park in a hilly section forested in oak and bordered on one side by the Old Pinnebog River Channel and the other by M-25. Many sites have a partial view of Saginaw Bay and 25 of them are right off the beach. These, understandably, are not only the most popular sites in the park but some of the most scenic on the east side of the state. They are in such high demand during the summer that the park has devised a lot-move procedure to allow campers to sign up for them after they have already arrived at the campground. Facilities include tables, fire rings, two restrooms with showers and a sanitation station.

Day-Use Facilities: The west half of the park is a day-use area and is separated from the campground and hiking trails by the Pinnebog River. The area includes two picnic grounds along the river, a shelter that can be rented near the beach, a fitness trail nearby and limited play equipment. A boardwalk leads from the shelter to the beach, one of the finest along Lake Huron, passing small decks with picnic tables perched on top of the low dunes.

Fishing: While Saginaw Bay is renowned for its walleye and perch fishery, the Pinnebog River is fished by shore anglers for bass, panfish and northern pike during the

A young hiker pauses at the base of a Port Crescent sand dune. The state park features the tallest dunes on the east side of Michigan.

---

summer and occasionally for Chinook salmon in September and October by tossing spoons and spawn. In the day-use area there is a launch for hand-carried boats and some barrier-free fishing piers over the river. Perch anglers should head to Port Austin and catch the morning or afternoon run of the perch party boat, *Miss Port Austin,* (☎ (989) 738-5271).

Hiking: Port Crescent has three miles of foot trails in an isolated area between the Pinnebog River and the Old Pinnebog River Channel. You can reach one trailhead by a beach access next to site 119 and then tiptoe through the channel where it empties into the bay. On the other side is a yellow trail marker. The entire loop is a 2.3-mile walk that passes several scenic viewing points of the shoreline and the Pinnebog River. By using the cutoff spur you can shorten it to a 1.3-mile walk.

Season: Port Crescent is open from April 15 to Oct. 15. The campground is filled most weekends during the summer and often daily from mid-July to early August. The best time to check in without a reservation is Sunday and Monday. You can reserve a site in advance by calling the state parks Central Reservation System at ☎ (800) 44-PARKS or online at *www.michigan.gov/dnr.*

9 Pinconning
County Park

Campground: Modern
County: Bay   **Nearest Community:** Pinconning
Sites: 42   **Reservations:** Yes
Fee: $11.50 to $15.50 plus vehicle entry fee
Information: Bay County Recreation ☎ (989) 879-5050

One of the most pleasant and, best of all, least crowded modern campgrounds along Lake Huron is Pinconning County Park on the Saginaw Bay. The park is only three miles from I-75 but most likely too far south for many campers to consider stopping for the night.

Too bad. This is a scenic park with a beach, improved boat launch, some short but interesting hiking trails and many sites that overlook a small bay and peninsula bordering Saginaw Bay.

Directions: From I-75 turn off at Pinconning (exit 181), 21 miles north of Bay City. Head east on Pinconning Road, through the town of Pinconning, and in three miles the road ends at the park entrance.

Campground: Pinconning is a single loop of 42 sites in an open grassy area that is shaded by giant oak trees. Half the sites are along the Bay and some of them have a clear view of the water while the others are tucked behind a wall of cattails. The rest border the forest that surrounds the campground. Facilities include electric hookups, fire rings, tables, a restroom with showers and a sanitation station. Also located in the campground are six rental cabins ($40 a night) equipped with electric lights and propane heaters.

The nightly fee is $10 Sunday through Wednesday and $14 Thursday through Saturday. There is also a $1.50 vehicle entry fee into the park.

Day-Use Facilities: Pinconning has a sandy beach but in recent years the water level had dropped in the Bay making it muddy and unattractive to swimmers. Bay County plans to rectify the situation, however, by extending the beach. Also within the picnic area is a shelter, tables, pedestal grills, play equipment and an open view of Saginaw Bay.

Fishing: There is also a cement boat launch and dock in the day-use area. Again the low water level has hampered boaters but officials plan to dredge a channel for them into deeper water from the launch. Saginaw Bay is renowned for its walleye and perch fisheries while in the small bay off the campground anglers target mostly large and smallmouth bass.

Hiking: The park has four posted trails, all short excursions into the surrounding woods and marshes. The most interesting by far is the *Marsh Trail*, a round trip of 0.6 mile through the extensive cattail marshes that enclose the bay. The path passes views of the water and a small observation deck before turning around at a wooden bridge.

Season: The campground is open year-round although the hookups and restrooms may be closed during the off season. Reservations can be booked in advance by calling the park office at ☎ (989) 879-5050 but this is a lightly used facility that fills up only on an occasional weekend during the summer.

10 Tawas Point
State Park

Campground: Modern
County: Iosco   **Nearest Community:** Tawas City
Sites: 195   **Reservations:** Yes
Fee: $23 plus vehicle entry fee
Information: Park office ☎ (989) 362-5041

Tawas Point is a popular state park that combines a beautiful beach within walking distance of a large campground crowned by a classic lighthouse. The 200-acre park is the end of a sandy spit that separates Tawas Bay from Lake Huron and prompts a few people to call it "the Cape Cod of the Midwest."

That's stretching it a bit but Tawas Point is definitely a scenic area and even has a short trail to the end of the spit and back. The area also attracts birders from around the state as it is an important landfall for birds migrating across Saginaw Bay. The contact station can provide a birding checklist.

Directions: The park is 3.5 miles from East Tawas. Follow US-23 just northeast of the town and then turn east onto Tawas Point Road and follow signs to the park entrance.

Campground: Tawas Point is an open campground with little shade or privacy between parties. A handful of sites overlooks a small beach along Tawas Bay while a foot trail leads from the back of one loop to the day-use area beach along Lake Huron. Facilities include two restrooms with showers, play equipment and a sanitation station within the campground and fire rings and tables at each site.

Day-Use Facilities: The park's day-use beach is along Lake Huron where the sand is almost pure white and stretches more than 300 feet from where you park your car to where the waves are gently washing ashore. Located here is a bathhouse, picnic shelter and more play equipment. The area is surrounded by several small ponds that occasionally attracts the interest of young anglers.

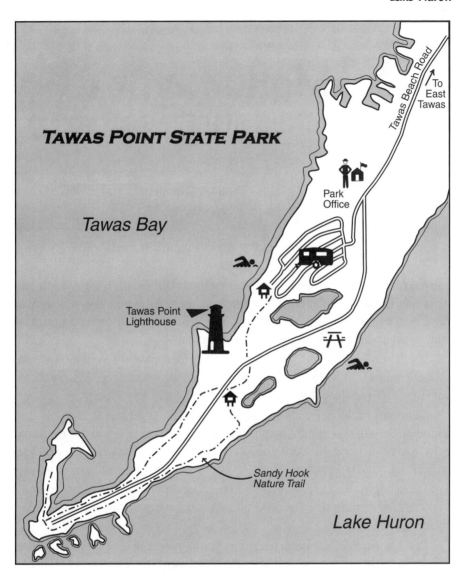

Hiking: Beginning at the day-use parking lot, near the lighthouse, is the *Sandy Hook Nature Trail*, a 1.5-mile loop to the end of the point. Its most scenic portion by far is along Lake Huron where you pass several small islets and skirt the tops of some very small dunes.

Season: The campground is open from mid-April to mid-October and through most of the summer it's filled from Thursday until Sunday. In July, expect it to be filled any day of the week. Reservations are important if you want to plan a vacation around this campground. You can reserve a site in advance by calling the state parks Central Reservation System at ☎ (800) 44-PARKS or online at *www.michigan.gov/dnr*.

11 Monument
Huron National Forest

Campground: Rustic
County: Iosco   **Nearest Community:** Tawas City
Sites: 20   **Reservations:** No
Fee: $8
Information: Huron Shores Ranger Station ☎ (989) 739-0728

As a campground, Lumbermen's Monument is only fair, basically 20 sites in a red pine plantation. But the nearby interpretive center, museum, trails and scenic overlooks make this facility an excellent place to spend a weekend. There's much to do at the monument and most of it is only a short walk from the campground.

Directions: From Tawas City head west on M-55 for a mile and then north (right) onto Wilber Road for 1.5 miles to reach Monument Road. Head northwest on Monument Road until it ends at River Road. The entrance to the campground is east (right) on River Road.

Campground: Monument is a single loop in a red pine plantation. The sites are well spread out but, as is typical with pine plantations, there is little undergrowth to isolate one party from another. Sites have tables and fire rings with sliding grills while within the loop are vault toilets and spigots for water.

The entrance to the interpretive center is a quarter mile west of the campground but the back of the loop borders the visitor center picnic area and from here a paved path winds past the museum and overlooks.

Day-Use Facility: Lumbermen's Monument is an impressive bronze statue of three loggers that was erected in 1931 and is now the centerpiece of the Huron National Forest's most popular attraction. The interpretive area includes a small museum and outdoor hands-on exhibits devoted to Michigan's logging era at the turn of the century and a stairway that leads to where a replica of a cook's raft is tied up on the river. The overlooks of the AuSable River valley are spectacular in the fall. The visitor center is open daily from 10 A.M. to 7 P.M. during the summer and until 5 P.M. to mid-October. There is no admission.

Just to the west on River Road is Iargo Springs, another interpretive area where a long stairway leads down the riverside bluff to the freshwater springs that were once a popular resting place for Chippewa Indians on the Saginaw-Mackinac Trail.

Hiking: Crossing the campground's entrance drive and marked in blue diamonds is the *Highbanks Trail*, a seven-mile point-to-point path that extends from Iargo Springs to

Sidtown. The trail is named from the fact that it skirts the high bluffs above the AuSable River and along the way you pass many spectacular vistas of the river valley. To the west of Iargo Springs is a 3.6-mile walk from the campground and along the way you pass the eagle viewing point in 1.8 miles.

Canoeing: AuSable River is a noted waterway for canoeists (see Keystone Campground page 133) but Monument Campground is not a place to launch a boat due to the steep bluffs.

Season: The campground is managed Memorial Day to Labor Day but may be open earlier or later depending on weather and demand. Lumbermen's Monument is one of the most popular attractions in Huron National Forest and thus the campground is a popular facility, often filled on weekends as early as Thursday evening.

IARGO: SPRINGS OF MANY WATERS

Traversing the steep river bluffs overlooking the AuSable River—and passing through Monument Campground—is the *Highbanks Trail*.

The linear footpath stretches seven miles beginning in the west at Iargo Springs, where most people begin their walk with a 300-step descent to the AuSable River.

At the bottom of the bluff you'll find a quarter mile of boardwalk that winds through towering cedars to eight observation decks; half of them perch above the gurgling springs, the rest overlook the AuSable.

Iargo is the Chippewa word for "many waters" and it's believed that Native Americans gathered here once for tribal powwows where they would drink the cold, clear water for medicinal powers.

Today Iargo is still a tonic. No matter how many leaf peepers are zipping along River Road, the springs are always a quiet and tranquil spot that soothes the soul.

From Monument Campground Iargo Springs is a one-way hike of four miles or a round trip of eight miles that passes the overlook known as Canoer's Monument halfway there.

Iargo Springs near the AuSable River

12 Rollways
Huron National Forest

Campground: Rustic
County: Iosco
Sites: 19
Fee: $8

Nearest Community: Hale
Reservations: No

Information: Huron Shores Ranger Station ☎ (989) 739-0728

Located on high bluffs above the AuSable River is Rollways National Forest Campground, an alternative if Lumbermen's Monument is full, which it quite often can be. Rollways picks up its name from the turn of the century when lumbermen used to roll logs down the steep banks to the river below and then floated them to sawmills on Lake Huron.

You can spend an afternoon learning about Michigan's incredible lumber era at the Monument only eight miles to the east. Then return to camp at Rollways, which features the same spectacular panoramas of the AuSable Valley as seen elsewhere along River Road.

Directions: Rollways is posted and located right off M-65 on Rollaway Road. From I-75 depart at exit 188 and take US-23 through Standish and Omer. Two miles out of Omer turn north on M-65, passing through the towns Whittemore and Hale. The campground is posted roughly seven miles north of Hale.

Campground: Rollways is a single loop of 19 sites with paved spurs, tables and fire rings with sliding grills. The campground, lightly forested in large oaks and red pines, is located near the edge of the river bluff. Most sites do not have a clear view of the valley below. The exception is site number 8 where from your picnic table there is an incredible overlook of the river below and the ridges to the north. Vault toilets and hand pumps for water are in the middle of the loop.

Day-Use Facilities: Rollways has a scenic day-use area featuring tables, pedestal grills, and a classic log picnic shelter with fieldstone fireplaces at each end. Many of the tables are within view of the AuSable River and Loud Dam Pond to the east. Nearby a staircase leads down to the river though care should be used when descending. The picnic grounds are open from 6 A.M. to 10 P.M.

Fishing: Rollways is located where the AuSable River flows into Loud Dam Pond. This is no Holy Waters. Upstream from the campground the river is 50 to 75 yards wide and so deep you can't wade it in most places. But anglers say this is where the river yields some of its biggest brown and rainbow trout. Loud Dam Pond is known primarily for smallmouth bass but also yields walleye and pike.

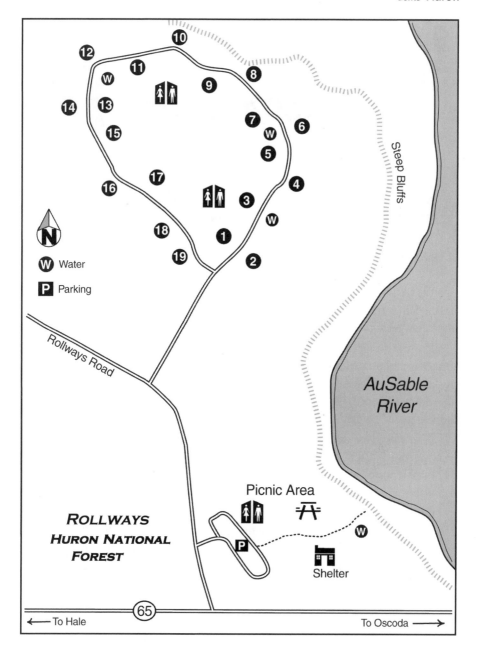

Canoeing: For paddlers, across the road from the campground is *Rollways Resort* (☎ (989) 728-3322), which runs a canoe livery during the summer. Most paddlers are taken upriver to either Alcona County Park, a 23-mile, five-hour trip, or Stewart Creek, a 13-mile, two-hour paddle from the campground.

Season: Rollways' managed season is from the end of May through mid-September. This is a lightly used facility and a site is easy to obtain here even on most weekends.

13

Horseshoe Lake

Huron National Forest

Campground: Rustic

County: Alcona **Nearest Community:** Glennie

Sites: 9 **Reservations:** No

Fee: $8

Information: Huron Shores Ranger Station ☎ (989) 739-0728

The brown national forest sign on M-65 simply says "Campground." It doesn't say if it is modern or rustic, if it's on a lake or how many sites there are. Go ahead, take a chance and follow the sign.

The best things in life are always unexpected and Horseshoe Lake Campground, located in the heart of the Huron National Forest, turned out to be a real gem the first time my family stayed there. It's a small facility with only nine sites, located on a wooded bluff above a undeveloped lake. And it's a lightly-used facility. Though we arrived in mid-July, the height of Michigan's camping season, only one other site was occupied.

Directions: Horseshoe Lake is 3.5 miles north of Glennie on M-65. From Harrisville head west on M-72 for 22 miles and then south on M-65 for a mile to the Forest Service Road 4124 that is posted with a "Campground" sign. Head a mile west on the dirt road to the entrance.

Campground: Horseshoe Lake is a single loop of nine sites with gravel spurs, tables, and fire rings with sliding grills. The campground is lightly shaded and several sites are in a semi-open grassy area but the loop is enclosed by the hilly and heavily forested terrain. Three sites (1, 3 and 4) are on the edge of the bluff with a view of the lake and a direct path down to the water. Other facilities include vault toilets and a hand pump for water.

Fishing: Within the campground is an unimproved launch that's strictly for carry-in boats. But you really don't need anything more for the 16-acre lake that is indeed shaped like a horseshoe. The west half of the lake is the best for fishing and quite deep in the middle. At one time Horseshoe was stocked with rainbow trout but that program has since been discontinued. I've always found it a fun lake to catch bass, even though few are of legal size.

Hiking: Near the fee pipe is a marked trailhead for a 1.3-mile loop that winds around the lakeshore to a bench on the opposite shore and then circles back through the rolling hills.

Season: Horseshoe Lake's managed season is mid-April to the end of November. This is a small but lightly used facility.

14 Jewell Lake
Huron National Forest

Campground: Rustic
County: Alcona   **Nearest Community:** Barton City
Sites: 32   **Reservations:** No
Fee: $8
Information: Huron Shores Ranger Station ☎ (989) 739-0728

One of the largest campgrounds in the Huron National Forest is Jewell Lake, offering not only numerous sites but several other attractive features. There's a pleasant beach and swimming area, a mile-long nature trail ideal for children, a separate picnic area and fishing opportunities in the large lake.

Very little of Jewell Lake is on National Forest land so expect a shoreline ringed by cottages and heavy traffic for boaters and anglers. Otherwise this is a delightful place for a weekend camping trip.

Directions: From US-23 in Harrisville, head west on M-72 for 14.5 miles then north on Sanborn Road for 1.7 miles and left on Trask Road for 0.7 miles. Jewell Lake has a posted entrance on Trask Road.

Campground: Jewell Lake has 32 gravelled-spur sites with numbers 1-15 on Aspen Loop and 16-32 on Pine Loop. Both loops are lightly shaded and although there are no sites directly on the lake, most of Aspen Loop is only a short walk from the beach and swimming area. Facilities include a handful of vault toilets, two hand pumps for water, tables and fire rings with sliding grills.

Day-Use Facilities: The campground has a small picnic area next to its boat launch, separated from the campground by a marsh. Next to Aspen Loop is a delightful beach and marked swimming area with shallow water and a sandy bottom. Be aware that the lake once had a problem with swimmer's itch.

Fishing: Jewel Lake has 193 surface acres and is exceptionally clear. Only the southeast corner of its shoreline is part of the National Forest; the rest of it is privately owned. A cement slab boat launch is located in the picnic area with parking for additional cars and trailers. The lake is best known for panfish but anglers also work its waters for largemouth bass and northern pike.

Hiking: Departing from the beach area is a delightful mile-long loop that in its first half crosses a bridge over a beaver dam and then follows the shoreline of Jewell Lake. The second half winds through an enchanting paper birch forest.

Season: Jewell Lake's managed season is Memorial Day through Labor Day and fills only on the holidays and a rare weekend.

15 Harrisville
State Park

Campground: Modern
County: Alcona   **Nearest Community:** Harrisville
Sites: 195   **Reservations:** Yes
Fee: $21 plus vehicle entry fee
Information: State park office ☎ (989) 724-5126

Harrisville State Park is proof that Lake Michigan campgrounds do not have a monopoly on wide sandy beaches. The outstanding feature of this 107-acre park is its half-mile-long stretch of Lake Huron shoreline where its sugar-like sand is more than 30 yards wide in most places. Here you take a refreshing dip in the cooling waters of the Great Lake, lay out in the sun or, if you're lucky, set up camp at a beachfront campsite.

Although the park has a day-use area and even a nature trail, its relatively small size limits the facilities that other larger units offer. But there is a bike path that connects it with Harrisville, a quaint town during the summer with small restaurants, ice cream parlors, gift shops and the Harrisville Harbor where you can watch charter fishing boats return with their daily catch of salmon and trout.

Directions: The state park is on US-23, a half mile south of Harrisville.

Campground: The park has a single campground of several paved loops in a lightly forested area of pine and cedar. Sites feature hookups, tables and fire pits and are within view of each other but not crammed together. By far the most popular sites are located right along the lake where your tent or trailer would be in the shade of the trees but your beach blanket only a few yards away. These are some of the best places to camp along Lake Huron and obtaining a site usually requires changing sites once you have arrived. Along with a pair of bathroom and shower buildings, the campground features mini-cabins that families can reserve in advance through the Central Reservation System.

Day-Use Facilities: At the south end of the park is a day-use area with a bathhouse, shelter, picnic tables, playground equipment, and, of course, more of that wide, beautiful beach and Lake Huron surf. Here you can set up a lounge chair, take in the sun or watch iron ore freighters pass by on the horizon. The bike/foot path begins near the entrance of the campground and is a paved trail that extends a half mile north to Harrisville, ending near First Street.

Fishing: Lake Huron is a noted deepwater fishery for salmon and lake trout and charters can be arranged at the Harrisville Harbor or bait shops in town. There is an unimproved launch for cartop and other hand-carried boats next to the park's day-use area but you need to go to town for anything bigger. Actually the only fishing activity within the park is surf anglers who work the beaches during the fall for salmon and brown trout feeding in the shallows.

Hiking: Departing and returning from the campground is the *Cedar Run Nature Trail*, a mile-long loop that takes 30 to 45 minutes to enjoy. There are 14 numbered posts on the trail and an interpretive brochure, obtained from the contact station, points out different species of trees.

Season: Harrisville is open from mid-April to the end of October. The campground is often filled on the weekends by Friday afternoon and sometimes by Thursday afternoon. For reservations call ☎(800) 44-PARKS.

16 Ess Lake
Mackinaw State Forest

Campground: Rustic
County: Montmorency   **Nearest Community:** Hillman
Sites: 28   **Reservations:** No
Fee: $10
Information: Atlanta DNR Office ☎ (989) 785-4251

Almost since the earliest days of automobile travel, a small peninsula jutting out into Ess Lake has been a popular spot for campers to pull up and an official state campground since 1938. This midsize lake, with its productive fishing, clear water and fine beach still draws campers today.

The Forest Management Division enlarged the state forest campground in 1968 with a second loop of 13 sites but the campground still fills on weekends during the summer and sometimes by Thursday evening at the height of the camping season. Anglers are especially attracted to this lake because of its no-wake regulations during the prime fishing hours in the morning and evening.

Directions: The campground is 16 miles northeast of Atlanta in Montmorency County. From Atlanta head north on M-33 and then east on County Road 624, reached just after passing Jackson Lake State Forest Campground. The entrance to Ess Lake is 9.5 miles east on CR 624.

Campground: Ess has 28 sites divided on two loops situated almost across from each other on the lake. The first loop is connected to the beach and day-use area by a foot path and features 13 sites well secluded in a forest of mixed pine and hardwoods. Two sites overlook the water.

The second loop is farther from the beach but on a point that gives Ess its horseshoe shape. Almost all of these sites are on the water and 19-25 are on a low bluff with a scenic view of the lake. Both loops have tables, fire rings, hand pumps for water, and vault toilets.

Day-Use Facilities: Off the first loop is the day-use area with parking for additional vehicles. Ess features a beach and grassy area and a marked swimming area with a sandy bottom and a gentle slope. A few tables and vault toilets are also located here.

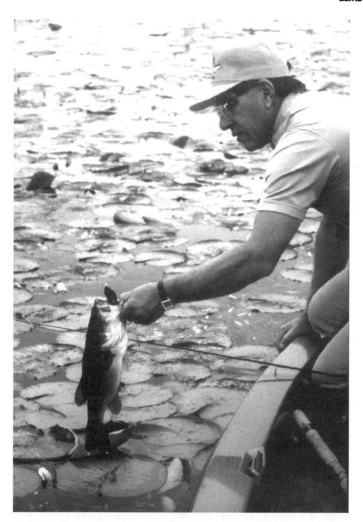

Ess Lake is a favorite among anglers for smallmouth and largemouth bass as well as walleye. The Ess Lake Campground includes an improved boat launch.

Fishing: The 114-acre lake is heavily developed with cottages and boating traffic can be moderate to heavy on the weekends. For this reason a no-wake regulation is imposed on Ess from 7:30 P.M. to 11 A.M.

Near the second loop is an improved boat launch with a cement ramp, dock and limited parking for a handful of vehicles and rigs. Ess has no outlet and ranges in depth up to 50 feet in the middle of the west bay. The lake has been planted with walleyes in the past and anglers also target smallmouth and largemouth bass, perch and pike.

Season: From mid-July through late August Ess Lake can be filled on any weekend and often is at least half filled by Thursday afternoon.

17 *Ossineke*
Mackinaw State Forest

Campground: Rustic	
County: Alpena	**Nearest Community:** Ossineke
Sites: 42	**Reservations:** No
Fee: $10	
Information: Atlanta DNR Office ☎ (989) 785-4251	

The only state forest campground on Lake Huron is a delightful facility that most travelers heading north on US-23 don't even realize is there. The tendency when passing through the hamlet of Ossineke is to overlook the small brown campground sign and that's too bad.

The rustic campground is separated from the town, off by itself and is a place where you can wander undeveloped stretches of beaches for miles, right into Negwegon State Park if so desired. The facility offers a beautiful beach, sandy swimming area, and even a mile-long pathway where it's possible to spot deer in the early morning.

Directions: The campground is posted at the corner of US-23 and Ossineke Road but the sign is easy to miss. Turn east onto Ossineke Road and follow it to another state forest sign at the corner of State Road. Turn right on State Road and drive to the entrance at the end.

Campground: Ossineke has 42 rustic sites on two loops winding along Lake Huron. The first loop has sites 1-26 of which 19 of them, including 18-26, are right off the water. Most have a thin line of trees or brush separating them from the sandy beach but three are out in the open with a clear and beautiful view of the Great Lake. These sites for the most part are in a stand of white and red pine with little undergrowth and thus little privacy.

The second loop is situated in an oak/maple forest and sites 27-42 are more spread out and secluded from each other but not as close to the stretch of beach favored by swimmers. Fire rings, tables, hand pumps for water and vault toilets are on each loop.

Day-Use Facilities: A small picnic area with a handful of tables and pedestal grills is located within the west loop and closes at 10 P.M. The beach here is beautiful; most years there is a wide sandy strip with shallow water and a soft bottom ideal for young swimmers even if there is no marked swimming area. On a clear summer day you can enjoy a view from the water towers of Alpena to Scarecrow Island of the Michigan Island National Wildlife Refuge to the south. The campground has no boat launch on the lake.

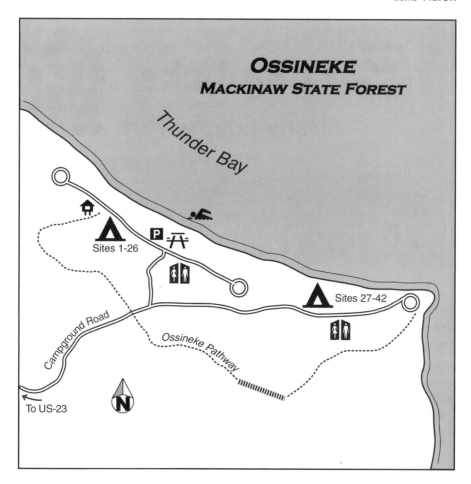

Hiking: *Ossineke Pathway* is a one-mile trail that begins next to site 14 and ends near site 42 of the second loop. You start off in an upland forest of a wide variety of trees ranging from white and red pine to oak, beech, paper birch and maple. The trail winds across the entrance drive and then swings through a low-lying forest, passing several grassy meadows and even crossing a boardwalk through a swamp.

You can also hike the beach south along one of the most undeveloped stretches of Lake Huron, and within six miles reach South Point in Negwegon State Park. The shoreline switches from beautiful sandy bays and beaches to rocky shorelines. Two miles beyond South Point is the state park's parking area and water pump.

Season: Ossineke experiences moderate use on weekends in mid-July through mid-August but getting a site anytime during the summer is usually possible.

18 Long Lake
Alpena County Park

Campground: Rustic/Modern
County: Alpena   **Nearest Community:** Alpena
Sites: 124   **Reservations:** Yes
Fee: $11 to $19
Information: Park Office ☎ (989) 7595-2401

Who says only the state or federal governments know how to run a campground? Long Lake County Park is an example of a pleasant modern campground that isn't filled every day of the summer like state parks and offers more amenities than national forest campgrounds.

An Alpena County park, Long Lake is a spot where you spend a few days fishing, boating and exploring the surrounding area, particularly the lighthouses of Presque Isle just to the north. To the south the city of Alpena is only 10 miles away and features museums, bike paths, an interesting canoe trail and an opportunity to board a glass-bottom boat to tour shipwrecks in Thunder Bay.

Directions: From Alpena head north on US-23 for 10 miles and then west on Long Lake Park Road.

Campground: Long Lake has 124 sites located on East Bay in the northeast corner of this large lake. The campground is well shaded but not wooded and the sites are close together with little privacy, even the rustic tent sites. Many of them are right on the water, so close to the shoreline that campers pull their boats up to the edge of their sites.

Sites No. 1 through No. 80 are modern with water and electricity hookups with 12 of them right on the lake and commanding a higher nightly fee. Sites No. 81 through No. 124 are tent sites with 10 of those overlooking the shoreline.

The daily fees are $11 for a tent site, $16 for a modern site and $19 for a modern site on the water.

Day-Use Facilities: Long Lake has picnic areas, shelters, volleyball courts and play equipment in two day-use areas, each with its own small beach for swimmers. There is also a small store in the park with limited supplies.

Fishing: The park has an improved boat launch and a large parking area for trailers, a testimony to Long Lake's popularity among anglers. There is a $3 fee to launch a boat.

Long Lake covers 5,200 acres and generally is a long, shallow body of water, its

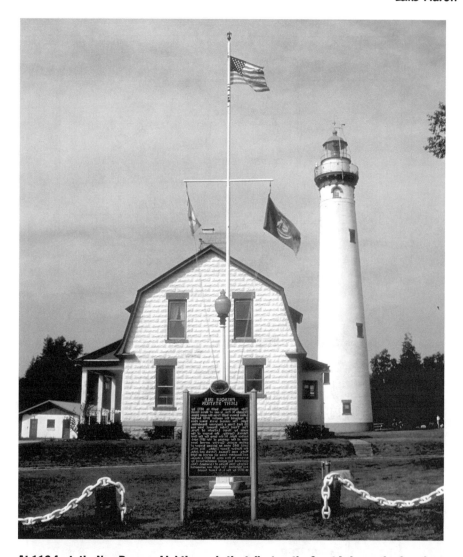

At 113 feet, the New Presque Lighthouse is the tallest on the Great Lakes and only a short drive from Long Lake County Park. Summer visitors can climb the tower for the spectacular view at the top.

---

deepest point being only 25 feet. The lake has good smallmouth bass and perch fishing but anglers also target walleyes, northern pike and bluegills.

Season: Long Lake is open to camping May 15 through October 1 and is filled on many weekends in July and August. Reservation can be made after May 1 by calling the park office at ☎(989) 595-2401.

For more information on the shipwreck tours, lighthouses or trails in the area contact the Alpena Convention and Visitors Bureau at ☎(800) 4-ALPENA or *www.alpenacvb.com*.

The Heartland

 Coldbrook

 Deep Lake

 Newaygo

 Henning

 White Cloud

 School Section

 Tubbs Island

 Paris

 Merrill Lake

 Herrick

 Gladwin

 Island Lake

 Wagner Lake

 Leverentz

 Silver Creek

 Hemlock

 Goose Lake

 Long Lake

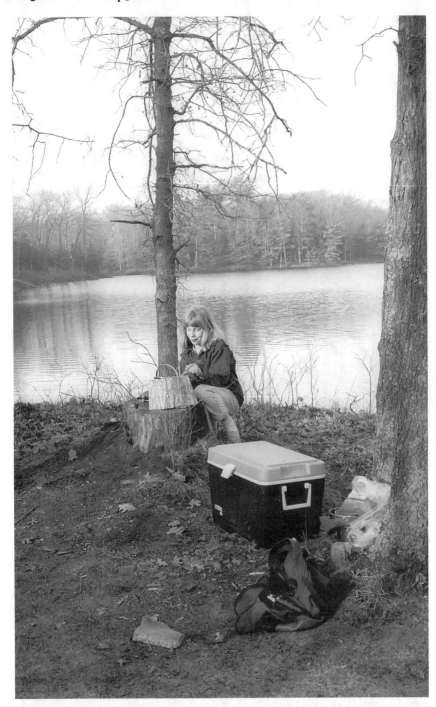

A camper cooks dinner at a rustic lakeshore site. Scattered throughout Michigan's heartland region are many rustic lakeside campgrounds, such as Deep Lake, where it is easier to secure a site on the weekends.

19 Coldbrook
Kalamazoo County Park

Campground: Modern and rustic
County: Kalamazoo   **Nearest Community:** Climax
Sites: 51   **Reservations:** Yes
Fee: $15 to $20
Information: Kalamazoo County Parks ☎ (269) 383-8778

At the headwaters of the Portage River are Portage and Blue Lakes, a sprawling body of water of many peninsulas, bays, channels and the site of a modern campground that lies just a few miles off I-94 between Battle Creek and Kalamazoo. Coldbrook County Park is a 275-acre facility operated by Kalamazoo County with both rustic and modern sites.

The park is spread along the south and east shore of Portage Lake and totally encloses Blue Lake. Much of the west half of the lakes are shallow marshy areas filled with lily pads and other aquatic plants that attract a variety of waterfowl during the spring and fall migrations.

Directions: Coldbrook is just south of I-94, eight miles east of Kalamazoo along MN Avenue. From the east, depart at exit 92, Business I-94 for Battle Creek, but head south for the town of Climax. In two miles you'll merge onto MN Avenue and the entrance of the park is a mile west along the road.

Campground: Coldbrook has both modern sites and a rustic loop, each on a small peninsula of their own on the southwest corner of Portage Lake. The 29 modern sites are close together in an open grassy area with only a few small trees and little shade. There is a single restroom with showers along with grills, tables, a sanitation station and limited play equipment. A bridge crosses the narrow channel into Blue Lake to the picnic area on the other side.

The rustic portion of the campground has 22 sites in a wooded area of small hardwoods with the sites well shaded but still close together. This loop has vault toilets, fire grills, table and a hand pump for water.

Day-Use Facilities: A pleasant picnic area with a large shelter, play equipment and tables and grills is located on a wooded hill overlooking both Blue and Portage Lake. Farther up the park road is another shelter, ball field and finally the beach area with its bathhouse, parking for additional vehicles and more tables and grills. On the east side of Portage Lake, where the beach is located, the water is deep and clear. The beach contains very little sand but is bordered by a pleasant grassy area.

Fishing: An improved boat launch with cement ramp and dock is situated next to the beach and includes its own parking area. There is a no-wake regulation between the narrow channels of the lakes and no high speed boating or water skiing is allowed from 7:30 P.M. to 11 A.M. The shorelines of these lakes are completely undeveloped and anglers will work the east side of Portage for a variety of fish, including bass and panfish.

Hiking: A posted trail system departs from the beach area and skirts the park shoreline, passing through the picnic area and both campgrounds before crossing a dike at the rustic loop to woods on the west side.

Season: Coldbrook is open from Memorial Day through October and is often filled on summer weekends. Nightly fees are $15 for a rustic site and $20 for a modern one. Call the Kalamazoo County parks office to reserve sites but they must be booked two weeks in advance and there is a $5 reservation fee.

20 Deep Lake
Yankee Springs
Recreation Area

Campground: Rustic	
County: Barry	Nearest Community: Middleville
Sites: 120	Reservations: No
Fee: $10 plus a vehicle entry permit	
Information: State park office ☎ (269) 795-9081	

Yankee Springs Recreation Area is a 5,017-acre state park between Kalamazoo and Grand Rapids and its main campground is Gun Lake, a large, modern facility that is often filled during the summer. But even if it's full, you don't have to leave the park.

Head east on Gun Lake Road and stake out a site at Deep Lake, the largest rustic campground in the Michigan State Park system. With 120 sites along this lake, you can usually count on an open spot in this campground throughout the summer, even on the weekends.

Directions: From US-131, depart at exit 61 and follow County Road A42 east for seven miles to its junction with Gun Lake Road. Turn right on Gun Lake Road and follow it through the park and past the entrance to Gun Lake Campground. Turn left on Yankee Springs Road and the entrance of Deep Lake Campground is within a mile.

Campground: Deep Lake is a very scenic section of Yankee Springs. The campground has 120 sites with most of them well spread out in a wooded setting. None are directly on the lake but a few are within view of the water and several sites have direct access to the park's mountain bike trail system.

Day-Use Facilities: The swimming is poor in Deep Lake but there are good beaches and a scenic picnic area on Murphy's Point Peninsula, which juts into Gun Lake near the modern campground. The peninsula features three beaches, picnic shelters, bathhouses and a concessionaire that rents out rowboats and canoes.

Fishing: Deep Lake is a shallow, 36-acre body of water with no-wake regulations and good fishing for bluegill and other panfish. The campground has a small boat launch and new fishing pier for shore anglers.

Mountain Biking: The campground is a popular destination for mountain bikers. Next to the campground is the trailhead for the *Deep Lake Mountain Bike Trail*, arguably one of the busiest off-road biking areas in western Michigan. The 13-mile trail system consists of two single-track segments; a two-mile loop north of the campground for beginners and an 11-mile expert loop south of it.

Hiking: There are 17 miles of hiking trails in Yankee Springs Recreation Area, including a segment of the *North Country Trail*. One of the most scenic is *Hall Lake Trail*, which begins across from the entrance to the Long Lake Outdoor Center. The trail forms a two-mile loop that skirts the shoreline of the lake and continues onto Graves Hill before returning.

Season: The campground is open from May through October and will fill on an occasional weekend during the summer. Unlike the modern campground on Gun Lake, sites cannot be reserved in advance.

21 Newaygo
State Park

Campground: Rustic	
County: Newaygo	**Nearest Community:** Oxbow
Sites: 99	**Reservations:** Yes
Fee: $10 plus a vehicle entry permit	
Information: State park office ☎ (231) 856-4452	

Newaygo is one of the few units of the state park system with a rustic campground and where there is actually a little space and privacy between sites. For these reasons the 257-acre park is also one of the few rustic facilities that can easily be filled on almost any weekend in the summer.

Located on the shores of Hardy Dam Pond southwest of Big Rapids, the park features little beyond its campground and a boat launch. But the fishing is moderately good in the man-made lake and the campground is a splendid place to park a trailer in October when the facility is empty and the surrounding hardwoods are at the peak of their autumn blaze of color.

Directions: The park is 43 miles north of Grand Rapids and can be reached from US-131. Depart west on Jefferson Road at the Morley exit for seven miles and then head north on Beech Road to the park's entrance.

Campground: Newaygo has 99 sites spread out on two loops. *Oak Campground* features sites 1-48 in a forest of young hardwoods and moderate undergrowth, providing privacy that is usually not associated with state parks. No sites are on the water but a path from the back of the loop leads to a bluff where you view most of the reservoir. Depending on the water level, a small beach lies below the bluff here.

Sites 49-99 are located in *Poplar Campground* where campers set up in a forest of slightly older hardwoods. A couple of sites are a few feet from the edge of the bluff overlooking the lake but the rest, like Oak Campground, are tucked into the trees and out of sight of the water. Both loops have limited playground equipment, vault toilets, hand pumps for water, tables, and fire rings.

Fishing: Newaygo features an improved boat launch along with a dock and parking for 50 additional vehicles and trailers on a small inlet of Hardy Dam Pond. The lake, often cited as "the third largest earthen-filled dam in the world," is six miles long and features more than 50 miles of shoreline that is dotted with campgrounds and boat ramps. It's stocked annually with walleyes and also was one of a handful of lakes where an experimental early bass season was held.

Season: Newaygo is open from May through October and, despite being a rustic facility, often fills up on weekends from mid-July to early August. During the week it's easy to obtain a site as well as before July 4 and after mid-August. You can reserve a site in advance by calling the state parks Central Reservation System at ☎ (800) 44-PARKS. After the summer the campground contact station is closed and you must call ☎ (231) 745-2888 for park information.

22 Henning

Newaygo County Park

Campground: Modern	
County: Newaygo	Nearest Community: Newaygo
Sites: 60	Reservations: Yes
Fee: $20 plus vehicle entry fee	
Information: Park office ☎ (231) 652-1202	

Just a half mile from Newaygo and M-37 and only a 40-minute drive from Grand Rapids is Henning Park, a 60-acre Newaygo County park with a range of facilities. They include a modern campground that attracts canoeists in the summer and salmon and steelhead fishermen in the fall thanks to its location on the Muskegon River.

Directions: From downtown Newaygo, head north on M-37 and turn east on Croton Road just after crossing the Muskegon River. The park entrance is a half mile east on Croton Road.

Campground: Henning Park has 60 modern sites that are situated close together in three loops in an open grassy field. None of them are directly on the river. Campground amenities include electric and water hookups, a large modern restroom and a dump station for recreational vehicles.

Day-Use Facilities: The park has an extensive day-use area that includes a baseball field and courts for basketball, tennis, beach volleyball and horseshoes. There is a picnic area with tables and grills and a pond with one end developed as swimming beach. Due to strong currents, swimming is not recommended in the Muskegon River.

Fishing: The park also maintains an improved boat launch and a fish cleaning area. This portion of the Muskegon River is well known for its steelhead and salmon fishing after Labor Day and walleye fishing in Croton Pond and downstream from Croton Dam in spring and early summer.

Canoeing: A popular canoe trip is to put in just below Croton Dam and pull out at Henning Park. This is a 16-mile float that most paddlers cover in three to five hours. Croton Dam Float Trips (☎(231) 652-6073) is a canoe livery that can arrange both rental canoes and transportation. Shorter trips are also possible.

Season: Henning is open for camping from April 15 through September 30. The campground experiences moderate use but will fill up on a handful of weekends throughout the summer. Sites can be booked in advance when the campground office is open. Contact Henning Park, 500 Croton Rd., Newaygo, MI 49337; ☎(231) 652-1202. There is a $10 fee for every reservation made.

23 White Cloud
City Campground

Campground: Modern and Rustic
County: Newaygo   **Nearest Community:** White Cloud
Sites: 104   **Reservations:** Yes
Fee: $13 to $15
Information: Park office ☎ (231) 689-2021

If White Cloud City Campground has the look of a state park to you that's because it used to be a state park. The 99-acre park that borders the White River in Newaygo County was designated White Cloud State Park in 1920. In 1940 a small portion was given to the city of White Cloud and in the late 1950s the rest of the park was handed over.

But the campground has always retained that "state park" appearance and today is a pleasant modern campground within easy walking distance of the shops and restaurants in this small town. White Cloud City Campground does have one feature that is unique to most state park campgrounds, however. You can usually get a site there during the summer, even on the weekends.

Directions: From M-37, turn west onto Wilcox Avenue to reach the campground entrance within a block.

Campground: White Cloud has 104 sites divided among modern sites with electric hookups, rustic sites and group camping. The sites are close together but well shaded by large hardwoods. None of them are directly on the river. The campground also has a bathhouse with showers and a dumping station.

In 2005 the city has plans to renovate the campground by upgrading the electricity and possibly adding sewage and water hookups at some sites.

Day-Use Facilities: The campground has a picnic area, play equipment, horseshoe courts and an enclosed pavilion with a fireplace and kitchen.

Hiking: There is a nature trail that departs from the campground and follows the river west to Flowing Well Park, a city park with a natural mineral springs.

Tubing: Bring an inner tube! Upstream from the campground are Smith and Raceway Parks located off Walnut Avenue and right below Lake White Cloud, an impoundment of the White River. During the summer it's common for children and families to tube from these parks back to the campground.

Season: The campground is open from April 15 until the first weekend of the firearm deer season. It only fills on holidays and an occasional weekend during July or early August. Modern sites are $15, rustic $13 and can be reserved by calling the campground office at ☎(231) 689-2021.

24 *School Section Lake*

Mecosta County Park

Campground: Modern
County: Mecosta   **Nearest Community:** Mecosta
Sites: 166   **Reservations:** Yes
Fee: $17 plus vehicle entry fee
Information: Park office ☎ (231) 972-7450

At School Section Lake Park in Mecosta County you have a lake, a campground and a lot of history. Some of the earliest settlers in Mecosta and Isabella County were African-American farmers and woodsmen who arrived in 1860 from southern Michigan and Ohio. Their pioneering spirit eventually led to the Old Settlers Reunions that began in 1890 at the homestead of one of the early families. That farm was on School Section Lake and today is the 85-acre county park and a Michigan Historic Site.

This interesting park also contains Little River School, a classic one-room schoolhouse from the early 1900s, a giant oak tree in the picnic area that is probably 200 years old, an excellent day-use area and a large campground.

Directions: From Mecosta head south on M-20 and then west on Nine Mile Road, which reaches the park in two miles.

Campground: School Section Lake has 166 modern sites that are situated close together in a semi-open area away from the lake. Each site has water and electricity and there is a dump station in the middle of the campground.

The park also has five rental cabins that are off by themselves and overlook the lake from a gently sloping hill. The 12-by-12-foot cabins sleep six each in a pair of bunks and a loft and contain a table and benches inside. Outside there are picnic tables, fire rings and wooden "easy chairs" that allow you to relax with a view of the lake.

The campsites are $17 per night, the cabins $35 per night. A vehicle entry fee is also required that is $20 for an annual pass, $12 for the weekend and $5 a day.

Day-Use Facilities: School Section has a large, shaded picnic area with tables, grills and five shelters that overlook the beach. Also within the park is a baseball field and courts for basketball, beach volleyball and horseshoes. There is a long sandy beach on the lake that borders a designated swimming area.

Fishing: There is no boat ramp in the park but hand-carried boats such as a canoe can easily be launched. School Section Lake is fished primarily for bass and bluegill.

Season: The park campground is open from May 1 to October and during the summer is often filled during holidays and the weekends. You can reserve a site or a cabin by calling the park office (☎ (231) 972-7450) after May 1. For information from October to May call Mecosta County Park System at ☎ (231) 832-3246.

25 Tubbs Island

Pere Marquette State Forest

Campground: Rustic
County: Mecosta   **Nearest Community:** Barryton
Sites: 12   **Reservations:** No
Fee: $10
Information: Mecosta County Parks ☎ (231) 832-3246

There are two state forest campgrounds on Tubbs Lake in Mecosta County. The first is located on the east shore and is called, simply enough, Tubbs Lake Campground. It has 21 sites, many of them right on the water, and all of them secluded in a well forested area that is typical of most state forest facilities. It's a nice place to spend a weekend but the second campground is nicer. It's an island.

What was originally a hill overlooking the west side of the lake became Tubbs Island when the surrounded areas were flooded to create a waterfowl habitat known as Martiny Flooding. But you don't need a boat to reach it.

Tubbs Island is reached by driving across a narrow dike and once on the island you'll discover a delightful state forest campground where there is a view of water or marshes from every site. The state forest facility is managed by Mecosta County Park Commission, no doubt the reason it's so well maintained. While there are only 12 sites, two are walk-in and often are available for tent campers when the rest of the loop is filled.

The only drawback is the lack of swimming in the campground and the large number of cottages along the south shore of Tubbs Lake.

Directions: From US-10, head south on M-66, pass through the town of Barryton and in 12 miles turn west on 17 Mile Road for 1.5 miles. Turn south of 45th Avenue and then

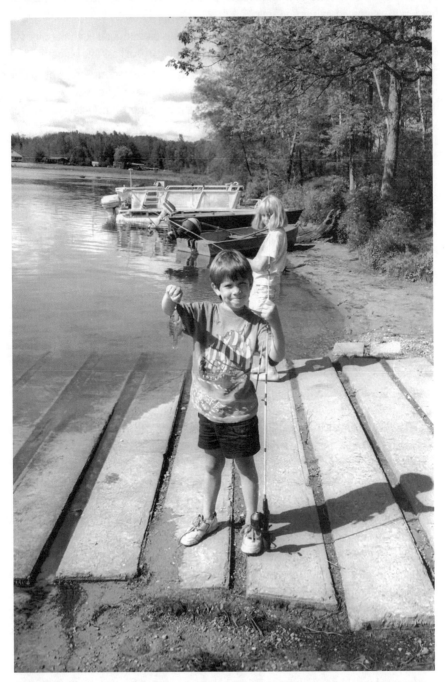

An angler with his first bluegill from Tubbs Lake. Tubbs Island Campground provides an excellent opportunity for children and families to fish from shore for bluegill and other species of panfish.

west on Madison Road and in a little over a mile you'll pass the posted entrance to Tubbs Lake State Forest Campground. The posted drive to Tubbs Island State Forest Campground is another two miles west.

Campground: It's easy to understand the popularity of Tubbs Island; every site overlooks the water. There is a single loop of 10 drive-in sites, located in a lightly forested area of hardwoods with views of either Tubbs Lake or marshy Lost Lake to the west. The last two sites are designated as walk-in and are located at the top of the island in a semi-open area that has a great view of the lakes as well as all your neighbors below. Campers park their vehicles along the loop and walk 30 yards to where they can pitch their tent. All sites have tables and fire rings while vault toilets and hand pumps for water are along the loop.

Fishing: The 116-acre lake is an excellent fishery that includes northern pike, perch, largemouth bass, and black crappies. But it's best known as a panfish lake with bluegills and pumpkinseed sunfish. Tubbs Lake isn't stocked and hasn't been since 1941.

There is a fish cleaning station and an improved boat ramp on the island along with parking for a few vehicles and trailers. Bluegills and sunfish can also be caught from shore with simple bobber rigs, making the lake an ideal fishery for children. In all, there are six public boat ramps accessing the Martiny Flooding, which is composed of six lakes, though many are little more than a small opening in a cattail marsh.

Season: The campground is generally open from early April through mid-November, closing when it's too hazardous to drive across the dike. It is often filled weekends from late June through August.

26 Paris
Mecosta County Park

Campground: Modern
County: Mecosta   **Nearest Community:** Paris
Sites: 70   **Reservations:** Yes
Fee: $12 plus vehicle entry fee
Information: Park office ☎ (231) 796-3420

In 1881, Michigan opened its second fish rearing facility near the town of Paris because of its excellent railroad connections with the rest of the state and the abundant water source of the nearby Muskegon River. Biologists raised salmon and brown trout fingerlings that were then placed in milk cans (painted red so as not to confuse them with real milk cans) and shipped all over Michigan on railroad baggage cars.

The Paris Fish Hatchery went on to become the state's major supplier of salmon and trout and was renovated and expanded in the mid-1930s before the Department of Natural Resources shut it down in 1964 as an outdated facility. But the impressive white building, ponds and raceways are still there and make the Mecosta County park so unique.

Where else can you camp at a fish hatchery, look at huge trout, feed trout, even catch an 18-inch rainbow trout for dinner? The 15-acre park, which opened in 1976, also features a large picnic area, a canoe launch area, one of the state's newest rails-to-trails passing through, even a replica of the Eiffel Tower.

This is Paris, after all, isn't it?

Directions: Paris Park is six miles north of Big Rapids on Old US-131 (also labeled Northland Drive). From US-131 depart at exit 142 and head east on 19 Mile Road and then north on Northland Drive.

Campground: The modern facility has electric and water hookups along with heated restrooms and showers. The 70 sites are located in a semi-open grassy area with scattered hardwoods. It's well shaded but offers little privacy and none of the sites are near the Muskegon River or have a view of the water. A site is $12 per night; the vehicle entry fee is $12 for three days or $5 a day.

Day-Use Facilities: Across from the campground is a large day-use area with a shelter, tables, pedestal grills, swings and other playground equipment. Park here and stroll through the old hatchery ponds and raceways. These have been converted into an interesting wildlife area where you see a variety of semidomesticated ducks, Canada geese and swans or some very impressive rainbow trout, some up to 10 pounds in weight. Both bird feed (dry corn) and fish feed (pellets) are available from dispensers and sidewalks, bridges and stone fences wind through the area and past a small replica of the Eiffel Tower.

Fishing: The Muskegon River is a renowned fishery and this far upstream anglers target trout in spring and fall and smallmouth bass during the summer.

But even of more interest to visitors are the trout ponds within the park. The old fish hatchery building is now occupied by a local trout farmer who stocks the ponds and runs a "fish-for-fee" concession. He supplies poles, bait and a net and aspiring anglers are allowed to fish the first trout pond. It looks easy but it's not. Those trout know when you're just tossing a pellet in and when there is a hook embedded in it. The experience is lots of fun for children, no fishing licenses are needed and the trout are excellent to eat. Most fish run between 12-14 inches but there are a few 18 inches and larger swimming around. The concession is open 10 A.M. to 6 P.M. Thursday through Sunday from June through August and weekends in May and September.

Canoeing: The park includes a canoe launch on the Muskegon River and parking for a limited number of vehicles for a trip down the Muskegon River. The paddle from Paris to Highbanks Park in Big Rapids is a 13-mile, four-hour trip through a mostly wide and easy river. Canoes can be rented in Big Rapids at *Sawmill Canoe Livery* (☎ (231) 796-6408),

Hiking: The newest linear state park, the White Pine Trail State Park, is the longest rail-trail in the Lower Peninsula and passes through the middle of Paris Park on its way from Cadillac to Big Rapids.

Season: The campground is open from May to October or sometimes later depending on the weather. On the weekends it is busy but rarely filled and there is no problem obtaining a site Sunday through Wednesday. You can reserve a site or a cabin by calling the park office (☎ (231) 796-3420) after May 1. For information from October to May call Mecosta County Park System at ☎ (231) 832-3246.

WHITE PINE TRAIL STATE PARK
A PARK WITHIN A PARK

Passing through Paris Park is White Pine Trail State Park, one of Michigan's four linear state parks. The White Pine stretches 92 miles from Cadillac south to Comstock Park near Grand Rapids, making it the longest rail-trail in the Lower Peninsula.

It was dedicated in July 1995 and within two years Friends of the White Pine Trail was formed to work toward paving its surface. The longest stretch that has been paved so far is a 13-mile segment from Big Rapids, through Paris Park to Reed City.

The converted abandoned railroad corridor makes for a relatively straight trail with very gentle grades. There are no heart-pounding hills here to confront cyclists or in-line skaters and it's extremely scenic.

The main staging area in Big Rapids is a train depot on the corner of Maple Street and M-20 that was built a month after the Grand Rapids & Indiana Railroad arrived in 1870.

From the depot you head north and within a mile cross the Muskegon River on the 319-foot-long Whites Bridge. The railroad trestle is the longest of the 14 bridges the trail utilizes and provides an excellent vantage point to gaze up and down the river.

Paris is another scenic stretch. A half mile south of the small town, the trail sidles a bluff to put you right above the swirling currents of the Muskegon River and alongside wooded hillsides that come alive in the spring with skunk cabbage and wildflowers. Beyond the park, the White Pine winds another 6.5 miles through a rural landscape, woodlots and Reed City to US-10, the end of the paved portion.

For a trail map or more information, call William Mitchell State Park at ☎ (231) 832-0795).

27 Merrill Lake

Mecosta County Park

Campground: Rustic
County: Mecosta
Nearest Community: Barryton
Sites: 145
Reservations: Yes
Fee: $15 plus vehicle entry fee
Information: Mecosta County Parks ☎ (231) 382-7158

Situated between two lakes in the heart of the Lower Peninsula, Merrill Lake Park is an excellent campground in a natural setting. Best of all, there always seems to be a site available. The park has a wide range of facilities including modern sites, rustic sites and even rental cabins. The two lakes, Gorrel and Merrill, double the opportunities for anglers while children can explore the surrounding woods and swamps that give this 90-acre Mecosta County park a Northwoods appearance.

Directions: Merrill Lake is located in the northeast corner of Mecosta County with an entrance off M-66 just a mile south of the Osceola County Line.

Campground: Merrill has a total of 145 sites. There are 119 modern sites with both water and electric hookups located close together in an open setting. The modern sites are split between two loops, one overlooking each lake but not directly on the water. The 26 rustic sites are off by themselves in a stand of woods that is almost entirely surround by a marsh. This can be a beautiful spot to pitch the tent in the fall and a little buggy in late May and June.

The park also has two rental cabins located side-by-side near the modern sites on Gorrel Lake. The cabins sleep six with two sets of bunk beds and a loft. Other amenities include a table, benches and a cooking counter inside.

A modern site is $15 per night, a rustic site $3 per person per night and the cabins are $35 per night. A vehicle entry fee is also required and is $20 for the season, $12 for three days or a weekend and $5 per day.

Day-Use Facilities: The park has a pair of beaches with one on each lake along with a picnic area, playground equipment and a shelter on Merrill Lake. Near the modern sites is also a baseball field and horseshoe courts.

Fishing: There is a boat launch with additional parking for trailers on each lake along with a fishing pier for shore anglers on Gorrel Lake and a fish cleaning station in the modern campground. Merrill Lake is the larger of the two and is fished for bass, perch, crappies and even northern pike. Gorrel Lake is smaller, totally undeveloped and restricts the size of motors to 10 horsepower. It's a very scenic place to cast for bass and panfish.

Season: The park is open for camping from May 1 to October. Other than an occasional holiday weekend, this campground is rarely filled. You can reserve sites or cabins in advance by calling the park office (☎(517)382-7158) and then sending in the full payment at least three days before your arrival.

28 Herrick
Isabella County Park

Campground: Modern
County: Isabella   **Nearest Community:** Clare
Sites: 73   **Reservations:** Yes
Fee: $11 or $18
Information: Park office ☎ (989) 386-2010

Herrick County Park is a 70-acre unit of Isabella County that protects four spring-fed ponds. In 1991-92 the park underwent a $300,000 renovation that included everything from building a new play area for children to installing electrical hookups to what was then a rustic campground. Park officials have also worked with biologists of the Department of Natural Resources in recent years to improve the fishing in the ponds.

All of the improvements have made Herrick a pleasant weekend getaway for campers while its location just south of Clare means it is also an easy-to-reach park for people in Lansing, Flint, Saginaw and Midland.

Directions: Herrick is 2.5 miles southeast of Clare. From US-27, turn east on Herrick Road to the park entrance.

Campground: Herrick has 73 sites that in 1992 were converted from rustic to modern with the addition of electrical and water hookups. A portion of the sites is in a stand of red pine, the rest in a semi-open setting. On a hill overlooking South Pond are five rental cabins that sleep four persons in two rooms. Each cabin has electric outlets, an outside faucet for water and a covered porch overlooking the pond.

A campsite is $11 per night for Isabella county residents, $18 for non-county residents. Cabins are $25 for county residents and $32 for non-county residents. No vehicle entry permit is required when camping.

Day-Use Facilities: Herrick features an elaborate railroad-theme play area for children along with additional play equipment within the campground. The Swimming Pond includes a beach and a modern bathhouse and two pavilions in the large picnic area can be reserved in advance.

Fishing: All four ponds within the park can be fished and have access sites on them for anglers. The South Pond is the largest and has a place to launch small boats. Anglers fish for primarily bluegill and other panfish and park officials have worked with DNR biologists in recent years in an attempt to eliminate the problem of stunted fish. Because of the numerous but small panfish, the ponds are excellent places to introduce young children to fishing.

Season: Camp sites and cabins can be reserved by calling Isabella County Parks and Recreation Commission at ☎(989) 772-0911, ext. 233.

29 Gladwin
City Park

Campground: Modern	
County: Gladwin	Nearest Community: Gladwin
Sites: 61	Reservations: Yes
Fee: $16	
Information: Park Office ☎ (989) 426-8126	

Entering Gladwin City Park can be a little discomforting. From M-61 you turn into the entrance drive where on one side is the Gladwin County Courthouse and on the other the Gladwin County Jail, complete with coils of razor wire on its roof. Once past the jail you enter one of the most delightful campgrounds in mid-Michigan. This is a place where anybody not on a 10 Most Wanted List can relax.

Originally a state park, the city acquired the 25-acre facility in 1983 and turned it into a modern campground that is a short walk from downtown Gladwin. The fact that it's right behind the county jail, a place swarming with police cars, is a good thing. "We never have any problems down there," said one city official.

Directions: From I-75 depart at exit 190 and head west on M-61 to reach Gladwin in 23 miles. The entrance drive for the park is on the south side of M-61 between the Gladwin County Courthouse and the County Jail.

Campground: You may be in downtown Gladwin—only a five-minute walk from a steamed latte at the Northern Espresso Shop—but you would never know it from your campsite. The park is set in the bottomlands of the Cedar River and well shaded by a scattering of mature maple, ash and beech trees. The grassy sites are bordered on one side by the river, on the other by a forested bluff. What you hear from your campsite is the gurgle of the Cedar, not the traffic on M-61.

The campground has 61 sites, all of them with electric hookups and 16 sites with water hookups. A few of them in the Lower Campground (No. 23 through No. 26) are right on the river. The 16 sites in the Upper Campground are on a bluff above the river. Other amenities include a restroom and dump station for recreational vehicles. Camping is $16 per night any day of the week.

Day-Use Facilities: The park also has courts for tennis, basketball, volleyball and horseshoes along with play equipment and a special Tot Lot. One spot of the Cedar has been developed into a small beach and swimming area. Within the picnic area are two pavilions that can be reserved in advance.

Hiking: Departing from site No. 28 is *Riverwalk*, a footpath that skirts the Cedar River for more than a mile. There is also a short path that leads from the park to downtown Gladwin.

Fishing: Anglers fish the Cedar River for trout and often follow Riverwalk to holes and runs downstream from the campground.

Tubing: The most popular activity in the park during the summer is tubing. Young floaters will drop their inner tubes into the Red Cedar near the park office, drift past the picnic area and campground and then continue on for another half mile or so, using the Riverwalk to return to their campsites.

More adventurous floaters will load their gear into the car and drive six blocks north of the campground on Bowery Road and then west on First Street to the city's North Park. By beginning here you can enjoy a three-mile float and only know you're in Gladwin when you drift underneath M-61.

Season: The campground is open from May to December, remaining open for the entire firearm deer season. There are discounted rates in October. You can mail in reservations beginning January 1 for the current camping season and request them by phone when the campground office opens on May 1. For reservations in advance contact Gladwin City Park, 1000 W. Cedar, Gladwin, MI 48625; ☎(989) 426-8126.

30 Island Lake
Huron National Forest

Campground: Rustic	
County: Oscoda	**Nearest Community:** Rose City
Sites: 17	**Reservations:** No
Fee: $10	
Information: Mio Ranger District ☎ (989) 826-3252	

First impressions can be misleading. Take Island Lake Campground for example. The first thing many people notice driving through the Huron National Forest campground are the cottages bordering the loop.

And then maybe the cottages across from the small beach, cottages all along the shoreline of the 65-acre lake, cottages everywhere.

Ugh! How do you escape?

You pitch your tent in one of the lightly shaded sites that overlook the water, throw swim suits and towels in a small pack and lose yourself along the Island Lake Nature Trail on your way to Loon Lake Recreation Area. Within minutes you're trudging up a ridge, deep in a woods of impressive oaks and an occasional towering white pine and seemingly miles from anywhere, not a cottage in sight.

The campground and nearby day-use area are linked together by foot trails and make for an excellent place to camp, providing opportunities for limited hiking, fishing, boating or just wiggling your toes in two different beaches.

Directions: From I-75 depart onto M-33 (exit 202) and head north through Rose City. Six miles north of the town turn west on County Road 486 to first pass the entrance of Loon Lake. The campground is another half mile along CR 486.

Campground: The campground is a single loop located on a gently sloping hillside leading down to Island Lake. The 17 sites feature paved parking spurs, fire rings with sliding grills and tables while nearby are four vault toilets and two hand pumps for water. The sites are lightly shaded with little privacy between them and cottages border each side of the campground. But one rents out canoes, rowboats and pedalboats to campers and the other sells firewood.

Day-Use Facilities: There is a small day-use area within Island Lake composed of a parking area, grassy area with tables and pedestal grills and a thin strip of beach overlooking a marked swimming area. Hours are 6 A.M. to 10 P.M.

Loon Lake Recreation Area is far better and worth the two-minute drive or the 0.8-mile hike. The 90-acre lake has few visible cottages on it as most of the north and west shore is national forest. The beach is also wider than at Island Lake. There is a bathhouse with flush toilets, tables, pedestal grills, and drinking fountains. There is no fee to enter Loon Lake in a vehicle.

Hiking: Island Lake Nature Trail is basically a one-mile loop with a spur near post number 14 leading off to Loon Lake, crossing County Road 486 along the way. It is a 1.4-mile round trip to the lake through an area laden with glacial evidence in the form of morainal hills and potholes. Along the way you pass 20 numbered posts that correspond to a pamphlet available from the campground manager. Posts point out everything from where a lightning bolt struck a red pine to an 1890 logging trail.

Fishing: There are no boat ramps at either facility although hand-carried boats could be easily launched. Island Lake is 65 acres large with fair fishing for perch, rock bass, bluegill and largemouth bass, though it's rare to see any bass larger than 12 inches here. There is a ban on boat motors in the lake.

Loon Lake is larger, more clear and generally considered to have a better fishery, particularly for largemouth bass but also yellow perch and bluegill. Although there is no public boat ramp here, *Loon Lake Campground* (☎(989) 685-2407) off M-33 has bait and boats for rent.

Season: Island Lake is open from mid-May to mid-September and is often filled on weekends during July and early August.

31 Wagner Lake
Huron National Forest

Campground: Rustic	
County: Oscoda	Nearest Community: Mio
Sites: 12	Reservations: No
Fee: $10	
Information: Mio Ranger District ☎ (989) 826-3252	

Wagner Lake is a small body of water seven miles south of Mio and completely surrounded by national forest land. Bordering its east side is a small campground. One compliments the other extremely well and a stay here is usually a quiet, relaxing night on the shore of a scenic lake. The key is getting a site.

With only 12 sites, Wagner Lake tends to be full most weekends from late June through mid-August. The facility is rustic but its paved interior road and spurs make it especially popular with RV campers. Site availability is on a first-come, first-served basis and to ensure getting a spot, plan on arriving Wednesday evening or Thursday morning.

There are no hiking trails nearby and the beach is limited but there is good bluegill fishing in a lake small enough for canoes or cartop rowboats.

Directions: From Rose City head north on M-33 for nine miles then turn west (left) on Wagner Lake Road, a dirt road that passes the paved entrance of the campground in 1.2 miles. Wagner Lake Road is seven miles south from M-72 in Mio.

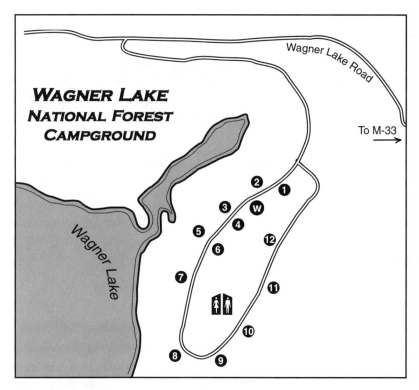

Campground: The campground is a single loop of 12 paved sites in an area wooded in both pines and towering hardwoods. Both the loop and sites can be easily handled by the largest motor homes and in the middle of the loop is a pair of vault toilets and a hand pump for water. Half of the sites are just up from the shoreline with a full view of the lake. The other half is located on a gently sloping hillside and still provide partial views of the water.

Day-Use Facilities: The campground features a small sandy beach with a shallow marked swimming area. Though there is a visitors' parking lot near it, the beach is limited to campers only.

Fishing: Wagner Lake has 26 surfaced areas and is free from cottages or docks, so provides a pleasant angling experience in a scenic setting. The fishing must be good at times as a few locals often stash a small boat along the shore here and there. Forest Service rangers report fisheries of bluegill, bass and perch but without a doubt this is primarily panfish waters. Bluegill fishing is good while most bass landed tend to measure less than 10 inches in length.

There is no boat launch within the campground, making hand-carried boats ideal here. Children and other boatless anglers can follow a sandy path along the north side of the lake and have few problems reaching any stretch of the shore.

Season: The managed season is from Memorial Day through Labor Day but if spring weather is warm the park hosts begin collecting fees earlier. This campground is often filled on the weekends in July and August.

32 Leverentz Lakes

Pere Marquette State Forest

Campground: Rustic
County: Lake
Sites: 17
Fee: $10
Nearest Community: Baldwin
Reservations: No
Information: Baldwin DNR office ☎ (231) 745-4651

Is this one or two campgrounds? There are two separate loops, each with its own entrance, each its own lake, with its own vault toilets and other facilities. Yet the numbering system that begins on the sites along Big Leverentz Lake finishes on Little Leverentz Lake.

Does it matter? Either way this is a delightful place to camp with lake-view sites, good fishing opportunities and a trail system that wanders into the woods. Best of all, despite its close proximity to Baldwin, it does not receive an overload of campers and other users.

Directions: The campground is northeast of Baldwin and can be reached by heading east on US-10 for two miles and then north on Mud Trail. Immediately turn west (left) on Campground Road and follow signs to either lake. The campgrounds are posted along both US-10 and on Campground Road.

Campground: Big Leverentz has 10 sites on two loops along the south side of the lake. Eight sites are situated on one loop with most of them on a low rise for a nice view of the water. The other two are off by themselves near the boat launch and all of them are well spread out in a mixed stand of pines and hardwoods with moderate undergrowth.

Little Leverentz is to the south and has seven sites on a single loop. The area is a little more forested in pine but only one site is on the water while within view are the backsides of several cottages. Both feature vault toilets, hand pumps for water, fire rings and tables.

Fishing: On Big Leverentz there is an unimproved dirt boat launch and additional parking for two or three vehicles within the campground. Next to the launch is a very nice T-shaped dock and, in a lake this small, you can reach a lot of water with a good cast from here. The lake is completely undeveloped and its west side is heavy weeded with aquatic plants and lily pads but the rest is clear. For the most part Big Leverentz is panfish waters with an occasional bluegill reaching nine to 10 inches but most of them small. Every once in a while somebody will also pull out a largemouth bass.

LEVERENTZ LAKES
STATE FOREST
CAMPGROUNDS

Overlook

40th Street

Baldwin River

Big
Leverentz
Lake

River Loop
2.3 Miles

Little
Leverentz
Lake

Lake Loop
1 Mile

Mud Trail

Lakeview Rd

Sheep Ranch Pathway

Campground Rd

Whalen
Lake

Sandborn Creek

10

← To Baldwin

There is no launch on Little Leverentz but a pathway next to site number 14 leads to the shoreline. The lake is the better of the two though it is slightly smaller at 5.6 acres. It has a weedy shoreline but the middle is 30 feet deep. Little Leverentz contains bluegill, pumpkinseed and perch along with largemouth bass and northern pike and attracts moderate pressure in the summer.

Hiking: The trailhead for *Sheep Ranch Pathway* is posted in Big Leverentz. It's composed of several loops including the River Loop, a 2.3 mile trek to an overlook on the Baldwin River to the north. Because of clearcuts and cars and other trash dumped in the woods, this pathway is a far better ski trail in the winter than it is for hiking during the summer.

Season: Big Leverentz is the more popular of the two lakes and occasionally will fill up on a July or August weekend but not often due to the large number of state and national campgrounds in the Baldwin area.

33 Silver Creek
Pere Marquette State Forest

Campground: Rustic
County: Lake   **Nearest Community:** Luther
Sites: 25   **Reservations:** No
Fee: $10
Information: Baldwin DNR office ☎ (231) 745-4651

No matter how you arrive at Silver Creek State Forest Campground, whether it's in the bow of a canoe or the backseat of a car, this is a delightful spot to spend a night or even a few days.

The Pine River is one of the state's blue ribbon trout streams as well as one of the most popular canoe routes during the summer. You can paddle downstream, hike along its banks upstream or just sit in your riverbend campsite dabbling a worm in hopes of landing a trout.

The rustic facility features many sites along the water along with a handful of walk-in sites and is not nearly as busy as the national forest campgrounds downstream. The only drawback for some people is the off-road vehicle trail that passes nearby. But most ORV riders, and thus their activity, tend to congregate a mile to north at Lincoln Bridge State Forest Campground.

Directions: Silver Creek is located north of Baldwin and west of Cadillac. From US-131 the campground is reached by exiting onto Luther Highway and heading west for Luther, a town on the banks of the Little Manistee River. At Luther head north on State Road for six miles to the posted entrance of the facility.

Campground: Situated along a single loop are 25 sites in a forest of young beech and other hardwoods with a thick undergrowth. The sites are well spread out and secluded from each other while a handful are right on the river, some so close people set up lawn chairs in front of their trailer and fish for trout. All sites feature the usual fire rings, tables, hand pumps, and vault toilets.

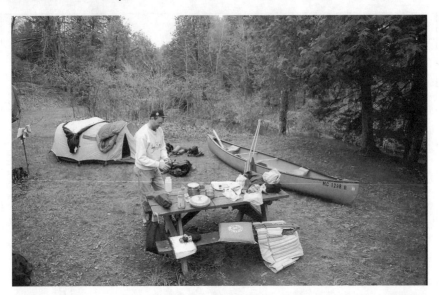

A canoist prepares dinner at his Silver Creek campsite after a day of paddling the Pine River.

Another nine sites are walk-in or canoe sites located on a point formed by a big horseshoe curve in the Pine River. Most overlook this gentle river and no. 23 is one of the best riverbank sites in the Lower Peninsula as it's shaded by several tall cedar and spruce trees and lies above a small stretch of rapids. The parking lot is less than 25 yards from the walk-in sites.

Fishing: The Pine is regarded as a good to excellent trout stream with brook and rainbow trout last planted in the early 1970s. This far up the river the Pine is 10-15 yards wide and wadeable in most places while fishing pressure is moderate. Most anglers toss worms or small spinners into deep pools, under log jams and past undercut banks for primarily brown trout. Brook trout tend to dominate the river upstream near Skookum Bridge. Use the Silver Creek Pathway to gain access to the river downstream.

Hiking: Silver Creek Pathway was rerouted in the late 1990s and is now a two-mile trek that begins at Silver Creek State Forest Campground and ends downstream at Lincoln Bridge State Forest Campground. The pathway begins near site no. 10 and quickly crosses the creek near its confluence with the Pine, a popular swimming spot for children staying in the campground. Once on the other side you enter the most scenic stretch by far. Here the pathway parallels the river for almost a mile, providing an excellent view of the Pine from a bluff above, before arriving at a side trail to State Road. The trail can be turned into a 1.5-mile loop by using the side trail and returning along State Road.

Canoeing: The Pine originates near LeRoy in Osceola County and flows 60 miles before merging with the Manistee River. Almost 40 miles of it is floatable in a canoe, making the entire river an ideal three-day float. The first put-in is Edgett's Bridge on

Raymond Road and from here it's a five-hour paddle to Silver Creek. The last takeout point is Low Bridge on M-55, a nine-hour paddle.

A permit for each canoe is required for paddling the Pine in the Manistee National Forest between May 1 and September 30. With less than 700 permits available per day for both private and livery canoes, reservations are mandatory for any weekend from mid-June through August. For more information or to reserve a permit for the Pine River call the Baldwin Ranger Station (☎(231) 745-4631). Canoe Liveries that service the river include Pine River Paddlesport Center (☎(231) 862-3471), Jarolim Canoe Rental (☎(231) 862-3475) and Sportman's Port (☎(231) 862-3571).

Season: The only time this campground is filled on the weekends is when a large group of canoeists pass through but that is rare this far upstream.

34 Hemlock
Manistee National Forest

Campground: Rustic
County: Wexford **Nearest Community:** Cadillac
Sites: 19 **Reservations:** No
Fee: $12
Information: Manistee Ranger District ☎ (231) 723-2211

A rustic and much more quiet alternative to the William Mitchell State Park is Hemlock on a back bay of Lake Mitchell just five miles east of Cadillac. Unlike the large and compact campground at the state park that borders M-119, an extremely busy road during the summer, Hemlock is a considerably smaller facility with a wooded appearance that still provides access to fisheries of Lake Mitchell and Lake Cadillac.

The drawback is the national forest campground does not have a swimming area of any kind and it tends to fill up as often as the state park, where at least you can book a site in advance.

Directions: From US-131, head north on M-115 and then just before reaching Mitchell State Park, turn west on M-55. Within a mile turn right on Pole Road and the campground entrance is reached in another mile.

Campground: Hemlock is a managed campground of 19 rustic sites. The loop is paved and so are the spurs with many of them pull-throughs ideal for large RVs. The sites are well separated and secluded in an area that includes both a pine plantation and a stand of spruce and hardwoods.

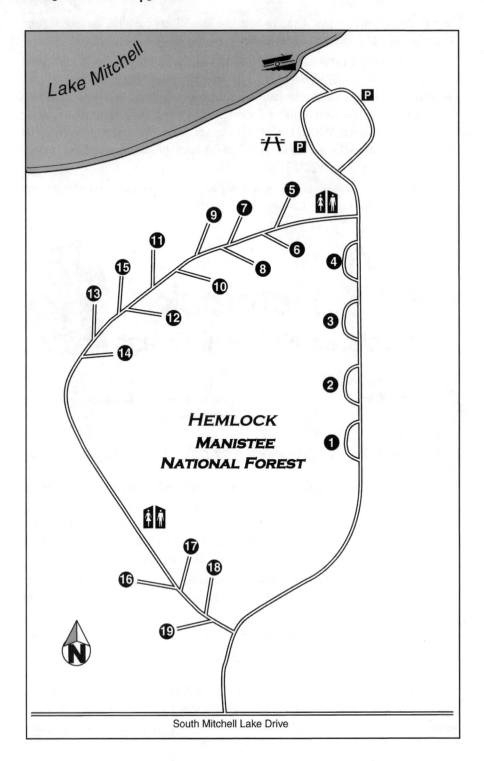

Six sites (5, 7, 9, 11, 13, and 14) are labeled lakefront and but only a few of them actually overlook the water and provide direct access to the lake. The others, most notably site 14, overlook the heavy growth of cattails along the shore.

Day-Use Facilities: Near the boat launch are a few tables and fire rings including two on each side of the ramp that overlook the entire back bay. Otherwise there is no swimming area nor any hiking trails.

Fishing: An improved ramp with a metal grate bottom is situated on the lake along with parking for a handful of vehicles. The back bay is for the most part undeveloped except for cottages and docks near its entrance. Most of the shore supports a heavy growth of cattails, reeds and other aquatic plant life, the reason, no doubt there is always a good number of anglers.

Both Mitchell and Cadillac are known as fine walleye fisheries and are heavily fished during the summer. The 1,150-acre Lake Cadillac is an extremely busy body of water as it lies totally within the city limits of Cadillac and its shoreline is totally developed. For that reason many anglers prefer the 2,580-acre Mitchell that also supports walleyes as well as perch, various panfish and bass. You can put in at Hemlock and reach Cadillac by a quarter-mile canal that runs along the state park and connects the two lakes.

Season: Hemlock is open from mid-May through September. Because of its close proximity to Cadillac, the facility fills up most weekends July through August and often during the middle of the week.

35 *Goose Lake*
Pere Marquette State Forest

Campground: Rustic
County: Missaukee   **Nearest Community:** Lake City
Sites: 54   **Reservations:** No
Fee: $10
Information: Cadillac DNR Office ☎ (231) 775-9727

Goose Lake is the largest state forest campground in the Lower Peninsula and when combined with Long Lake provides almost 70 sites on the neighboring lakes. A lot of campsites, yet on many summer weekends these facilities are nearly filled. Located just northwest of Lake City in a hilly and scenic section of the Pere Marquette State Forest, Goose Lake offers everything most campers seek in a rustic facility. There are good swimming and fishing opportunities and a choice of sites with many overlooking the sandy shoreline of this horseshoe-shaped lake. If this facility has too many campers for you, then just continue along the forest road to Long Lake, a much smaller campground.

Directions: From Lake City head north on M-66 and then west (left) on Sanborn Road to Al Moses Road. Here state forest signs direct you west along Goose Lake Road, a well-graded dirt road that leads a mile to Goose Lake.

Campground: Strung out along the northern shore, Goose Lake has 54 sites with most of them gathered in a half dozen small loops. Many sites are located right on the water or within view of the lake and a few are even situated on a high shoreline bank, an especially scenic spot from your tent.

Most of the sites along the lake are close together and lack privacy but those on the other side of the road, away from the water, are well separated and secluded in a young hardwood forest. Vault toilets and hand pumps for water are scattered throughout the campground but many tables and fire rings are missing.

Day-Use Facilities: There isn't a marked beach area but much of the lake's shoreline is sandy and shallow, making it pleasant for swimming.

Fishing: An improved boat ramp with a cement slab is located within the campground but small boats can be launched from many shoreline sites. Goose Lake is a horseshoe-shaped body of water with a point in the middle and an island on its west side. Its eastern arm is narrow and very weedy but the west arm is free of heavy aquatic growth in the middle and holds the deepest sections. Panfish are plentiful, though a bluegill over 10 inches seems to be a rare catch. Anglers also target smallmouth bass and occasionally catch small northern pike.

Season: Goose Lake is managed by a campground host and on July and August weekends can be more than three-quarters filled by Saturday afternoon. The first sites to go, naturally, are those along the lake's sandy shoreline.

36 Long Lake
Pere Marquette State Forest

Campground: Rustic
County: Missaukee   **Nearest Community:** Lake City
Sites: 16   **Reservations:** No
Fee: $10
Information: Cadillac DNR Office ☎ (231) 775-9727

Long Lake is reached by first driving through Goose Lake campground and then following a one-way loop past several ponds before arriving at the small lake. On the way

Long Lake in Pere Marquette State Forest near Lake City.

back you skirt a bluff with an overlook of Goose Lake, all part of this very hilly and scenic area just northwest of Lake City.

If you want a large campground with lakeview sites and lots of sandy shoreline for swimming, stop at Goose Lake. If you want a small, somewhat remote and quieter facility on a lake of its own, continue on to Long Lake. Many people do, the reason Long Lake is occasionally full on a summer weekend while Goose Lake has open sites.

Directions: From Lake City head north on M-66 and then west (left) on Sanborn Road to Al Moses Road. Here state forest signs direct you west along Goose Lake Road, which in a mile arrives at the entrance of Goose Lake State Forest Campground. You have to drive through the campground and continue on the forest road to reach Long Lake.

Campground: Located on the northeast corner of the lake are 16 sites. Half of them are right on the shoreline with a scenic view of the length of this long and narrow body of water. The forest here is hardwoods with little undergrowth and sites tend to be close together. There is no marked swimming area or beach, but the edges of Long Lake are sandy and shallow, making it possible for children to enjoy some swimming activity.

Fishing: There is an unimproved boat launch near the end of the campground. The middle of Long Lake is free of heavy aquatic plants but lily pads are thick at the north end. The lake supports smallmouth bass, bluegill and some pike. Overall there is less fishing pressure here than Goose Lake because of the size of the campground. Most anglers arrive with canoes or small rowboats and the lake is so narrow it could even be tackled in a belly boat.

Season: Long Lake usually has its own campground host and because of its limited number of sites will occasionally fill up on a July or early August weekend.

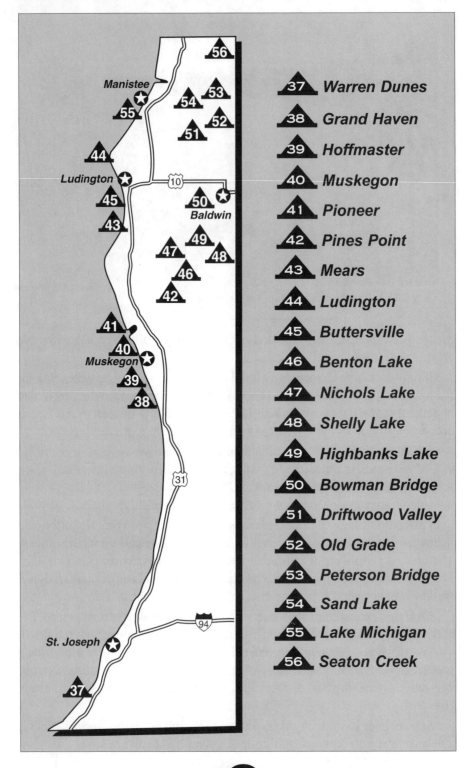

37 Warren Dunes
38 Grand Haven
39 Hoffmaster
40 Muskegon
41 Pioneer
42 Pines Point
43 Mears
44 Ludington
45 Buttersville
46 Benton Lake
47 Nichols Lake
48 Shelly Lake
49 Highbanks Lake
50 Bowman Bridge
51 Driftwood Valley
52 Old Grade
53 Peterson Bridge
54 Sand Lake
55 Lake Michigan
56 Seaton Creek

Lake Michigan

37 Warren Dunes
State Park

Campground: Modern and rustic
County: Berrien **Nearest Community:** Bridgman
Sites: 185 **Reservations:** Yes
Fee: $10 to $25 plus vehicle entry fee
Information: State park office ☎ (269) 426-4013

Warren Dunes may be a Michigan state park but every summer it's invaded by Hoosiers and Chicagoans. The 1,952-acre unit is the first preserve along Lake Michigan and only 12 miles north of the state border. Thus of the 1.3 million visitors Warren Dunes draws every year, more than 80 percent of them are from outside of Michigan. For this reason Warren Dunes is the only park in the state that charges a higher entry fee for nonresidents.

Still, they pack this beautiful stretch of dunes and shoreline and the reason is clear. The park has 2.5-miles of undeveloped lakeshore, 200-foot high sand dunes that lure an occasional hang glider and a modern campground that still provides a little space between parties. The trick here is getting a site and sometimes during the summer just getting inside the park.

Directions: Warren Dunes is reached from I-94 by departing at exit 16 and following Red Arrow Highway south to the park entrance.

Campground: Warren Dunes has 185 sites located well away from the beach. This facility is two loops in a wooded area on the backside of the dunes, offering shade and, surprisingly, for the number of sites in it, a small degree of privacy between campers. On the southern loop are three mini-cabins, two Rent-A-Tipis and a foot trail that leads around Mt. Randal to the day-use area on Lake Michigan. Along with tables and fire rings, each loop has a restroom with showers. A sanitation station is located near the registration station.

In 2000, Warren Dunes also changed its organizational camp into a 20-site rustic campground located in the woods north of the modern campground. A modern site is $20 a night, a rustic site is $9.

Day-Use Facilities: Separated from the rest of the park by several towering dunes is the day-use beach areas of the park. There is parking for 1,500 cars along Lake Michigan but the area still fills up on summer weekends and occasionally the staff sets up overflow parking for another 600 vehicles before they start turning people away. The popularity of the beach is easy to understand. The wide sandy beach is bordered by towering dunes on one side and the light blue waters of Lake Michigan on the other. In between are three bathhouses. The park also has a wooded picnic area bordered on one side by a windblown dune.

Hiking: There are more than five miles of maintained hiking trails in Warren Dunes with most of them forming a four-mile loop through the dunes in the park's interior, along Lake Michigan and back to the modern campground. The trail passes through both wooded terrain and open dunes and can be picked up from the northern parking lot of the day-use beach area, the organization camp and a small trailhead near the modern campground. Plan on three hours for the loop.

Another trailhead is located at the end of Flora Lane, north of the park entrance on Red Arrow Highway, where there is a small parking area, trash cans and a trail sign. From here there is a mile loop to the north that was originally built as part of the cross country ski system. After the park constructed a 400-foot boardwalk over a marsh, hikers began using the loop, especially in the spring when it is possible to sight a variety of birds.

Part of the trail system is posted as the *Warren Dunes Nature Trail*, a one-mile loop featuring 10 interpretive stops that correspond to a brochure. Pick up the nature trail at the small trailhead parking lot just south of the modern campground. Finally, a popular hike in early spring is to simply walk the beach from the park's day-use area north to Weko Beach, a City of Bridgman park that adjoins the state park. Round-trip to Weko Beach and back to the day-use area is a five-mile hike.

Season: The campground is filled 90 percent of time during the summer and every weekend from the beginning of May through October. Best bet is to make reservations far in advance of your trip. You can reserve a site by calling ☎ (800) 44-PARKS or online at *www.michigan.gov/dnr.*

38 *Grand Haven* State Park

Campground: Modern
County: Ottawa   **Nearest Community:** Grand Haven
Sites: 174   **Reservations:** Yes
Fee: $23 to $25 plus vehicle entry permit
Information: State park office ☎ (616) 847-1309

Sites at Grand Haven State Park are little more than a cement slab with no trees, no vegetation to keep the blowing sand at bay and little privacy from your neighbor who is but four feet away. There are no maintained trails at this park, no boat launch and it's located in one of the most popular tourist towns along Lake Michigan. But what a beach! Many

Grand Haven State Park features open sites that overlook one of the best Lake Michigan beaches in the heart of Grand Haven.

consider Grand Haven's 2,500-foot strip of Lake Michigan the finest beach in the state and that is one reason why this park draws more than 1.3 million visitors annually. The other is Grand Haven, the town. The park is connected to the restaurants and shops of downtown Grand Haven by Lighthouse Connector Park, a delightful boardwalk along the Grand River that ends with a popular fishing pier and picturesque Grand Haven Lighthouse.

If an urban campground is what you like, Grand Haven is a gem.

Directions: The park is a mile southwest of US-31 in Grand Haven along Harbor Drive. From US-31 follow directional signs to "Downtown."

Campground: Grand Haven has 174 modern sites in a setting that is open with no shade and little space between campers. A few sites actually border the beach with an open view of Lake Michigan and all of them are a short walk away from the surf. Each site has a table and hookup but no fire rings or grills of any kind. Showers, modern restrooms and a sanitation station round out the facilities.

Day-Use Facilities: Grand Haven's beach possesses some of the finest sand along Lake Michigan and during the summer is a colorful scene with wind surfers, swimmers, sunbathers and kite flyers. There is day parking for 800 vehicles but often on weekends in July and August the lot fills and additional cars are turned away. People are then encouraged to park downtown and hop the city trolley bus to the beach for a small fee. Also located within the day-use area are picnic facilities, play equipment, bathhouse and a concession store.

Fishing: Adjacent to the park is Grand Haven Lighthouse and a pier connecting it to the boardwalk along Grand River. This is a popular Great Lakes fishing pier with anglers jigging for perch during the summer and casting spoons and plugs for brown trout, steelhead and salmon during the fall and spring.

The park maintains a fishermen's parking lot with a posted entrance off Harbor Drive and it opens at 5 A.M. as often the best fishing is in the early morning. Lake Michigan is a noted deepwater fishery for salmon and steelhead although in recent years the catch has been down. There is no ramp facility in the park but there are public boat ramps and marinas in the city. A number of charter boat captains work out of Chinook Pier.

Season: Grand Haven's campground is open from April to November with electricity and water available, but restrooms are closed by mid-October. The facility is full daily from mid-June to the end of August, and on weekends throughout June and most of September. Due to the park's overwhelming popularity, there is little chance of getting a site during the summer without a reservation. You can reserve a site by calling the State Parks Central Reservation System at ☎ (800) 44-PARKS or online at *www.michigan.gov/dnr*.

39 P.J. Hoffmaster State Park

Campground: Modern
County: Muskegon
Sites: 293
Fee: $25 plus vehicle entry fee
Information: State park office ☎ (231) 798-3711

Nearest Community: Muskegon
Reservations: Yes

Like many Lake Michigan state parks, P.J. Hoffmaster features a wide and sandy beach and a rolling terrain of both wooded and open dunes. But unlike most units along Michigan's Gold Coast, P.J. Hoffmaster is large enough to be more than a campground and a beach.

The 1,043-acre park includes 2.5-miles of shoreline, a 10-mile network of trails, even a "quiet area" where often it's possible to escape the summer crush of tourists found elsewhere along this side of the state. P.J. Hoffmaster also has a huge campground of several hundred modern sites that, despite the large number, still maintains something of a rustic wooded appearance.

What P.J. Hoffmaster does share with the other Lake Michigan state parks is the

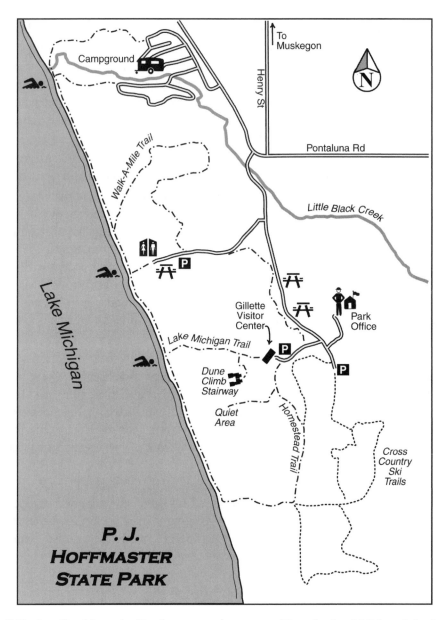

To Muskegon

Henry St

Campground

Walk-A-Mile Trail

Pontaluna Rd

Little Black Creek

P

Gillette Visitor Center

Lake Michigan Trail

Lake Michigan

P

Park Office

Dune Climb Stairway

Quiet Area

Homestead Trail

P

Cross Country Ski Trails

P. J. HOFFMASTER STATE PARK

difficulty of booking a site. Don't expect to show up on a Thursday in mid-July and obtain a site. Advance reservations are strongly recommended during the summer season but they are far easier to book here than at Grand Haven State Park just down the shore. And P.J. Hoffmaster is definitely worth a little pre-vacation planning.

Directions: The park is located just south of Muskegon. From I-96 depart at exit 4 and head south on 148th Avenue, then immediately turn west (right) onto Pontaluna Road, which ends in six miles at the park entrance.

Campground: Located at the north end of the park in a wooded valley, the campground has 293 sites on four loops. The loops are well forested in hardwoods and pines and being dune country the sites are in a sandy area covered with needles but little undergrowth.

The largest loop, the only one on the south side of Little Black Creek, is especially nice as many of the sites back up to a steep wooded dune while others overlook the clear, gently flowing stream. The trees here are older pines and hardwoods for a more natural setting than the red pine plantation where two other loops are located. A 0.25-mile trail leads from the back of this loop to a camper's beach on Lake Michigan.

Sites have tables, fire rings and electric hookups while four shower/restrooms service the campground. A sanitation station for trailers is located just beyond the contact station.

Day-Use Facilities: P.J. Hoffmaster maintains a day-use area on Lake Michigan with parking for 550 cars. The facility includes a bathhouse, concession store and picnic areas near a golden stretch of Lake Michigan beach. Farther south along the park road are additional picnic areas in a wooded setting and Gillette Nature Center. Built in 1976 as Michigan's sand dune interpretive center, the two-story building is overshadowed by a huge, windblown dune. The center features an exhibit hall, 82-seat theater and a hands-on display area, all related to dunes and the biological zones that surround them. Gillette (☎ (231) 798-3573) is open year-round Tuesday through Sunday. In the summer, the hours are 10 A.M. to 5 P.M.

Hiking: The park is large enough to be laced by a 10-mile network of foot trails that loop through the wooded dunes and along the Lake Michigan shoreline. The most popular walk is *Dune Climb Stairway* that departs from Gillette Nature Center and follows a long stairway to the top of a high sand dune for a panorama of the park. The best hike in the park is *Homestead Trail*, a 3.5-mile loop that also departs from the nature center and winds through a designated natural area, passes a spur to the park's Quiet Area and ends up on Lake Michigan.

Season: Like most other Lake Michigan state parks, P.J. Hoffmaster fills up daily from Wednesday through Sunday mid-June through most of August. On Monday and Tuesday the campground is generally 75 percent full throughout most of the summer. You can reserve a site six months in advance by calling the state parks Central Reservation System at ☎(800) 44-PARKS or going online at *www.michigan.gov/dnr*.

40 Muskegon

State Park

Campground: Modern
County: Muskegon   **Nearest Community:** Muskegon
Sites: 110   **Reservations:** Yes
Fee: $24 plus vehicle entry fee
Information: State park office ☎ (231) 744-3480

One of the oldest campgrounds on the west side of the state is at Muskegon State Park. The park's Lake Michigan Campground was constructed in the 1930s, before the advent of motor homes and pop-up trailers. As a result, this modern facility is atypical, lacking that plowed-out, paved-over look of many state park campgrounds. If you can maneuver your trailer into the site, this is a delightful place to camp.

The 1,165-acre park is a peninsula surrounded by Lake Michigan on one side and Muskegon Lake on the other and is best known as the home of the only luge run in the Lower Peninsula. But of more interest to summer campers is the trail network that winds through the dunes and the three miles of wide, sandy beach.

Directions: The park is five miles west of North Muskegon. From US-31 depart at M-120 and head southwest, following park signs to Memorial Drive, which terminates at the park's south entrance. Lake Michigan Campground is closer to the north entrance reached by Scenic Drive from Whitehall.

Campground: The Lake Michigan campground has 110 sites on a loop of several lanes. The pre-motorhome era facility is neither level nor is it easy to pull trailers into many of the sites and large RVs are sent down to Muskegon Lake campground at the south end of the park. The gently rolling area at Lake Michigan campground is well wooded in deciduous trees and bordered to the west by windblown sand dunes. Within the campground is a pair of Mini-Cabins. There are no sites directly on the water but the beautiful Great Lake shoreline is only a short walk away. The facility has a sanitation station and two restrooms with showers.

Day-Use Facilities: The park has two day-use areas. The most popular one is on Lake Michigan where there is parking for 600 vehicles, a bathhouse-store and a wide sandy beach that is typical for this side of the state. The second is on Snug Harbor on Muskegon Lake near the south entrance of the park. Snug Harbor has tables, pedestal grills, a shelter and a small sandy beach, though the water here is not nearly as desirable as Lake Michigan.

Fishing: There are two improved boat launches with docks and cement ramps within the park. Both are on Muskegon Lake, one in the Snug Harbor day-use area and the other

The Blockhouse along Scenic Drive provides a view of Muskegon State Park's rugged interior and serves as a trailhead.

in the nearby modern campground. Boaters then use Ship Canal to gain quick access into Lake Michigan. Fishing opportunities abound in this park. The 4,150-acre Muskegon Lake is noted for its perch and bass as well as being stocked annually with walleye. Shore anglers can use piers in Snug Harbor or along Ship Canal or follow the beach south to reach a rocky breakwall where the catch is perch during the summer and steelhead and salmon in the spring and late fall.

Hiking: The park maintains 12 miles of foot trails through a terrain of mostly well-forested lowlands and dunes. Most of the network is a series of loops and side trails spread between Muskegon Lake Campground and the East Campground but you can also enter the system at the Blockhouse on Scenic Drive south of Lake Michigan Campground and from the Snug Harbor day-use area. Often the trails involve steep climbs to the crest of dunes where there are scenic views, particularly in the southern half of the park, or past such interesting spots as Devil's Kitchen, the village site of Old Bay Mills or Lost Lake, a small, isolated inland lake in the northern half. There is no mountain biking on the trails.

Season: Lake Michigan Campground is not quite as popular as the one on Muskegon Lake but both campgrounds fill on the weekends from July through Labor Day and are usually near capacity during the week. You can reserve a site by calling ☎ (800) 44-PARKS or online at *www.michigan.gov/dnr*.

41

Pioneer
Muskegon County Park

Campground: Modern
County: Muskegon   **Nearest Community:** Muskegon
Sites: 213   **Reservations:** No
Fee: $18 plus vehicle entry fee
Information: Park office ☎ (231) 744-3580

Located north of Muskegon State Park on Lake Michigan, Pioneer County Park is the most popular unit in the Muskegon County park system. But unlike the state park, reservations are not accepted at Pioneer so you're more likely to find an open site on a Thursday or Friday afternoon.

Directions: Pioneer is three miles north of Muskegon State Park on Scenic Drive. From US-31, depart at M-120 and head north to Giles Road. Turn west on Giles Road and follow it to Scenic Drive. The park entrance is a quarter mile north on Scenic Drive.

Campground: Pioneer has 213 modern sites equipped with both electric and water hookups. The sites are close together but most of them are well shaded by red pines. Three restrooms service the campground and a sanitary station for recreational vehicles is located in the middle. None of the sites has a view of Lake Michigan but all are a short stroll from the beach. Along with a nightly camping fee, a $4 daily or $20 annual motor vehicle permit is also required to camp.

Day-Use Facilities: A boardwalk with a series of observation decks skirts the bluff above the Lake Michigan shoreline, providing a pleasant view and access to the park's 2,200-feet of surf and sand. Like Muskegon State Park to the south, the beach here is wide and beautiful. The park also has a picnic area with tables, grills, play equipment and a log lodge that can be rented out in advance. Near the picnic area are basketball, tennis and volleyball courts as well as a softball field. There are no hiking trails in Pioneer.

Season: Although the campground is full most weekends during the summer, sites are often still available on Thursday afternoon and even Friday morning and generally on Sunday and Monday. When the campground is full, new arrivals are given a number by the park staff beginning at 8 A.M. and a drawing is held at 10 A.M. to fill any sites being vacated that day.

42 Pines Point

Manistee National Forest

Campground: Rustic
County: Newaygo   **Nearest Community:** Hesperia
Sites: 33   **Reservations:** No
Fee: $12
Information: Baldwin Ranger District ☎ (231) 745-4631

In many ways, Pines Point is your typical national forest campground. It's rustic with vault toilets, hand pumps for water and well spread and wooded sites. Your typical national forest campground with one exception. Pines Point has a tuber's loop where people can float the South Branch of the White River in an inner tube, ending where they began: in the campground.

There are opportunities to fish, hike, even go backpacking, but what most campers enjoy best about this Manistee National Forest facility is spending a hot afternoon cooling off in the gin-clear waters of the White River and never worrying about special transportation or arranging a drop-off, as is necessary on other rivers.

Directions: From White Cloud head west on M-20 to Hesperia where you turn south on Maple Island Road. In a mile turn west on Garfield Road for five miles and then south on 168th Avenue where the campground is posted. Follow the blacktop for 2.5 miles to the campground.

Campground: Pines Point has 33 sites along a paved loop on a high bluff above the South Branch of the White River. The area is heavily forested and the sites are well spread out and secluded from each other. Ten sites are on the edge of the bluff with a view of the river and log stairways nearby that lead down to the water. The gravelled parking spurs make this facility ideal for large RVs while other amenities include fire rings with sliding grills, tables, drinking fountains and a flush toilet along with vault toilets.

Day-Use Facilities: A picnic area is situated in a grove of red pine on the bluff above the water and includes a separate entrance, tables, pedestal grills and a large parking lot. Both the trailhead for the *White River Foot Trail* and the departure point for tubers is located here.

Fishing: The White River is the southernmost major trout stream draining into Lake Michigan. At Pines Point you'll find fall and spring steelhead fishing as well as fall salmon, which is extremely popular among anglers. White River Trail can also be used to access more remote sections of the river. Other species caught during the summer include smallmouth bass and northern pike.

PINES POINT
CAMPGROUND
MANISTEE
NATIONAL FOREST

White River

Canoe and
tube launch

White River
Trailhead

White River

Tubing: The South Branch of the White River forms an oxbow at Pines Point Campground where tubers can put in at the canoe launch and then get out at the picnic area for a 30- to 40-minute float. This far upstream the South Branch is 20 to 30 yards wide and so shallow in many stretches that even children can stand up.

Canoeing: Pines Point has a canoe landing along the South Branch with boat racks and a pull-through drive for vehicles. Designated "Country Scenic River" by the state, the White River flows through primarily wooded and agricultural land. Most paddlers begin in the town of Hesperia and from there it's a six-mile, two-hour paddle to the campground. The next takeout is Sischo Bayou, a seven-mile, three-hour journey. Canoes and transportation can be arranged through *Happy Mohawk Canoe Livery* (☎ (231) 894-4209).

Hiking: Departing from the day-use area is *White River Trail*, a trail system that is being developed by the U.S. Forest Service. Currently there are 12 miles of paths marked by blue blazes. The first two miles of the trail follow the high banks overlooking the river much of the way.

Season: Pines Point has a campground manager that collects fees from Memorial Day through Labor Day and possibly earlier if there is a demand. It's rarely filled in midweek and only full on holidays and an occasional weekend.

43 Charles Mears
State Park

Campground: Modern
County: Oceana   **Nearest Community:** Pentwater
Sites: 179   **Reservations:** Yes
Fee: $23 plus vehicle entry fee
Information: State park office ☎ (231) 869-2051

It might be small at only 50 acres in size, but Charles Mears State Park is still one of the most popular campgrounds in the entire state. As an urban campground, it's hard to match. It's tucked away on a beach of its own, away from the traffic of Business US-31, but within a short walk are the shops, stores and restaurants of downtown Pentwater, a popular resort town.

Mears is a "destination campground" as opposed to a stopover on the way up north. People work so hard or wait so long to get a site they end up staying here four to five days on the average. Plan ahead if you want to make this park a part of your summer vacation.

Directions: From US-31, follow Business US-31 through Pentwater and look for state park signs. Mears is four blocks from the downtown area.

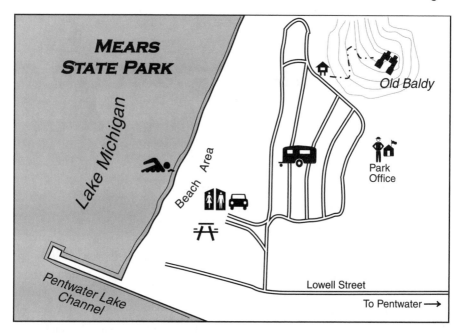

Campground: Mears has 179 sites that feature not only electric hookups but also paved pads for recreational vehicles because the campground is little more than an open sandy area with little to no shade. Nor do any of the sites overlook Lake Michigan like at Grand Haven because a string of dunes separates them from the beach. Within the campground are two modern restrooms with showers, a sanitation station and a fish cleaning hut.

Day-Use Facilities: Mears has a beautiful beach while the small dunes that border it are a great place to catch a Great Lakes sunset. The day-use area has a shelter, bathhouse, beach volleyball courts and play equipment, concession store and picnic area. Often on summer weekends the parking lot will fill and all other visitors must park elsewhere in town and walk in.

Fishing: Adjacent to the park is Pentwater Pier, where anglers cast for perch and smallmouth bass during the summer. There is no boat ramp in the park but public facilities are located downtown and Pentwater is a popular port for deepwater fishing for salmon and steelhead in Lake Michigan. If you don't have a boat, several charter captains work out of Pentwater.

Hiking: There is a half mile of trail that winds around to the top of Old Baldy, a wooded and partially windblown sand dune that provides an excellent view of the Lake Michigan shoreline, the town of Pentwater and its extensive boat harbor.

Season: The campground is filled every day from mid-June to late August. Sites can be obtained without a reservations on weekends in April and May and usually in September and October...just don't plan to do too much swimming in Lake Michigan at that time of year. Otherwise a reservation is necessary to camp here and should be booked four to six months in advanced by calling ☎(800) 44-PARKS or online at *www.michigan.gov/dnr*.

44 Ludington

State Park

Campground: Modern
County: Mason   **Nearest Community:** Ludington
Sites: 299   **Reservations:** Yes
Fee: $23 to $25 plus vehicle entry fee
Information: State park office ☎ (231) 843-8671

Like many state parks along Lake Michigan, Ludington State Park is a popular unit and a tough place to get a site without a reservation or waiting a day or two. Unlike most other parks, however, once you have set up camp, it's easy to escape the crowds in this wonderful stretch of shoreline, dunes and forest.

At 5,202 acres, Ludington is the largest state park on Lake Michigan and second largest in the Lower Peninsula. It includes 5.5 miles of Great Lake shoreline, another four miles along popular Hamlin Lake and a 1,699-acre Wilderness Natural Area that is undeveloped and forms a border with Nordhouse Dunes Wilderness to the north.

The popularity of this park is easy to understand. There are paved bike paths, the Great Lakes Interpretive Center to visit, an 18-mile network of hiking trails and Big Point Sable Lighthouse, a photographer's delight with its distinctive black and white tower. All this accounts for the more than 750,000 visitors annually with the vast majority arriving from May through September. But if the crowds turn you off then just start hiking the Lake Michigan shoreline north and eventually the beach towels, bikes, bustle, and even the footprints in the sand disappear.

Directions: The state park is 8.5 miles north of Ludington at the end of M-116.

Campground: The park has three separate campgrounds that stretch from Lake Michigan to Hamlin Lake on the north side of the Big Sable River. All three are well wooded, offering shady sites, and are connected to the day-use areas by the paved bike paths. There is little privacy between sites but there is just enough space and trees to avoid a campground that looks like a used RV lot.

Pines Campground has 97 sites and is closest to Lake Michigan, separated by the golden beach by only a sand dune, thus the popularity for the west side of the loop. *Cedar Campground* is a pair of loops of 105 sites located in the middle and *Beachwood Campground* has 97 sites located just north of the Hamlin Lake day-use area. Beachwood is my personal choice when setting up camp. It's a figure-eight loop where the sites surround forested knolls and low dunes in the middle. On the east side the sites border a low dune that can be climbed for a pleasant view of Hamlin Lake and its many islands and

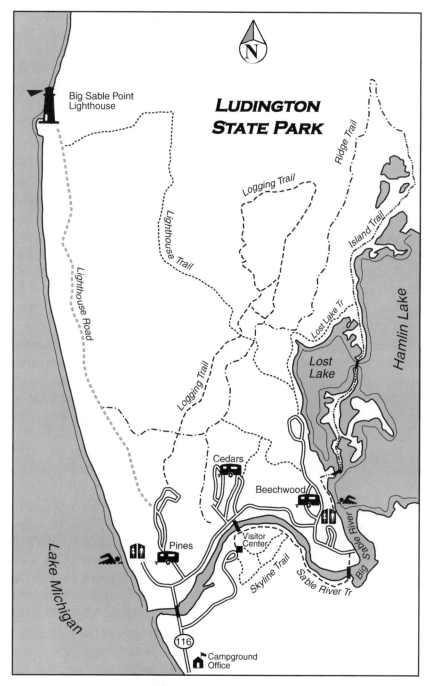

lagoons as well as provide direct access to the Beachwood Trail. A handful of sites at the northeast corner of the loop actually look out onto Lost Lake, the only place in the park where a waterfront view is possible. Sites include tables and fire rings while four restroom/shower buildings service the campgrounds.

Day-Use Facilities: There are two beaches in the park, one on Lake Michigan, just north of where the Big Sable River empties into the Great Lake, and the second on Hamlin Lake. Both have parking and a bathhouse but early in the summer the Hamlin beach is more popular because its water warms up quicker. M-116 follows Lake Michigan for almost three miles after entering the park and it's common for visitors to just pull over along the road to enjoy a stretch of beach.

The Great Lakes Interpretive Center, on the south side of Big Sable River, has exhibits and a slide presentation focusing on Michigan's most famous lakes. The center is open daily from Memorial Day to Labor Day from 10 A.M. to 5 P.M.

Fishing: Hamlin Lake, with its many coves, inlets and bayous, is a renowned warm water fishery. There is heavy spawning of northern pike and tiger muskellunge in the shallow coves, and anglers frequently have landed muskies over 15 pounds. The 4,490-acre lake, which is nearly 10 miles long, is noted for bass and bluegill as well. The lake has been stocked with tiger muskies since the early 1980s and in 1987 a walleye stocking program began. The park maintains an improved boat ramp on the inland lake near the day-use area with parking for 75 trailers and vehicles and a fish cleaning station near the Lake Michigan beachhouse. Other fishing activity in the park includes surf fishing in the early spring and October for salmon and trout off the Lake Michigan shoreline.

Hiking: The park boasts a well-posted trail network, featuring a number of stone shelters that make for an ideal place to enjoy lunch. There are 11 named and color-coded trails within the 18-mile network with the shortest and most spectacular located south of the Big Sable River. The *Skyline Interpretive Trail* is less than a half mile long but involves a steep winding stairway to the top of a dune where a boardwalk has been constructed along the crest. How steep is the dune? Helicopters were needed to carry the lumber to the top. But the view from the boardwalk is spectacular and along the way there are numbered interpretive posts that correspond to a brochure available at each of the three stairways.

The rest of the trail system is north of the river with posted trailheads located in the campgrounds or the Hamlin Lake Day-Use Area. Several trails can be combined for day-long loops through the unique terrain of the park's Wilderness Natural Area. The *Ridge* and *Island Trails* make a 5.2-mile loop that features viewing the perched dunes above Hamlin Lake and winding around the inlets and bays along the lake. Plan on three to four hours for the trek. Equally scenic is the *Logging* and *Lighthouse Trails* out to Big Point Sable Lighthouse with a return along the beach. The 4.8-mile hike would include climbing the historic lighthouse, which is open 10 A.M. to 6 P.M. daily from May through October.

Season: Ludington's campgrounds are booked daily July through Labor Day and are full on weekends beginning in Memorial Day. Late April is a particularly pleasant time to camp as reservations (☎ (800) 44-PARKS) are unnecessary and the park is practically empty at that time of year. The campground is open year-round but the modern restrooms are available only from April 15 to November 1.

45
Buttersville

Pere Marquette Township Park

Campground: Modern
County: Mason **Nearest Community:** Ludington
Sites: 44 **Reservations:** No
Fee: $18
Information: Pere Marquette Township ☎ (231) 845-1277

Buttersville Park is a small lakeshore bluff campground located south of Ludington. Because it is a township park you're more likely to find an open site here than other better-known Lake Michigan campgrounds such as Ludington or Mears State Parks.

Directions: From US-31 south of Ludington, exit north onto Pere Marquette Highway and then head west on Iris Road for 1.4 miles. Turn north on Lakeshore Drive and follow it past White Pine Historic Village to the park.

Campground: Buttersville was originally a rustic campground that featured restrooms and showers. In 2002 the township upgraded the site with electric hookups for trailers and then increased the nightly fee to $18. The sites are well shaded and not jammed together like those at Ludington State Park. Seven sites have a view of Lake Michigan from the edge of the bluff and from any of them you can enjoy the breeze off the Great Lake that will keep you comfortable even on the hottest summer night.

Day-Use Facilities: A stairway leads down to the beach, where you can relax with a view of the Ludington North Breakwall Lighthouse. In the evening you can watch the ferry, *S.S. Badger*, return from Wisconsin and then stick around for the sunset.

Within the campground is a shelter and play equipment and at the north end of the park is a small day-use area with a few picnic tables and a separate parking area. There are no hiking trails in the park but you can stroll the beach along Big Sand Bay for more than three miles.

Season: The park is open for camping from Memorial Day to Labor Day. Although it tends to be full on most weekends from early July to mid-August, sites are often still available on Thursday afternoon. It is not possible to reserve a site in advance.

46

Benton Lake
Manistee National Forest

Campground: Rustic

County: Newaygo

Nearest Community: Brohman

Sites: 24

Reservations: No

Fee: $10

Information: Baldwin Ranger District ☎ (231) 745-4631

What was a turkey farm in the 1940s is now a lightly used campground in the Baldwin District of the Huron-Manistee National Forest. Benton Lake is a midsize facility of 24 sites located on the south shore of this 33-acre lake. Half of the sites are in the wooded area but the other half are in an open, grassy area, remnants of the poultry farm here.

The farm also had a profound effect on the lake itself. Until the 1950s, Benton Lake was private water that was rarely fished and that, say some locals, is the reason for the Benton Lake's excellent bluegill fishery.

Directions: The campground is an hour drive north of Grand Rapids. From M-37 in Brohman turn west on Pierce Drive (also labeled Forest Road 5308) and drive 4.5 miles to the posted entrance of the campground.

Campground: There are 24 sites on two loops with sites 1-12 located in an area forested in young hardwoods with moderate undergrowth. Much of the second loop is open, however, and the grassy sites are closer to the lakes. There are none directly on the water but several are only a few steps away. Sites feature a table, fire ring with sliding grill, lantern post and paved spurs, making them ideal for RVs. Both loops have vault toilets and hand pumps for water.

Day-Use Facilities: The campground has a pleasant picnic area with some of the tables and grills on a grassy hillside overlooking the lake. Although a beach and swimming area is marked on handouts, it's little more than a small clearing in the aquatic vegetation, just enough for young children. There is additional parking and a vault toilet at the picnic area.

Fishing: Beyond the picnic area is an unimproved boat launch on the northwest corner of the lake. Benton is a 33-acre lake that lies completely in national forest land thus free of any cottages or other development. It's not large and attracts only light fishing pressure throughout most of the summer. There is a drop-off 15 to 20 yards off shore and during the summer anglers who fish the edge of it with wax and leaf worms can often entice a variety of panfish. Some bluegills that have come out of the lake have easily exceeded a pound.

Hiking: There is a trailhead for the *North Country Trail* located off Pierce Drive, two miles east of the campground entrance. To the north along the NCT it's approximately a four- to five-mile trek to Nichols Lake Campground, to the south a three- to four-mile hike to Loda Lake Wildflower Sanctuary.

Season: The campground is managed by a concessionaire from Memorial Day to Labor Day. Sites are occupied on a first-come, first-served basis and have a capacity of eight people and two vehicles.

47

Nichols Lake
Manistee National Forest

Campground: Rustic
County: Newaygo **Nearest Community:** Brohman
Sites: 28 **Reservations:** No
Fee: $12
Information: Baldwin Ranger District ☎ (231) 745-4631

Of the eight national forest campgrounds located between White Cloud and Baldwin, Nichols Lake is one of the most popular because it's one of the nicest. Overlooking a scenic lake, the facility is wooded with well spread out sites and paved spurs. You can sneak into the woods on the North Country Trail, fish for bluegill in Nichols Lake or trailer your boat to dozens of other lakes in the area.

Little wonder then that this facility is often filled on a summer weekend. No reservations are accepted but Nichols Lake is well worth arriving a day early to beat the Friday night crowd.

Directions: From White Cloud, head north on M-37 for 13 miles and then turn west on 11 Mile Road. The posted entrance of the campground is reached in 4.5 miles or three miles beyond the community of Woodland.

Campground: Nichols Lake is a single loop of 28 sites situated on a bluff wooded predominantly by oaks. Sites are well spread out but within sight of each other due to thin undergrowth. One side of the bluff borders the lake and a few sites have a partial view of the water. On the other side several sites overlook a grassy marsh, an excellent area to watch for deer in the early evening.

Sites include not only fire rings with sliding grills and tables but also lantern posts. Sites 16 and 17 are large two-family sites. Within the loop are both vault and flush toilets and three spigots for water. The other nice aspect about Nichols Lake is the bluff catches any breeze at all on the lake, making the campground a little less bug infested during the summer.

Day-Use Facilities: A ramp next to site number 17 leads to the small peninsula that ~ives Nichols Lake its horseshoe shape. At the base of the point is small strip of sand with ~ted swimming area. From here the path climbs to the end of the point for nice overview ~tire lake and who's fishing where. On the northwest corner of the lake is a separate ~ that is reached from Cleveland Road via Bitely.

Fishing: Before entering the campground you pass a separate spur that leads to the trailhead for the *North Country Trail* and an improved boat launch. There are parking areas for both here. Also next to the swimming beach is a fishing pier. Nichols Lake has a 160 surface acres and is horseshoe-shaped with cottages and developed shoreline limited almost entirely to the northeast corner. The prime species are bluegills and the lake receives moderate fishing pressure.

Hiking: The *North Country Trail* passes through the campground and has a trailhead near the boat launch. The most scenic section by far is north past the Nichols Lake Picnic Area and across Cleveland Road. In the next three miles the trail winds past five lakes.

Season: The managed season is from Memorial Day to Labor Day. If arriving on a Friday or Saturday afternoon be prepared for the possibility of this campground being full.

48

Shelley Lake
Manistee National Forest

Campground: Rustic
County: Newaygo   **Nearest Community:** Brohman
Sites: 9   **Reservations:** No
Fee: Huron-Manistee National Forest vehicle pass
Information: Baldwin Ranger District ☎ (231) 745-4631

Spending a night at Shelley Lake in Manistee National Forest is something that falls between hiking in and pulling up to your site with a car full of coolers, lawn chairs and a deluxe, three-burner Coleman stove. The U.S. Forest Service calls it a "dispersed recreation area," which means it's non-developed—no toilets, no fire rings, no facilities whatsoever. It means you're out in the woods and off on by yourself, all by careful design.

The recreation area was set up after unrestricted use of the scenic area began causing irreversible damage to the small, 15-acre lake. So barriers were built across the old logging roads leading up to the shoreline and nine campsites were designated. You can pull right up to a couple of the campsites away from the lake. But the best ones are along the shoreline, overlooking the water, and those you have park and walk to. Not far, just enough to make you cringe at the thought of carrying in a cooler full of ice and soda pop.

Directions: From White Cloud head north on M-37 and look for a gravel parking area to the east. From the parking lot a very rough forest road (not recommended for large recreation vehicles) heads east to the lake.

Campground: The facility has nine designated sites around the small lake and you have to walk into seven of them. Site No. 3 is on a point in the southwest corner in a stand of paper birch with a 180-degree view of the water. Site No. 7 is another a gem. It is reached by a footbridge from the boat launch and is off by itself on a small peninsula. You camp beneath towering white pines with a view that includes the entire lake. One site is on the east side of lake and reached from M-37 by heading east on Hayes Road and then south on Centerline Road. From a parking area on Centerline it's a quarter mile walk through the forest where you break out at a small sandy beach. There are no tables, fire rings, vault toilets or safe water sources within the campground.

Fishing: At the north end of the lake there is an unimproved boat launch onto the lake and parking for two or three vehicles. The 15-acre lake is completely surrounded by national you can catch the sun dipping behind the shoreline bluff in the evening or watch fishermen enticing bluegills.

Fishing: Near the beach you can launch a hand-carried boat. Canoes are perfect for this 20-acre lake, haul one along. Panfish, most notably bluegill, and bass are the species most anglers are targeting here. Shore fishermen can follow a foot path along the shore at the east end of the lake and this little inlet can be especially productive when bluegills are spawning in May.

For a little angling adventure try fishing

Amaung Lake. The lake lies east of Highbank but there is no ramp on it or even a road to it. Follow Roosevelt Drive (also Forest Road 5396) past the entrance of the campground for another quarter mile and then just head into the woods. The lake is only a few hundred yards away and it's hard to miss as it is considerably larger than Highbank. Amaung offers less fishing pressure and seems to have a better population of largemouth bass and panfish. Haul a canoe or belly boat in and it could be a rewarding afternoon for the extra effort.

Hiking: There are no designated trails from the campground but traversing along the bluff that borders the west side of the lake is the *North Country Trail*. This is one of the most scenic stretches of the Baldwin Segment of the NCT. North of Highbank is a small lake that can be reached only on foot while to the south the trail winds around Condon and Leaf Lakes before reaching a trailhead on Cleveland Road. From its perch over Highbank Lake to Cleveland Road is a trek of 3.5 miles. To reach the trail, follow the anglers trail around the east side of the lake and then climb to the top of the west shore bluff. On the bluff the trail is a well-beaten path marked by blue diamonds.

Season: The managed season is from Memorial Day through Labor Day but if sp weather is warm the concessionaire will begin collecting fees earlier. The campgr often fills on weekends. If you want a site here plan on arriving early in the day an an alternative campground picked out just in case.

Canoeists can paddle 66 miles of the river. From M-37 in Baldwin, it's a 12-mile, four-hour paddle to Bowman Bridge. The next take-out is Rainbow Rapids, two hours downstream. You can obtain rentals in Baldwin from either *Ivan's Canoe Rental* (☎(231) 745-3361) or *Baldwin Canoe Rentals* (☎(231) 745-4669).

Fishing: Bowman Bridge is the start of the "flies only" stretch of the Pere Marquette that extends 8.7 miles downstream to Rainbow Rapids. Heaviest use of the river by anglers is at the peak of the salmon spawning run in September and October and the height of the steelhead run in March through mid-April. The river also supports brown trout, though many feel this fishery has diminished at the expense of the salmon.

Hiking: Along the group loop is a trailhead for a half-mile spur that is marked in blue diamonds and leads to the *North Country Trail*. On the NCT you can head north and in a mile reach the Bowman Lake Foot Travel Area. Bowman Lake is a 1,000-acre non-motorized preserve with a 2.2-mile pathway that circles the scenic lake. You can spend an hour hiking this area or carry in a fishing rod and some bait and spend an afternoon catching bluegills from the shore.

Season: The campground is managed from April 15 through Labor Day but may be open earlier or later depending on demand. Due mostly to canoeists, Bowman is a popular campground and will often be filled on the weekends and even midweek at the height of the camping season. Group sites can be reserved through the National Recreational Reservation Service at ☎(877)477-6777 or its website *www.reserveusa.com*. Individual sites are first-come, first-served.

51 Driftwood Valley

Manistee National Forest

Campground: Rustic
County: Lake   **Nearest Community:** Irons
Sites: 19   **Reservations:** No
Fee: $12
Information: Manistee Ranger District ☎ (231) 723-2211

The Little Manistee River is among the best known steelhead waters in the state. During the month of April the river is alive with both fish spawning upstream and anglers who toss spinners, plugs and spawn in an effort to entice the hard-fighting rainbows into striking. Of the three national forest campgrounds located along the river, the Bear Track facility downstream offers better canoeing along with hiking opportunities on the North Country Trail that passes nearby.

But Driftwood Valley makes for a more scenic place to camp, especially in the fall, while river fishermen will do well working this stretch of the Little Manistee. Canoeing is possible downstream from the campground but upriver the paddling is a challenge due to shallow water and overhanging brush.

Directions: From Wellston depart M-55 south on Bosschem Road (also labeled County Road 669) for four miles and then west (right) on 12 Mile Road for a half mile and south (left) on Bass Road for four miles where the road curves between Elbow and Harper Lake. Beyond the lakes turn west (right) on Forest Road 5357 and the posted entrance is less than a mile.

Campground: Driftwood Valley is a pair of loops on a high bank above the river. The area is forested in white pine and oaks and the 19 sites are well separated from each other. Although none are directly on the water, five of them are on the edge of the bluff from which you can look down at the Little Manistee gurgling past. Amenities include vault toilets, hand pumps for water, fire ring with sliding grill, and a group camping area for paddlers between the two loops.

Fishing: The river is best known by river anglers as a steelhead stream and fished hard in April. But Chinook and coho salmon can also be caught, primarily from October through November, and to a lesser degree brown trout. An angler's path runs along much of the river from the campground.

Canoeing: There is a canoe launch adjacent to the group campsite. The Little Manistee is not nearly as popular as the Pere Marquette or the Pine but still makes for enjoyable paddling. M-37 is the upper limit for canoeists and from there the river winds 85 miles to Manistee Lake near Lake Michigan. From Driftwood it's a two-hour paddle to Bear Track Campground, which also has a canoe launch. The next landing is Nine Mile Bridge, a five-hour paddle from Driftwood. Canoes are rented in Wellston from *Jarolim Canoes* (☎(231) 862-3475).

Season: The campground is managed from Memorial Day to Labor Day and except during the spring steelhead runs, is a lightly-used facility.

52 Old Grade
Manistee
National Forest

Campground: Rustic
County: Lake
Sites: 20
Fee: $12
Information: Baldwin Ranger District ☎ (231) 745-4631

Nearest Community: Wolf Lake
Reservations: No

The name for Old Grade Campground comes from a railroad grade that dates back to the logging era of the late 1800s and today parts of it can still be seen in the area. The campground is a lightly-used facility in the Manistee National Forest that will appeal to anglers, berrypickers and campers who want to avoid crowds and reservations. There is also a interpretive path that departs from the campground and provides an opportunity to spot wildlife, including whitetail deer, beavers and many songbirds.

But be forewarned—there is considerable low-lying forest and marshy areas nearby and the insects can be thick at times. Avoid this campground through much of June and early July. The trout fishing is good in late May in the Little Manistee River and the fall colors are spectacular in early October. Both are excellent times to pitch a tent here.

Old Grade Nature Trail

Little Manistee River

Old Grade Nature Trail

OLD GRADE
MANISTEE
NATIONAL FOREST

Railroad Grade

To M-37

Directions: From Baldwin, head north on M-37 for 11 miles. The campground entrance is reached just after crossing the Little Manistee River.

Campground: Old Grade has 20 rustic sites including several overlooking the Little Manistee River. The sites are well spread out in a wooded area, offering a good deal of privacy. Campground amenities include fire rings, tables, four vault toilets and hand pumps for water.

Hiking: The *Old Grade Nature Trail* is a 1.5-mile loop with eight interpretive displays and a trailhead near site No. 6. You begin in a low-lying woods and quickly cross a stream but within a quarter of a mile are on the banks of the Little Manistee River, one of the most beautiful trout streams on the west side of the state. Within a half mile the trail merges into the old railroad grade and leads you past patches of wild strawberries and raspberries on the way back to the campground.

Fishing: The Little Manistee is best known as a steelhead stream (see Driftwood Valley Campground) but this far upstream it is often fished for brown trout and rainbows. Below the campground the river is 25 yards wide with a mix of gravel and sand. The river is lightly fished through much of the summer and can be easily accessed from angler's paths that depart from the Old Grade Nature Trail. Fly fishermen will find inviting pools and good hatches of caddis, Sulphurs, brown brakes and Hexagenia here. Best of all, the river this far upstream is too shallow for canoeists. You should have it to yourself.

Season: Old Grade is open from Memorial Day to Labor Day. It is rare for this campground to be filled on a weekend much less in the middle of the week.

53 Peterson Bridge

Manistee National Forest

Campground: Rustic
County: Wexford   **Nearest Community:** Wellston
Sites: 30   **Reservations:** No
Fee: $12
Information: Manistee Ranger District ☎ (231) 723-2211

In 1925, Gideon Gerhardt stopped along the Pine River to do a little trout fishing but when he waded downstream to his favorite hole he found "No trespassing" signs. The incident triggered the *Collins vs. Gerhardt* case and eventually the Michigan Supreme

Court reversed a lower court in ruling that Frank Collins may have owned the land but the river and all streams, lakes and ponds in the state are public waters.

It was a historical decision for all outdoor enthusiasts and today that spot along the Pine River is part of Peterson Bridge Campground. The facility occupies both sides of the blue-ribbon trout stream, with a campground on the south side and a day-use and canoe landing on the north bank. It's a scenic and popular facility, especially with canoeists who can be seen paddling the river from June through August. Thanks in no small part to Gideon Gerhardt.

Directions: The campground is right on M-37, 1.5 miles south of M-55 or 21.5 miles north of Baldwin.

Campground: Peterson Bridge has a loop of 20 paved sites, well separated and secluded from each other in a mixed forest of hardwoods. Six sites along the back of the loop are enclosed by a towering wooded bluff while others are on the edge of a steep bank that leads down to the river. Number 20 is the only one with a view of the water as it overlooks where the river sweeps past the canoe landing.

An additional 10 walk-in group sites are located at the base of the bank along the river and can be reached by a stairway near the fee station though they are used mostly by canoeists. There are both vault toilets and one flush toilet, water spigots, tables and fire rings with sliding grills.

Day-Use Facilities: The picnic area and canoe landing is situated across the river from the campground and is a very pleasant, though often busy, place during the summer. Along with the canoe launch, there are tables and pedestal grills, some overlooking the river, vault toilets, a small shelter, canoe racks and additional parking for the large number of paddlers that depart from here. Next to a historical marker dedicated to the famous Michigan Supreme Court case, there is a group of benches in a stand of red pine where undoubtedly more than one tired paddler has sat down, glad that the day on the river is finally over.

Fishing: The Pine is regarded as a high quality trout stream, holding good populations of brown trout. The stretch upstream between Walker Bridge and Dobson Bridge was once considered the best stretch of water for trout in the Lower Peninsula. To avoid canoeists, fish before noon below Peterson Bridge.

Canoeing: The Pine flows 60 miles from near Leroy until it merges into the Manistee River near Stronach Dam in Manistee County. To paddle the river in national forest land, you need a free permit between May and October and they can be reserved in advance (see the Paddling The Pine asides on page 122) One popular put-in is Elm Flats and it's a 12-mile, four-hour paddle from there to the campground, passing Dobson Bridge along the way. Beyond the campground the final takeout is Low Bridge on M-55, an eight-mile, three-hour journey. Canoes and transportation can be arranged at *Pine River Paddlesport Center* (☎ (231) 862-3471) or *Jarolim Canoes* (☎ (231) 862-3475). River hours for paddlers are 9 A.M. to 6 P.M.

Season: The managed season for Peterson Bridge is May through September and the campground can be filled on any weekend from mid-June through mid-August.

PADDLING THE PINE

The Pine River, already an exciting river to paddle, is getting more exciting. Regarded by many as the fastest river in the Lower Peninsula, the Pine is picking up speed.

In 1997 Consumers Power and the U.S. Forest Service began removing the Stronach Dam in a gradual process called a "staged draw down." Every three months for the next six years, eight inches of the dam was removed, a little more of the backwater disappeared and farther upstream the river got a little faster.

How much faster is anybody's guess.

Mark Miltner of Pine River Paddlesport Center said if we're lucky the light rapids in this stretch could be bumped up a notch on the International Scale of River Difficulty. The Class I riffles could become legitimate Class II whitewater with two-foot standing waves and longer chutes and more obstacles.

Not that the Pine needs anything else to make it more appealing. The scenic, largely unspoiled river is already one of the most popular in the state. The river was attracting 6,000 to 7,000 paddlers on a summer weekend when in 1978 the U.S. Forest Service instituted a watercraft permit system, the first of its kind in Michigan, to eliminate the overcrowding.

A permit for each canoe is now required for paddling the Pine in the Manistee National Forest between May 15 and September 10. With only 658 permits available per day for both private and livery canoes, reservations are mandatory for any weekend from mid-June through August.

The Pine originates near LeRoy in Osceola County and flows 60 miles before merging with the Manistee River. Almost 40 miles of it is floatable in a canoe, making the entire river an ideal three-day float.

The Pine climaxes on the final day, a three-hour paddle from Peterson Bridge Campground to Low Bridge, the last access point just before the Pine flows underneath M-55 and into backwaters of Tippy Dam. The first half is nothing but whitewater; ripples, riffles and small rapids along every bend, sets of standing waves and a handful of small chutes that canoes glide through.

For more information or to reserve a permit for the Pine River call the Baldwin Ranger Station (☎(231) 745-4631) or Pine River Paddlesport Center (☎(231) 862-3471).

54 Sand Lake

Manistee
National Forest

Campground: Rustic
County: Manistee   **Nearest Community:** Wellston
Sites: 45   **Reservations:** No
Fee: $14
Information: Manistee Ranger District ☎ (231) 723-2211

Vault toilets get you down? So do modern campgrounds with their crowded sites? Sand Lake in the Manistee National Forest is an excellent compromise. Sites here are well spread out in a heavily forested area. Some are even off by themselves.

Yet at this national forest facility you can reserve a site in advance, though it is usually not necessary, not even on most weekends. Best of all for some people, Sand Lake has flush toilets as well as old-fashioned vault toilets. Sometimes that's all you need to get Mom to go camping.

Directions: From M-55 head to Wellston and then turn south on Seaman Road. Follow the road 4.5 miles as it passes through the village of Dublin. A mile south of Dublin, turn west on Forest Service Road 5728 where the campground is posted.

Campground: Sand Lake has three loops of 45 sites with tables, fire rings with sliding grills and paved spurs. The loops with sites 1 through 30 on them are in a hilly area forested in a variety of hardwoods. The sites here are well separated and some totally off by themselves without a neighbor in view. There are none directly on Sand Lake but a handful (sites 16-19) are conveniently located next to a stairway that leads directly to the campground's beach. Other facilities on the loops include flush toilets, vault toilets and spigots for water.

Day-Use Facilities: The campground has a beautiful and very wide beach with a marked swimming area, bathhouse and separate parking lot. During the summer a lifeguard arrives at 11 A.M. Located on a bluff overlooking the beach is a small picnic area with tables and grills. The campground managers charge $1 per adult and 50 cents per child as a day-use fee to non-campers.

Fishing: The campground has a ramp area for carry-in boats only with additional parking for anglers but it's $4 for non-campers to launch. Canoes and rowboats are available for rent during the summer.

Sand Lake has 50 surface acres and a shoreline that, except for the small portion in the campground, is privately owned. There are many cottages yet the lake doesn't appear to be

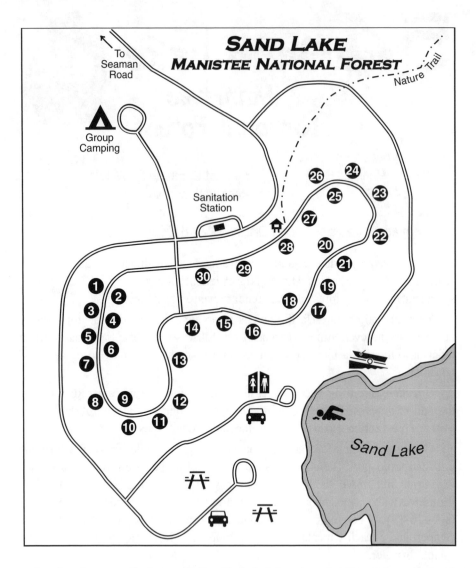

as developed as many further south. Sand Lake's fishery is a mixed bag. It's stocked with rainbow trout but many anglers target it for bass while others are just happy to catch a few perch or bluegill.

Hiking: There's a short nature trail here that is less than a mile long and begins across from site No. 28. It has 12 interpretive posts but you might be hard-pressed to find the corresponding guide.

Season: The campground is managed from Memorial Day through Labor Day. Sand Lake is rarely full in the middle of the week and open sites exist even on many weekends. You can reserve group sites ($17 per night) through the National Recreational Reservation Service at ☎ (877) 444-6777 or *www.reserveusa.com* but not individual sites.

55

Lake Michigan

Manistee National Forest

Campground: Rustic
County: Mason
Sites: 99
Fee: $13
Nearest Community: Manistee
Reservations: No
Information: Manistee Ranger District ☎ (231) 723-2211

Even though it's a rustic facility, the Lake Michigan Recreation Area is the most popular unit in the national forest and probably one of the most popular campgrounds anywhere in the state. Located 13 miles south of Manistee on the edge of the Nordhouse Dunes Wilderness, the U.S. Forest facility was once called by *Family Circle* magazine "one of the 20 best campgrounds in America."

It's easy to understand why.

The beach is beautiful, the dunes provide spectacular vistas, there are great hiking opportunities into the Nordhouse Dunes and just getting to the campground provides a sense of adventure. The recreation area is at the end of Lake Michigan Road (FR 5629), an eight-mile drive from US-31 through nothing but woods. Arrive at dawn or dusk and chances are you'll spot a handful if not a dozen or two of deer along the way.

About the only thing this campground lacks is good fishing opportunities but there are so many other things to do, you won't miss the rod and reel for a few days.

Directions: To reach the campground from Manistee head south on US-31 for 10 miles and then right at Lake Michigan Road. The recreation area is reached in eight miles at the end of the road. If coming from Ludington, Lake Michigan Road is 11.5 miles north of the junction of US-31 and US-10 in Scottville.

Campground: The 99 sites are located on four loops of 25 each. Hemlock and Orchid loops are the most popular due to their close proximity to the beach access point and their flush toilets. The other loops have vault toilets. The campsites are spacious and well spread out in an area forested in pines and hardwoods, especially oak trees. There is a fire ring, table and a lantern post at each site.

There are no showers but what a beach!

A forested dune separates the sites from Lake Michigan and access to the beach is where Porter Creek empties into the Great Lake. Stone and woodchip paths lead from all

A camper heads out to the beach at the Lake Michigan Recreation Area.

the loops to a wooden walkway that serves as entry to a beautiful stretch of golden sand and turquoise surf. If the night is clear you can sit on a bench or the small foredunes and watch a dying sun melt into the dark blue horizon of Lake Michigan.

Day-Use Facilities: North of Porter Creek is a day-use area with playground equipment, tables, pedestal grills and two small shelters as well as vault toilets and its own beach access. Paths and a footbridge allow campers to cross over and climb the observation deck in the day-use area, one of the two found here. It's 167 steps up to the top of a towering dune but well worth it. From the viewing platform on a clear day you can see miles of beach, acres of dunes and to the south the distinctive black and white tower of the Big Point Sable Lighthouse in Ludington State Park.

Hiking: The second observation deck is reached via a long staircase from the beach walkway near the campground. The view is not nearly as good but located next to the platform is the trailhead for the Nordhouse Dunes Wilderness, the only federally-designated wilderness in the Lower Peninsula.

There's a 10-mile network of foot paths in the 3,450-acre preserve, including *Arrowhead Trail,* a 0.8-mile loop that is ideal for families with young children. If a child can climb the 122 steps to the observation deck, he or she can handle this short trail. Even better is

LAKE MICHIGAN RECREATION AREA

the route that parallels the shoreline along the crest of a dune. At one time referred to as the *Michigan Trail*, this hike is an enchanting walk where you stroll while viewing the white sandy beach below or the endless blue of Lake Michigan on the horizon. Return on the first spur back from this trail and it makes for a 2.4-mile loop. Those up for an easy but all-day adventure can hike the beach all the way to the Big Point Sable Lighthouse, a round-trip of eight miles to the historical tower.

Season: The managed season is April 1 through October but the campground is open year-round unless the access road is closed by snowfall. The facility is often filled from Thursday through Sunday from July 4 through early August. Group sites ($35 to $50 per night) can be reserved at ☎ (877) 444-6777 or *www.reserveusa.com*. Individual sites are first-come, first-served only.

56

Seaton Creek

Manistee National Forest

Campground: Rustic
County: Wexford   **Nearest Community:** Mesick
Sites: 17   **Reservations:** No
Fee: $12
Information: Manistee Ranger District ☎ (231) 723-2211

Situated in a remote area on the backwaters of Hodenpyl Dam Pond, Seaton Creek Campground is hard to find, but once located is a very enjoyable spot to spend a weekend. The rustic campground is situated on a bluff above where its namesake creek flows into west end of this impoundment of the Manistee River.

This is a section of the Manistee National Forest with lots to do, including excellent opportunities for fishing, canoeing and morel hunting in the spring. Hikers have it even better. Located within the campground is the trailhead for the Manistee River Trail, an 11.5-mile route along the river, while nearby a footbridge leads across the Manistee River to a segment of the North Country Trail.

Directions: From Mesick head south six miles on M-37 and then turn right on 26-Mile Road near Yuma. Follow it for 1.7 miles then turn right on Fork Road (also labeled O'Rourke Drive on some maps) for 1.3 miles and right again on Forest Road 5993. The campground is 0.4 miles at the end of FR 5993.

Campground: Seaton Creek has 17 sites on a single loop in a wooded area that offers good privacy between campers. The sites are gravel spurs and 13 of them are pull-through making it easier for those who arrive in trailers and pop-ups.

Other amenities include four vault toilets, fire rings, tables and a hand pump for water.

Day-Use Facilities: There is a small picnic area closer to the edge of the bluff overlooking Seaton Creek. From here trails and steps lead to the water below and then upstream along the creek providing shore anglers with many places to cast.

Hiking: Within the picnic area is the trailhead for the *Manistee River Trail*, which extends 11.5 miles along the east side of the river to Red Bridge on Coates Highway. Built in 1990, this is a very scenic trail that passes many spots to view the river. It is also relatively level with few major hills or ridges to climb, unlike the *North Country Trail* on the west side of the river.

A popular dayhike is to a small waterfall along the trail, a round-trip trek of six miles

Forest Road 5993
To Fork Road

SEATON CREEK
NATIONAL FOREST
CAMPGROUND

from the campground. In the middle of the summer the falls are not overly impressive but in the spring or after a hard rainfall the cascade can be an eight-foot leap toward the river.

Within 1.25 miles of the campground you pass an impressive suspension bridge that spans 245 feet across the Manistee River just below the Hodenpyl Dam. On the other side of the footbridge is the Manistee Segment of the *North Country Trail,* which winds nine miles south to Red Bridge. Unlike the *Manistee River Trail*, this section of the NCT is a rugged trek with considerable climbing. When the two trails are combined, they form a 20-mile loop for backpackers, a two- to three-day trek from Seaton Creek Campground.

Canoeing: A trail and stairway lead from the picnic area to a small dock where paddlers can drop a canoe into Seaton Creek. The creek here is a sluggish body of water and easy to paddle. You can also dip into Hodenpyl Dam Pond but paddlers need to remember to stay well away from the nearby dam.

Fishing: Hodenpyl Dam Pond is a 1,798-acre, five-mile long impoundment of the Manistee River that was created in 1925. It reaches depths of up to 30 feet and is usually fished for walleye, smallmouth bass and northern pike. Seaton Creek also offers fishing opportunities, particularly for bluegills and black crappies, near the campground and at its mouth into the impoundment.

Season: Seaton Creek is open from mid-May through September. The campground can fill during weekends in July and August but otherwise sites are usually available.

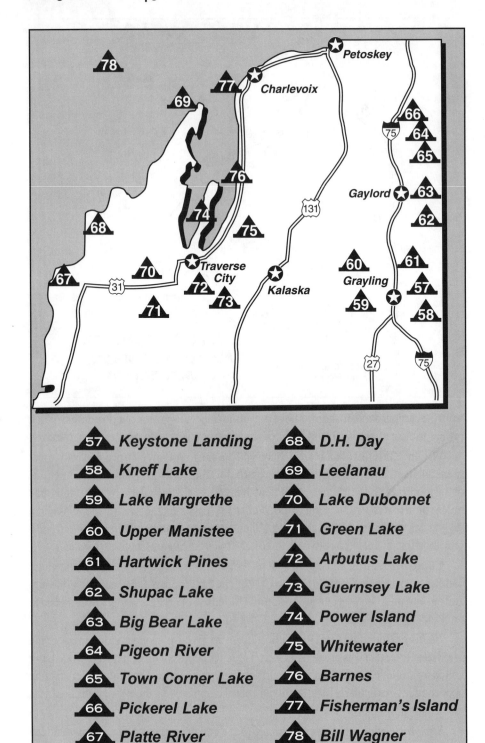

57 Keystone Landing
58 Kneff Lake
59 Lake Margrethe
60 Upper Manistee
61 Hartwick Pines
62 Shupac Lake
63 Big Bear Lake
64 Pigeon River
65 Town Corner Lake
66 Pickerel Lake
67 Platte River

68 D.H. Day
69 Leelanau
70 Lake Dubonnet
71 Green Lake
72 Arbutus Lake
73 Guernsey Lake
74 Power Island
75 Whitewater
76 Barnes
77 Fisherman's Island
78 Bill Wagner

Northwest Michigan

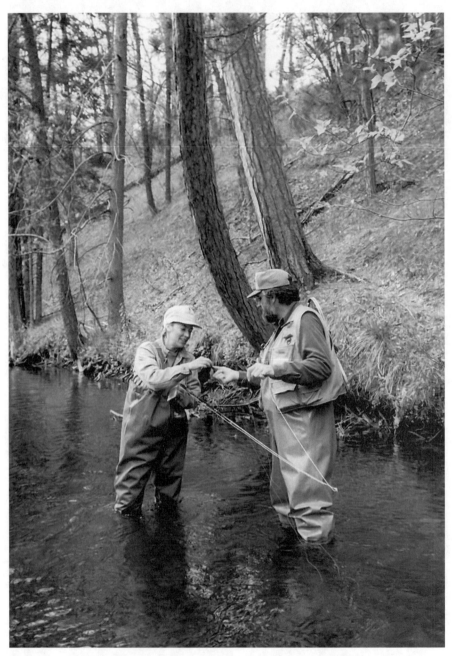

Fly fishers choose a fly on the Au Sable River near Keystone Landing State Forest Campground east of Grayling.

57 Keystone Landing
AuSable State Forest

Campground: Rustic
County: Crawford
Sites: 18
Fee: $10

Nearest Community: Grayling
Reservations: No

Information: Grayling DNR Office ☎ (989) 348-6371

A fly fisher's haven, Keystone Landing is one of several state forest facilities along the Au Sable River. It is a scenic facility overlooking Au Sable's legendary Holy Waters and utilized by both anglers and canoeists. But the campground is not big and at only 18 sites it's easy for Keystone Landing to fill up.

Directions: From the junction of Business Loop I-75 in Grayling, head east on M-72 and then in six miles turn north (left) on Keystone Landing Road.

Campground: Keystone Landing is a single loop of 18 sites located on a bluff along the south bank of the Au Sable. The area is heavily forested with the sites well spread out and secluded from each other. Yet you can wander to the edge of the bluff and spend a quiet evening watching fly fishermen work their magic. Tables, fire rings, hand pump for water and vault toilets are provided.

Fishing: This stretch of the Au Sable is part of the Holy Waters, a flies-only, no-kill quality fishing area with a year-round season. The river is 30 yards wide here, ranging from two to four feet in depth and for the most part can be waded. In May and June this is one of the most popular sections of the Au Sable for fly fishermen to catch both brown and brook trout.

A pair of stairs in the campground provide easy access down to the river for wader-attired anglers. You can also drive past the entrance of the campground and park at the end of Keystone Landing Road where there is a public access site.

Canoeing: The Au Sable is almost as famous a canoe route as it is a trout stream. The river makes for a 135-mile journey to Oscoda on Lake Huron and the most popular stretch is from Grayling to Mio. There are seven state forest campgrounds posted in the river for canoeists between Grayling and Mio. A number of canoe liveries work the Au Sable, including *Ray's Canoes* (☎(989) 348-5844) and *Carlisle Canoes* (☎(989) 348-2301) in Grayling.

Season: From early May through June this campground can be filled any weekend with fly fishermen. In July and August, it can be canoeists who take up all the sites. Getting a site midweek is rarely a problem.

58

Kneff Lake
Huron National Forest

Campground: Rustic
County: Crawford   **Nearest Community:** Grayling
Sites: 26   **Reservations:** No
Fee: $10
Information: Mio Ranger District ☎ (989) 826-3252

In an area of Michigan blessed with numerous campgrounds, Kneff Lake is a delightful little facility that is worth searching for. Although the national forest campground could be filled on a midsummer weekend, it doesn't seem to draw the heavy pressure seen by Hartwick Pines State Park to the north or some of the state forest facilities west of Grayling along M-72.

Yet Kneff Lake features an excellent beach and picnic area and a hilly terrain that allows sites to be well separated and secluded from each other. Kneff is also a designated trout lake but many anglers are dismayed once they arrive to discover that it lacks a boat ramp or any other kind of launch facility.

Directions: From the Business Loop I-75 in the heart of Grayling head east on M-72 for 6.5 miles and then south (right) on Stephan Bridge Road. In 1.4 miles turn east (left) on Forest Road 4003 and the entrance of the campground is reached in a half mile.

Campground: Sites 1-19 are located on Jack Pine Loop and 20-26 on Oak Loop. Both loops are on a bluff that surrounds the lake. Sites 10 and 12 actually have a partial view of the water but the rest are in a forest of predominantly oak with moderate undergrowth; while you can't see the lake, you can't see your neighbor either. A posted trail from each loop leads down to the beach and all sites have a table, fire ring with sliding grill, lantern post, and gravelled parking spurs. The campground also has vault toilets and spigots for water.

Day-Use Facilities: Kneff Lake has a picnic area separate from the campground loops with tables and pedestal grills that are well spread out. But the best part is the beach. The sand here is 15 to 20 yards wide and enclosed by extensive log terraces. A swimming area is marked off but beware—the water is cold and the bottom slopes off quickly.

Fishing: The 14-acre lake lies mostly in national forest land with the exception of a few cottages on the south end. It's a cold and deep lake, with depths of 40 to 50 feet, and once was stocked with grayling in a failed attempt to bring the fish back in the late 1980s. Today it's stocked with rainbow trout with most anglers using slip bobbers to fish worms right off

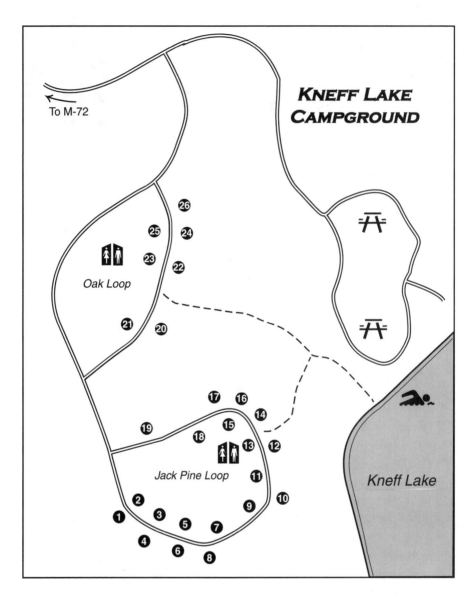

the bottom of the lake. There is no boat launch but it's easy to carry a canoe down to the water through the picnic area. A belly boat would be perfect here.

Hiking: A network of foot trails spans from site to site, down to the beach and through the surrounding hills.

Season: Kneff has a campground host and is managed from Memorial Day through Labor Day. Occasionally the facility will fill up on a weekend but usually you can count on getting a site.

59 Lake Margrethe

AuSable State Forest

Campground: Rustic
County: Crawford **Nearest Community:** Grayling
Sites: 40 **Reservations:** No
Fee: $10
Information: Grayling DNR Office ☎ (989) 348-6371

This might be the only campground in Michigan with signs along one side that say "Military Boundary." But don't worry about tanks from neighboring Camp Grayling rolling through the sites and missiles streaking overhead.

Lake Margrethe is a large but peaceful facility situated in the hilly terrain along the west shore of this popular lake. There is a variety of sites available, including some secluded walk-ins, others on the lakeshore and even a handicapped-access site. The only drawback of Lake Margrethe is its popularity—it's often filled on the weekends—and the lack of a boat launch.

Directions: The campground is five miles west of Grayling. From M-72 turn south onto McIntyre Landing Road.

Campground: Lake Margrethe has 40 sites spread out along many loops on the west side of the lake. The hilly shoreline makes this a beautiful campground with most of it forested in pine and hardwoods. More than half of the sites are situated right on the water with a fine view of this huge lake while others are merely across the park road.

A dozen of the sites, including seven of the first eight, are walk-in; you park your car and haul the tent to the site. Sites 1-3 are at the south end of the campground, off by themselves right on the lake, for a somewhat secluded setting. Sites 35-38 and a few others are up on a small hill from where you park the car and provide a unique overview of the lake.

Overall the sites are close together and lack the privacy of most state forest campgrounds. Site No. 32 is a handicapped reserved site, located next to a barrier-free vault toilet and near a special wood ramp and deck onto the lake. Facilities include vault toilets, hand pumps for water, fire rings and tables.

Day-Use Facilities: A beach and picnic area is located just north of the campground and consists of a separate parking lot and a handful of tables in an open grassy area. No real beach here but the swimming is excellent with shallow water and a sandy bottom in a lake that is gin clear.

Fishing: Unfortunately there is no boat launch within the campground and the nearest public facility is at the south end of the lake in Camp Grayling. Hand-carried boats can easily be launched from most sites.

The mile-wide Lake Margrethe is 1,920-acres large and well developed. An all-sports lake, there is considerable use by motor boaters, water skiers and jet skiers. The lake is a warm water fishery best known for smallmouth bass and muskies though the bulk of its catch by anglers is bluegill and other panfish.

Season: Lake Margrethe's location just off M-72 and the heavy recreational use of its waters makes it a popular facility. Expect it to be filled any weekend from July through August and occasionally in the middle of the week.

60 Upper Manistee River
AuSable State Forest

Campground: Rustic
County: Crawford   **Nearest Community:** Grayling
Sites: 50   **Reservations:** No
Fee: $10
Information: Grayling DNR Office ☎ (989) 348-6371

There are eight state forest campgrounds on the Manistee River and the most popular facility is eight miles west of Grayling where M-72 crosses the famous trout stream. If you camp to get away and value a little solitude in the woods, you don't want to stay at Manistee River Bridge. If nothing else, the fact that it is located across from a canoe livery should tell you something.

Instead, find your way to Upper Manistee River because this far upstream there is less development along the river and far less traffic on it. The campground is more of the wooded setting you expect up north and there's no M-72, a virtual interstate with travelers during the summer, 50 yards from your trailer.

Directions: From M-72, turn north on Manistee River Road, a dirt road that is reached from Graying right before you cross the river. Follow it six miles to County Road 612, turn west, cross the river and then turn south (left) on Goose Creek Road where the campground is posted. The entrance is a mile south.

The quickest way to reach the campground from I-75 is to skip Grayling altogether, depart at Frederic (exit 264) and head west on CR 612.

Campground: Upper Manistee River has 30 vehicle sites on two loops situated in a pine forest with an undergrowth of ferns. The sites are well spread out and a few are along the bank above the river but not within view of the water. There are also 20 more group and walk-in sites in an area lightly forested with little undergrowth. This is a very pleasant section, well worth the short walk in if you have a tent. Many sites are along the edge of the bank with a nice view of the Manistee gently flowing through a grassy area. Facilities include vault toilets, hand pumps for water, tables and fire rings.

Fishing: The upper Manistee is a popular fly fishing area for rainbow and brown trout. The river has been stabilized in many areas while log railings have been constructed along the banks in the campground. This far upstream the Manistee is 15 to 20 yards wide, more than enough to cast a fly rod at the raising rings. Most of the stream is less than four feet deep, and can be easily waded though you might encounter a few deep holes in this area.

Canoeing: Upper Manistee has a canoe landing within its group sites along with canoe racks. Another canoe landing is situated just upriver at the CR 612 bridge. From the county road it is an 18-mile paddle or four-hour trip to Manistee River Bridge Campground. The next state forest campground is CCC Campground, another 30 miles downstream. Canoes can be rented from *Long's Canoes* (☎ (989) 348-7224) and *Shel-Haven* (☎ (989) 348-2158) on M-72.

Season: Normally you can obtain a vehicle site and surely a walk-in at this campground even on the weekends. Just keep in mind that can change quickly if a large group of paddlers passes through.

61 Hartwick Pines
State Park

Campground: Modern
County: Wexford   **Nearest Community:** Grayling
Sites: 100   **Reservations:** Yes
Fee: $29 plus vehicle entry fee
Information: State park office ☎ (989) 348-7068

Loggers, lumber barons and towering white pines made Michigan the greatest lumber-producing state in the country between 1869 and 1900. Only a few parcels of virgin pine escaped the cutting and by far the most popular one is a 49-acre tract north of Grayling, the heart of Hartwick Pines State Park. Within this stand of 300-year-old trees are big wheels, a reconstructed logging camp, and a logging museum that recounts Michigan's White Pine Era.

The interpretive area is fascinating, but there is more to this Crawford County state park than big trees. At 9,672 acres, Hartwick is the largest unit in the Lower Peninsula and features four small lakes, the Au Sable River's East Branch, miles of hiking trails and the newest campground in the Michigan state park system.

Directions: From I-75, north of Grayling, depart at exit 259 and head north on M-93 for three miles to the park entrance.

Campground: Hartwick Pines' campground was rebuilt in 1994 and is now located in a much more isolated corner of the park. The modern campground is almost twice as large with 100 sites. Most of them are situated in an open grassy area but along the edge are wooded sites that offer a surprising amount of privacy for a modern campground.

Along with sanitation for RVers and modern restroom/shower buildings, the campground also has paved sites, many of them drive-through for larger recreational vehicles. Hartwick Pines is the only state park facility that offers full hookups with both water and electricity at 36 sites. Hartwick Pines also has a rustic cabin near Glory and Bright Lakes with a foot trail that connects it to the rest of the park. The stone and log cabin sleeps six and is just off M-93.

Nightly fees are $29 for a full hookup with either 20/30 or 50-amp service.

Day-Use Facilities: Hartwick Pines has no swimming area but there is a picnic area with shelters at the end of the park road. Departing from the parking lot are the trailheads for the *Mertz Grade Trail, AuSable River Trail* and the mountain biking system.

Interpretive Center: The park's stand of virgin pine is best enjoyed by first visiting the Michigan Forest Visitors Center. The history and growth of the Michigan forest is traced through a number of hands-on, computer generated exhibits, displays and photos of the men who cut the trees and the camps they lived in. During the summer the center is open 8 A.M.

to 7 P.M. daily except Monday. After Labor Day, the center switches to winter hours; 9 A.M. to 4 P.M. Tuesday through Sunday.

From the interpretive center you then follow *Virgin Pines Trail*, a paved path that winds through this rare stand of white pine. Along the way you pass a "big wheel," the device used to haul the massive logs out of the forest, The Monarch and a logging camp of several buildings that was constructed by the CCC. Within the camp there is a bunkhouse and mess hall you can walk through, the camp boss' quarters, blacksmith's shop and a steam-powered sawmill.

Fishing: The East Branch of the Au Sable River, which flows 16 miles from its source southwest into the main stream, is especially scenic in Hartwick Pines. Here the river is a crystal-clear stream that gurgles over gravel banks and undercuts the banks around deadheads and trees. Too narrow to be a good canoeing waterway, the East Branch is an excellent brook trout stream. Most anglers are spin or bait fishermen using worms to entice the brookies or the brown trout that have been known to exceed 20 inches at times. Access to the river is along the Scenic Trail, which crosses it twice, or the *AuSable River Trail*.

The state park also has four inland lakes of which three are stocked annually. Bright and Glory lakes lie side by side off M-93, south of the park entrance, and possess a good population of smallmouth bass and are stocked with trout. There is an unimproved boat launch to each lake and a fishing pier on Bright Lake. Hartwick Lake is a short walk from either M-93 or the campground and is stocked with a hybrid strain of sunfish.

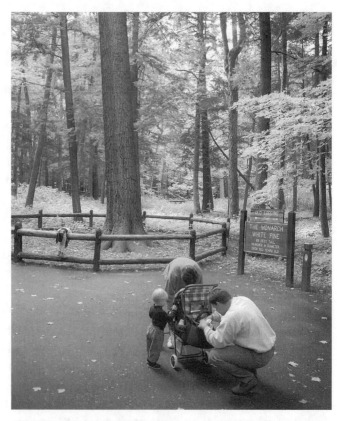

A family pauses on the Virgin Pines Trail at Hartwick Pines State Park.

A MONARCH NO MORE

The Monarch has died. The star attraction of the Hartwick Pines State Park and easily the most recognized and beloved tree in Michigan was a 350-year white pine that somehow escaped the swinging axes of the lumberjacks who marched through Crawford County in the late 19th century. In 1996, however, park naturalists noticed that what little green the tree had produced the year before had not returned. Basically the 155-foot tall white pine, the largest tree most people ever saw in Michigan, died of old age. It overwhelmed millions by its size and grandeur, especially children who would stand there and gaze at that massive trunk and unknowingly gain a sense, and maybe even an appreciation, for old growth forests. Plans are underway to crown a new Monarch, 130-foot tall white pine with a diameter of almost 44 inches, reroute the trail toward the tree and erect a fence around it.

Hiking: Hartwick has six miles of designated foot trails with the longest walk being the *Au Sable River Trail*. The three-mile loop has a trailhead at the day-use parking area and begins by immediately crossing M-93 and then Scenic Trail Drive. The trail passes through a hardwood and conifer forest, twice crosses the East Branch of the AuSable River and at one point reaches the height of 1,240 feet. The *Mertz Grade Trail* shares the same trailhead with the AuSable River Trail but swings south after crossing M-93. This two-mile trail loops around Hartwick Lake before recrossing M-93. The other designated foot trail is the popular *Virgin Pines Trail*, a mile loop through the tract of old growth white pines. All three paths are marked with numbered stops and corresponding trail brochures.

Mountain Biking: The ski trails at Hartwick Pines are open to mountain bikers spring through fall and make for a 10-mile system that basically forms a 7.5-mile loop with two crossover spurs. The route is a wide path through a rolling forested terrain and is rated for beginner and intermediate bikers. The bike trailhead is in the day-use area parking lot at the end of the park road.

Season: The campground is filled every weekend from late June through early October when the fall colors are peaking and 70 to 80 percent filled midweek throughout most of the summer. You can reserve a site by calling ☎ (800) 44-PARKS or online at *www.michigan.gov/dnr*.

62 Shupac Lake
AuSable State Forest

Campground: Rustic
County: Crawford   **Nearest Community:** Lovells
Sites: 30   **Reservations:** No
Fee: $10
Information: Mio DNR Office ☎ (989) 826-3211

Shupac Lake is a scenic body of water and a quiet one by law. Special regulations prevent high-speed boating while the limited number of cottages, mostly restricted to the southeast shoreline, allow the campers on the northwest corner to enjoy a little solitude in the woods.

The state forest campground is a longtime haven of trout fishermen who either take to the nearby North Branch of the Au Sable or fish Shupac Lake itself, which is stocked annually with rainbow trout.

But you don't have to fly fish to enjoy this rustic facility. Practically all the campgrounds have a view of the water, the beach is sandy, the swimming excellent, and there is even a perch fishery to entertain those anglers not interested in tossing around feathers on a hook.

Directions: From I-75, depart at exit 264 and head east. In eight miles you pass the posted side road to Jones Lake State Forest Campground at which point County Road 612 begins curving its way to the village of Lovells. Just before crossing the North Branch into town, turn north onto Twin Bridge Road and in two miles you'll reach the posted entrance to the campground.

Campground: Shupac has 30 sites located on a long loop with almost every one of them on the edge of a bluff overlooking the lake. Situated in a forest of predominantly oak with moderate undergrowth, the sites are well spread out and secluded from each other and many feature their own log staircase leading down to the water. The northern half of the loop is especially scenic as you look out over a small, undeveloped bay at the north end of the lake. Tables, fire grills, a hand pump for water and vault toilets are found along the loop.

Day-Use Facilities: A small picnic area with a few tables is located at the south end of the campground and features a narrow beach of sorts next to the boat launch. No marked swimming area but the water is extremely clear and the sandy bottom gently slopes into the lake.

Fishing: There is a cement ramp in the day-use area with a large parking area, attesting to the popularity of the lake to anglers. Boating regulations include a ban on water skiing and "no high-speed boating" that most locals interpret as no-wake. The deep lake is stocked with rainbow trout but also supports perch and a panfish fishery. During the summer anglers usually fish for trout with corn, live minnows or nightcrawlers about 20 feet down and rigged to a slip bobber.

Just before entering the campground, you cross Twin Bridge, an access point for fly fishermen entering the North Branch of the Au Sable. This is a Quality Fishing Area, meaning artificial flies only. The daily limit is six trout of which brook trout have to be a minimum eight inches, all others 10 inches. The North Branch fishery has long been considered one of Michigan's blue ribbon trout streams and attracts steady pressure. Fly shops in Lovells will be able to assist interested anglers with fly patterns and other access points.

Season: Occasionally this state forest campground can fill on a midsummer weekend but usually a site can be obtained throughout the summer.

63 Big Bear Lake
Mackinaw State Forest

Campground: Rustic
County: Otsego   **Nearest Community:** Vienna Corners
Sites: 44   **Reservations:** No
Fee: $10
Information: Gaylord DNR Office ☎ (989) 732-3541

The main campground on Big Bear Lake lacks a boat ramp as well as the privacy usually associated with state forest campgrounds. But it does have one feature most other units would be hard-pressed to match: a beautiful beach only a few steps from your site.

The clear water of the lake combined with the sandy strip at its north shore is no doubt the reason for its popularity. This is one of the few state forest units that can easily be filled on any summer weekend. Big Bear also features a foot trail, an opportunity to watch beavers and moderately good fishing for several species including walleye and pike.

Directions: From I-75 depart at exit 282 and head east through downtown Gaylord on M-32. The hamlet of Vienna Corners is reached in 19 miles where you turn south on County Road F-01 for 1.2 miles and then west on Little Bear Road to the posted entrance of the campground.

Campground: There are two loops on the lake, each with their own entrance off Little Bear Lake Road. The main loop is called Bear Bear Lake and has 30 sites on the northeast

BIG BEAR LAKE
CAMPGROUND AND PATHWAY

To M-32

County Road F-01

Beaver Lodge Loop

Little Bear Road

Eagle
Roost
Loop

Big Bear
Point

Big Bear Lake

corner of the lake with 15 of them overlooking the beach and lake. The area is lightly forested in hardwoods with little undergrowth thus the lack of isolation from your neighbors.

The smaller loop, called Big Bear Point, is on the northwest corner of the lake and has 14 sites in a thicker forest and heavier brush. Not only is there more privacy but four of the sites are situated on a low bluff above the water with a scenic view of the entire lake.

Day-Use Facilities: A small picnic area is situated along the beach in the main campground and has tables, pedestal grills and limited parking. The beach is nice—the reason this loop fills up first—and there is a large marked swimming area with a sandy bottom that gently slopes toward the deeper sections of the lake.

Fishing: The campground lacks a cement ramp but hand-carried boats are easy to launch from either loop and a few campers even use their trailers along the shore to put in something larger. Big Bear is primarily known as a good walleye fishery with most anglers working the drop-offs with jigs and crawlers to entice the popular gamefish. There is also northern pike as the small loop borders a pike spawning marsh, and of course, bluegill, pumpkinseed and other panfish. One of the best places for children to fish for bluegills from the shore is the sandy spit that extends out from the small loop.

Hiking: The *Big Bear Lake Pathway* is a 2.2-mile trail divided into two loops. Some sections are difficult to follow but it's hard to get lost because you are never very far from a road. One posted trailhead is near the picnic area in the large loop and from here it is a half-mile walk to reach a pond where there is usually one or two active beaver lodges. The trail also departs west from the opposite end of the large loop and from here you skirt the lake, cross Little Bear Lake Road and on the other side come to a much bigger pond with more beaver activity.

Season: This campground is popular and from mid-July to mid-August you might have difficulty getting a site on Saturday afternoon or even Friday evening. I've been here when it has even been filled in midweek but that is rare.

64

Pigeon River

Pigeon River Country State Forest

Campground: Rustic
County: Otsego   **Nearest Community:** Vanderbilt
Sites: 19   **Reservations:** No
Fee: $10
Information: State forest headquarters ☎ (989) 983-4101

Within the Pigeon River Country State Forest, a tract of more than 98,000 acres east of Vanderbilt, are seven rustic campgrounds. With the exception of Pickerel Lake, all are small, out-of-the-way campgrounds in this rugged corner of the Lower Peninsula, home of the largest elk herd east of the Mississippi.

This includes Pigeon River where it's easy to get turned around trying to find the rustic campground...or trying to find your way back to the highway. But that is also the nicest feature. If you camp to escape into the woods, Pigeon River is a good destination, a miles-from-anywhere campground with little more than fire rings, tables and vault toilets.

Directions: The campground is 13 miles east of Vanderbilt and reached by departing I-75 at exit 290. In downtown Vanderbilt turn east (left) on Sturgeon Valley Road and in 10 miles you will enter the state forest. After crossing the Pigeon River, turn north (left) on Osmond Road to arrive at the new forest headquarters, an impressive log lodge. Stop and get a map and then continue north on Osmond Road as it curves and winds its way past the posted entrance to the campground.

A fly fisherman relaxes at site in Pigeon River State Forest Campground while waiting for the afternoon hatch to begin.

Campground: Pigeon River is a single, one-way loop of 19 well-secluded sites spread out along the forested banks of its namesake river. Most of the sites are out of view of the water but a few are right on the bank, including site 19 that overlooks a river bridge and is a scenic spot to park a RV. Facilities include tables and fire rings at most sites and vault toilets and a hand pump for water.

Day-Use Facilities: A small, overgrown picnic area is at the south end of the loop with a table and a grill. The popular spot to picnic, however, is at the bridge. Here the river has been dammed up slightly to create a pool for wading and cooling off while open grassy banks lend themselves well to laying out in the sun on a hot August afternoon.

Fishing: Although many say the Pigeon is not supporting the trout populations it did a decade ago, the river still attracts a fair number of anglers. In June, half the sites here will have a pair of waders drying from a branch in mid-afternoon. In the campground the river is 30-40 feet wide and rarely more than four feet deep, making it easy wading with the exception of a few deep holes. Both brown and brook trout inhabit the Pigeon though you're most likely to catch a brown.

Hiking: The *Shingle Mill Pathway* passes through the campground and crosses the bridge over the Pigeon River here. The pathway is a series of loops that begins at Pigeon Bridge Campground on Sturgeon Valley Road and follows the river much of the way. The hike from the campground to Sturgeon Valley Road and back would be a six-mile trek.

Season: This campground is not nearly as popular as the smaller Pigeon Bridge Campground or Pickerel Lake. On an average July weekend it will be less than half filled. A campground host manages the facility during the summer.

65

Town Corner Lake

Pigeon River Country State Forest

Campground: Rustic
County: Otsego   **Nearest Community:** Vanderbilt
Sites: 12   **Reservations:** No
Fee: $10
Information: State forest headquarters ☎ (989) 983-4101

You'll never had a problem finding an open site in Pigeon River Country State Forest even when arriving on a Friday evening.

That's because spread across the 105,000-acre state forest are walk-in sites for backpackers, two-trail camps for equestrians and six campgrounds for people with a trailer on a hitch or a tent in the trunk. This makes Pigeon River Country an ideal destination when on Friday afternoon you suddenly decide to take the family camping.

If the first campground you pull into is full, just head to the next one. Eventually you'll find an open site. Or an entire campground.

This is particularly true about Town Corner Lake, one of the more remote campgrounds in the state forest. Like the others, Town Corner has sites overlooking a lake, fishing opportunities and a foot path passing through it.

But unlike the others, Town Corner is harder to find. It's best to begin any trip by stopping at the forest headquarters on Twin Lakes Road to pick up a map because there are few road signs in this area.

Directions: Town Corner Lake is tucked away in the southeast corner of the state forest. From the town of Vanderbilt follow Sturgeon Valley Road east to enter the state forest. Pass Pigeon Bridge Campground and stay on Sturgeon Valley Road until it ends at a stop sign. Head south on Tin Shanty Bridge Road (not posted) and in two miles veer southeast on Chandler Road, marked by a blue-tipped post at the intersection. The campground is reached in 2.5 miles on Chandler Road.

Campground: Town Corner is located on a low bluff along the south side of the lake. Seven of the 12 sites have a view of the water and all of them are located a short walk from the shoreline in a forested area with good privacy between sites.

Hiking: A spur connects Town Corner Lake to the *High Country Pathway*, the 70-mile backpacking trail that winds through four counties in the northeast corner of the Lower

PIGEON RIVER COUNTRY STATE FOREST CAMPGROUNDS

Peninsula. An excellent day hike from the campground is to head north on the pathway to reach the Pigeon River Lookout Tower in two miles.

The 55-foot tower is located on the top of a ridge and the view is spectacular, particularly in the fall. A round-trip outing to the tower is a four-mile trek with a bit of climbing.

Fishing: There is a boat ramp in the campground for anglers who want to fish the lake for bass and bluegill. Others, particularly fly fishermen, will fish nearby Black River in an effort to hook brook trout.

Season: This campground is rarely filled, even on the weekends.

66 Pickerel Lake
Pigeon River Country
State Forest

Campground: Rustic
County: Otsego   **Nearest Community:** Vanderbilt
Sites: 39   **Reservations:** No
Fee: $10
Information: State forest headquarters ☎ (989) 983-4101

How rugged is Pigeon River State Forest? On Pickerel Lake Road is a scenic pull-off with a view of nothing but forested ridges and hills for miles. From there it's a straight drop down to the campground that will have your children gripping the back of your seat and you worried about the trailer. That's how rugged.

The state forest contains almost 105,000 contiguous acres and includes 60 miles of foot trails, 27 miles of horse trail and the largest elk herd east of the Mississippi River. Of the campgrounds Pickerel is on the largest, most popular and, from an angler's point of view, the nicest lake.

Directions: From I-75 depart at exit 290 and in the town of Vanderbilt head east on Sturgeon Valley Road. Ten miles from Vanderbilt turn north (left) on Pickerel Lake Road to reach the posted campground entrance in two miles.

Campground: The north shore of Pickerel Lake was a camp for the Civilian Conservation Corps during the 1930s. There are enough trees for shade but not enough to isolate the sites for the kind of privacy you find in most state forest campgrounds. Three loops contain 39 sites but tables and fire rings are lacking on many of them. None of the sites are on the water or within view of the lake.

Day-Use Facilities: There is no beach on the lake but a grassy area serves as one; the water here is shallow for 30 or 40 yards with a sandy bottom.

Fishing: There is an unimproved boat launch with limited parking for a handful of vehicles. Pickerel Lake is completely undeveloped and has a ban on boat motors other than electric. Most anglers target bass and bluegill.

Hiking: Passing the boat launch area is *Pickerel Lake Pathway*, a two-mile hike that circles the lake. It's marked by blue blazes and mostly stays within sight of the water.

Elk Watching: Just east of Pickerel Lake Road on Sturgeon Valley Road is an elk viewing area. The bugle season, when the bulls emerge from the forests to call in their harem, is best from mid-September through October.

Season: With the exception of Fourth of July, it is rare for this campground to fill up during the summer and even if it did, there are several more nearby.

67 Platte River
Sleeping Bear Dunes
National Lakeshore

Campground: Modern and rustic
County: Benzie   **Nearest Community:** Honor
Sites: 174   **Reservations:** Yes
Fee: $12 to $21
Information: Park headquarters ☎ (231) 326-5134

The newest modern campground in Michigan is also one of the oldest campgrounds and certainly one of the most expensive facilities to build. Platte River Campground was originally Benzie State Park until the DNR deeded it over to the National Park Service in 1975 as part of Sleeping Bear Dunes National Lakeshore.

In 1992, the NPS spent almost $4 million in renovation and then opened what was then Michigan's newest modern facility. And what a facility! It's the state-of-the-art campground, providing modern, rustic and walk-in sites in one of the most beloved areas of the Lower Peninsula.

Directions: From the Sleeping Bear Dunes park headquarters (open daily 9 A.M. to 4.30 P.M.) on the corner of M-72 and M-22 in Empire, head south on M-22 and in 9.5 miles you'll reach the campground before crossing Platte River. From US-31, north of Beulah, head west on County Road 706 around the south side of Platte Lake and then north on M-22.

Campground: Platte River is a large facility of four paved loops in an area lightly forested predominantly in pines. Of the 174 sites, 96 of them have electric hookups and 53 others are rustic. None of the sites are near the water as Lake Michigan Road lies between the campground and the river. At the back of the campground there are 25 walk-in sites where you camp in a much more secluded, wooded area 50 yards from where you park your car. There are also group sites. Facilities include paved spurs, tables, fire rings, a sanitation station and modern restrooms with pay-to-use showers. The fee rate is $21 for modern sites, $16 for rustic and $12 for walk-in.

Day-Use Facilities: The major change in the campground was rerouting Lake Michigan Road and rebuilding the picnic area on the shores of the Platte River. The picnic area now lies across the road from the campground and includes tables and grills within view of the water.

There is no swimming area within the campground but one of the most scenic beaches in the state lies less than two miles away at the west end of Lake Michigan Road. Here the

PLATTE RIVER
SLEEPING BEAR DUNES
NATIONAL LAKESHORE

Esch Road

Otter Creek

Platte Bay

4 Mile Loop

White Pine Backcountry Campground

Otter Lake

Bass Lake

3.2 Mile Loop

6 Mile Loop

Peterson Road

Lake Michigan Rd

Platte River

22

N

Platte River Campground

Platte River empties into Lake Michigan, forming a delightful sandy split that is reached by wading through the shallow current. To the north is a view of undeveloped Platte Bay and Sleeping Bear Dune itself. One of the favorite activities at the beach is to float down the Platte River along the spit into Lake Michigan in an inner tube.

Fishing: The campground has a fish cleaning station because Platte Bay is renowned for its salmon and brown trout fishery during the spring and fall as the fish gather to spawn up the river. The deepwater fishery here is also very productive during the summer but the nearest Great Lakes boat launch is in Frankfort.

Hiking: Platte Plains Trail is a 15-mile network of trails with two trailheads in the campground. The one at the back near the walk-in sites provides the quickest route to the beaches of Lake Michigan, a walk of a little over a half mile. There is also a six-mile loop that begins and ends at Platte River and within 2.4 miles passes the backcountry campsites of White Pine Campground.

Canoeing: The lower Platte River from the campground makes for an easy, two-hour canoe trip while an equal number of people float it during the summer in an innertube. It averages only three feet in depth and along the way passes through a small lake before emptying into Lake Michigan. Riverside Canoes (☎ (231) 882-4072) can provide either canoes or innertubes and are located across the river from the campground. During the height of summer you may want to reserve a boat in advance.

Season: Platte River is open year-round but such facilities as restrooms and showers are seasonal. Since being renovated, the campground fills up almost daily from mid-June to late August. You can reserve a site through the National Parks Reservation System (☎ (800) 365-2267). Only 27 of the 96 modern sites, 10 rustic sites and six walk-in sites can be reserved in advance. The rest are handed out on a first-come, first-served basis.

68 D.H. Day
Sleeping Bear Dunes
National Lakeshore

Campground: Rustic
County: Leelanau   **Nearest Community:** Glen Arbor
Sites: 88   **Reservations:** No
Fee: $12
Information: Park headquarters ☎ (231) 326-5134

D.H. Day was the first chairman of the State Park Commission that, in the wake of a growing number of motorized campers in the 1920s, had the task of setting up Michigan's present system. Ironically, Day's name is attached to one of the most popular National Park Service facilities in Michigan, not a state park.

But the conservationist would hardly mind. D.H. Day Campground in Sleeping Bear Dunes National Lakeshore is an excellent facility, featuring somewhat secluded sites despite its size, nightly ranger programs during the summer and one of the finest beaches in a state known for great beaches.

All of this plus the popularity of the dunes themselves makes D.H. Day Campground one of the busiest public facilities in Michigan. To put it simply, it's filled nightly from June through Labor Day. Either show up early in the morning or keep heading north. There's rarely an open site for afternoon arrivals here.

Directions: From the park headquarters on the corner of M-72 and M-22 in Empire, head north on M-22 and veer left onto M-119. Within five miles you'll pass the Dune Climb and in another mile curve right toward the town of Glen Arbor. Before reaching the town you'll pass the posted entrance to the campground.

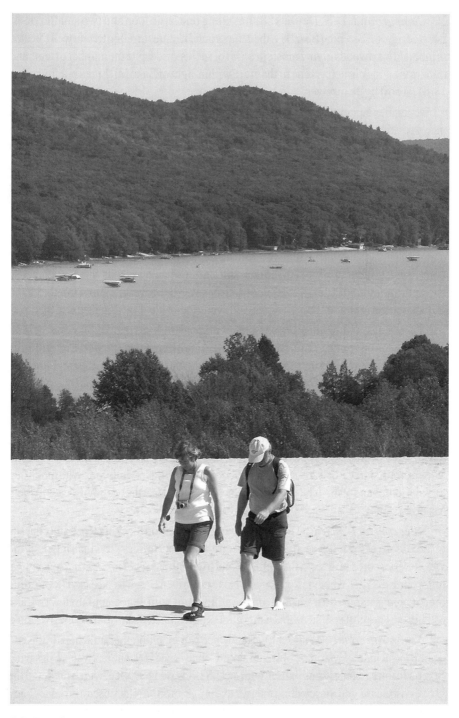

D.H. Day Campground is near the famous Dune Climb in Sleeping Bear Dunes National Lakeshore.

Campground: D.H. Day has 88 sites along one large loop and two smaller ones. Located right off Sleeping Bear Bay, the campground features a rolling terrain well forested in pine and hardwoods giving most sites a bit of seclusion despite the number of tents and trailers they pack in here. None of them are within sight of Lake Michigan but four sites, 58-61, are off by themselves.

Amenities include fire rings, tables, vault toilets and hand pumps for water. Although this is a rustic facility there is also a sanitation station for recreational vehicles along with pay phones and a firewood concession. Site 86 is a handicapped-accessible site and located next to a barrier-free vault toilet.

Day-Use Facilities: In the back of the campground is limited parking for day-use visitors located next to a warming cabin. From here a path leads north to quickly emerge at an incredible stretch of Lake Michigan beach. The sand is as fine as sugar, the water is shallow and turquoise in color and the view from your towel is a panorama second to none on any Michigan shoreline. To the west you can see Sleeping Bear Dune, to the east Pyramid Point rising straight out of the lake and due north are the Manitou Islands with the lighthouse on South Manitou Island easily visible on a clear day. The boat traffic, from freighters and sailboats to the Manitou Islands ferries, adds yet another pleasant dimension to this spot.

There is also an amphitheater, complete with a screen, in a wooded hollow on the west side of the campground. The National Park Service offers a variety of free interpretive programs throughout the summer; a schedule is posted at the entrance to the amphitheater.

Hiking: Although there are no trails that depart from the campground, the northern portion of the Sleeping Bears Dunes abounds with hiking opportunities. The closest and one of the most popular in the park is the *Dunes Trail* located a mile south on M-119. It begins with the steep Dune Climb and then continues another 1.5 miles out to Lake Michigan. Round trip is a good four miles and of moderate difficulty. West beyond the Maritime Museum on County Road 209 is *Sleeping Bear Point Trail*, a 2.8-mile loop with much of it through loose sand of moderately rolling dunes. A short spur at the beginning leads to Lake Michigan.

Alligator Hill Trail is located south of the campground on Stocking Road and consists of three loops of 2.5 miles each. These trails are better for Nordic skiers than hikers as the views are obscured by trees in the summer. Not true with *Pyramid Point Trail,* located 3.7 miles north of Glen Arbor via Port Oneida Road north then Basch Road east. The 2.6-mile loop includes a spur to a high point on Pyramid Point with a spectacular view of Lake Michigan. The bluff is so steep that hang-gliders occasionally take off from the overlook.

Nearby Attractions: Along with the renowned Dune Climb, other attractions in this end of the park include the Maritime Museum along County Road 209. The renovated Lifesaving Station features displays and exhibits on the U.S Lifesaving Service, which predated the U.S. Coast Guard, and a fascinating interpretive program on how they used a breeches buoy and a cannon to save distressed sailors. Pierce Stocking Drive is an eight-mile, one-way loop that you cover in your car or by bicycle. Along the way there is a covered bridge, interpretive posts and several scenic overlooks.

D.H. DAY CAMPGROUND

Lake Michigan

Log Shelter

Amphitheater

To Glen Arbor →

119

Season: The campground is managed by a host in site 82 from June through Labor Day. No reservations are accepted as all sites are handed out on a first-come, first-served basis. D.H. Day is filled daily during the summer, usually by 1 P.M. Plan on camping nearby the night before and arriving between 8-9 A.M. to stake out sites that are vacated. Pitch your tent and fill out a form; then you can continue your tour of Sleeping Bear Dunes.

Leelanau
State Park

Campground: Rustic
County: Leelanau   **Nearest Community:** Northport
Sites: 52   **Reservations:** Yes
Fee: $10 plus vehicle entry fee
Information: State park office ☎ (231) 386-5422

The campground at Leelanau State Park may be rustic but it's popular. Despite the lack of modern restrooms, showers or electrical hookups, the facility fills up daily throughout most of the summer due to both its location and scenery.

The campground is situated at the very top of the Leelanau Peninsula, providing splendid views of where the waters of Grand Traverse Bay merge with those of Lake Michigan. Lakeside sites are plentiful while a short walk away is Grand Traverse Lighthouse, which has been converted into an interesting museum. There is no beach at the tip but an enjoyable afternoon can be spent hiking into the park's separate Cathead Bay area for sand and surf.

Directions: The state park is split between two sections with the campground at the tip, eight miles north of Northport on County Road 629. Access to Cathead Bay is four miles north of the town and reached by turning off CR 629 onto Densmore Road and heading west to the trailhead at the end.

Campground: There are 52 sites along several loops at the tip of the peninsula. Most are situated in an area forested in pines and are not grouped together as tight as the average state park. Almost half of them have a view of the water and 11 sites are right on the shore, combining a little shade and easy access to Lake Michigan. These sites are very sandy but the beach is rocky, poor for swimming but great for Petoskey stone hunters.

The sites have tables and fire rings while nearby are vault toilets and hand pumps for water. Also located within the campground are the remnants of the first lighthouse on the point (1853-1857) in a fenced-in area next to site 47.

Day-Use Facilities: Away from the shore is an open grassy area with play equipment, shelter, picnic tables and pedestal grills. Nearby is Grand Traverse Lighthouse, which was built in 1858 as the most recent in a series of lighthouses that have been guiding ships around the peninsula since 1852. Inside there are displays in several rooms on the first floor and a staircase winds to the top of the tower for an immense view.

Hiking: Most of the 1,300-acre park is an area of wooded dunes and six miles of trails around Cathead Bay. Those intent on reaching the bay's beautiful sandy beach should follow the *Lake Michigan Trail*, a 1.5-mile loop.

Season: Leelanau State Park is open May through October and fills every day from the Fourth of July to Labor Day. Make reservations if possible at ☎ (800) 44-PARKS or *www.michigan.gov/dnr* for this very popular campground.

70 Lake Dubonnet

Pere Marquette State Park

Campground: Rustic	
County: Grand Traverse	**Nearest Community:** Interlochen
Sites: 50	**Reservations:** No
Fee: $10	
Information: Traverse City DNR office ☎ (231) 922-5280	

Lake Dubonnet is one of the largest state forest facilities in Michigan but come evening it can still be an enchanting place. A pair of loons nest here and after nightfall their eerie laugh can often be heard from every site. That wild call along with the fact that the lake, with the exception of one cottage, is totally undeveloped, gives the campground a Northwoods touch, a rarity for any facility this big and this close to Traverse City.

The lake was actually created in 1956 when a stream was dammed to improve fishing and waterfowl habitat. As a result the size of the lake nearly doubled as two lakes were merged into one by the rising water. Across the inlet on its north side is a rustic campground, built for hikers and equestrians following the Shore-To-Shore Trail that passes through the area. Lake Dubonnet also has a handicapped-accessible site located near a fishing pier that is accessible to the physically impaired but enjoyed by all who like tossing a fishing line from shore.

Directions: From Traverse City head west on US-31 and in 14 miles, or a mile past M-137, turn north on Wildwood Road.

Campground: The facility has four loops of 50 sites. But don't despair at its size. The sites are well spread in an area forested with a mix of maple, oak, aspen and even some paper birch with a good growth of undercover. Sites have tables, fire rings and angled spurs that make pulling an RV in and out easy. There are also hand pumps for water and vault toilets. None of the sites are directly on the lake but a handful are on the edge of the bluff overlooking the lake while a few more are located along an inlet. A special handicapped site is located in the second loop and includes a handicapped-accessible vault toilet nearby.

Fishing: There is an improved boat launch with a cement ramp and parking for a handful of cars near the entrance of the campground. Lake Dubonnet has bass and northern pike populations but is best for bluegill and other panfish, especially from the fishing pier that extends out at the mouth of the inlet that borders the campground. This close to shore the fish tend to be stunted but children still find them fun to catch.

Hiking: The *Lost Lake Pathway* begins in the campground near the handicapped site and includes several loops. At one point it was set up with interpretive markers but most of them are now gone and the path itself can be difficult to follow in places due primarily to forest roads and other trails passing through the area. The loop, a 5.5-mile trek, passes some interesting bogs, including one that surrounds Lost Lake.

Season: Lake Dubonnet can become busy during the height of the summer camping season but it is rare for this campground to fill up, even on a weekend.

71 Green Lake
Interlochen State Park

Campground: Rustic
County: Grand Traverse   **Nearest Community:** Interlochen
Sites: 60   **Reservations:** Yes
Fee: $10 plus vehicle entry fee
Information: State park office ☎ (231) 276-9511

Bach, Beethoven and a bass at the end of your line; only at Interlochen State Park. The 200-acre state park is Michigan's second oldest, preserved in 1917 after its virgin stand of white pine had somehow escaped the swinging axes of lumberjacks. But today it's best known as the park next to renowned Interlochen National Music Camp. This might be the only place in Michigan where you bed down to classical music as opposed to campfire songs from the site next door.

Interlochen is actually a thin strip of land between two lakes, Duck and Green, and features almost a mile of shoreline as well as its towering pines. Along Duck Lake is a modern campground and 430 of the park's 490 sites. My favorite, however, is the rustic campground along Green Lake where the sites are farther apart and more private than those across the road. Green Lake is also one of the few rustic campgrounds where you can make reservations.

Directions: Interlochen is located 15 miles southwest of Traverse City and is reached from the resort town by heading south on US-31. The park's entrance is on M-137, three miles south of US-31.

Campground: Green Lake has two loops of 60 rustic sites with tables, fire rings, vault toilets and hand pumps for water. Many of them are along the edge of a shoreline bluff with an excellent view of the water. All of them are spread out in a well forested area that is generally a little cooler at night than the other campground. You give up a shower but you get a lot more privacy in return.

To
US-31

Pines Nature Trail

Duck Lake

Beach Area

Park
Office

137

Duck Lake
Campground

Green Lake
Campground

Green Lake

**INTERLOCHEN
STATE PARK**

Day-Use Facilities: The park's picnic and swimming areas are on Duck Lake where you'll find a wide sandy beach, a designated swimming area, tables and a shelter that can be rented. There is also a boat rental concession that has rowboats on both Duck and Green Lake and is open daily in the summer.

Fishing: There is considerable fishing activity in the park as both lakes are considered excellent smallmouth bass waters with a number of tournaments staged here throughout the summer. Green Lake, however, has a wider variety of fish including perch, northern pike and brown trout as well as panfish. The park maintains three improved boat launches with cement slabs. Two are at the end of each loop in the modern campground and the third is in the rustic campground.

Hiking: The only path is *Pines Nature Trail*, a mile-long loop that winds through the towering stand of white pine and begins in the modern campground.

Season: The campground is open from mid-April to mid-October. The modern campground is filled weekends and often by Thursday from late June through late August. The demand on Green Lake is not nearly as great but it also fills most summer weekends. Either arrive in midweek or reserve a site in advance (☎ (800) 44-PARKS or *www.michigan.gov/dnr*).

72 Arbutus Lake

Pere Marquette State Forest

Campground: Rustic
County: Grand Traverse   **Nearest Community:** Traverse City
Sites: 40   **Reservations:** No
Fee: $10
Information: Traverse City DNR office ☎ (231) 922-5280

A mere 10 miles south of Traverse City is Arbutus Lake No. 4 State Forest Campground, which overlooks the shores of this chain of five lakes. The facility is no more than a 15-minute drive from downtown but a world away as far as this bustling tourist town is concerned.

The campground is unique, built on the side of a hill with many of the sites terraced lots above the water, and the lakes themselves are a haven of boating and fishing activities during the summer. There is also a beach and even a pathway and the only sign that Traverse City is on your doorstep is the lack of empty sites on the weekends.

Directions: From Traverse City head south on Garfield Road (M-611), then turn east (left) on Hobbs Highway. The road is a scenic and hilly drive around Arbutus Lake No. 5 before arriving at the junction with Arbutus Road. Head north (left) and in two miles a sign will direct you to turn west on a gravel road to the campground entrance.

Campground: This delightful campground is basically a loop around a prominent hill rising straight above the lake. Many of the sites can only be reached via a stairway from where you park your vehicle while others are situated on the edge of the bluff above the water and have been terraced to make room for a tent. The view of waves lapping against the shore almost straight below makes these the first sites to be picked.

Most of the hill is forested in maples and other hardwoods but a few sites on the back section are in a small clearing. All of them have a table and fire ring while nearby are vault toilets and hand pumps for water. Needless to say, much of the campground and certainly the most scenic sites are not conducive to recreational vehicles of any size.

Day-Use Facilities: The campground features a grassy area leading to a thin beach and a marked swimming area that is shallow with a sandy bottom. Also in the area are a few tables, vault toilets and a hand pump.

Boating: The campground lies on the fourth lake of a five-lake chain that is popular with boaters. To the north is Arbutus Lake No. 5 while to the south lie No. 1, 2 and 3. An East Bay Township ordinance limits high-speed boating and water skiing on Lakes No. 2, 3 and 4 from 10 A.M. until 6:30 P.M. each day and bans it entirely on Lakes No. 1 and 5.

A new boat launch has been built on Arbutus Lake No. 4 next to the campground. The access site has a separate entrance along Arbutus Road and parking for 20 cars and trailers. A foot trail connects it to the campground.

Fishing: Lake No. 4 has a lily-pad covered bay next to the campground and shore anglers can toss worms and crickets along its edges for bluegill, sunfish and other panfish. The chain as a whole has a mixed bag of a fishery including yellow perch, northern pike and black crappie. It is best fished for bass, with some largemouth exceeding 20 inches in length, and bluegill.

Hiking: The *Chandler Lake Pathway* departs from near the day-use area and is a loop that crosses a dirt road to the campground before passing a picnic area on Chandler Lake at the halfway point. The loop is a 1.5-mile hike through a wooded and hilly area while a spur shortens it to a one-mile trek before reaching the lake. You have to search around to find the trail at times.

Season: The campground is not managed during the summer and all sites are available on a first-come, first-served basis. Arbutus Lake's close proximity to Traverse City makes it a popular destination and often the campground will be filled on the weekends in July and August.

73 Guernsey Lake

Pere Marquette State Forest

Campground: Rustic
County: Grand Traverse   **Nearest Community:** Kalkaska
Sites: 30   **Reservations:** No
Fee: $10
Information: Traverse City DNR office ☎ (231) 922-5280

Located just eight miles west of Kalkaska, Guernsey Lake is a state forest campground overlooking an undeveloped lake with lots of opportunities for fishing, hiking, even an overnight backpacking adventure if you wish.

Small lakes abound in this part of the Pere Marquette State Forest. Surrounding the entrance of the campground are Little Guernsey Lakes, three small bodies of water within view of Campground Road. The more adventurous can explore, fish or camp along Sand Lakes, five lakes in the middle of the Sand Lakes Quiet Area, which has a trailhead in the state forest campground.

Directions: You can reach the campground from County Road 660 just south of Traverse City but once on Scenic Drive you'll find it a very rough ride. A smoother route is from Kalkaska where you turn west on Island Lake Road just north of the McDonalds on US-131. Within 5.5 miles you pass Island Lake then veer to the left on the dirt road and follow it 1.5 miles to Campground Road. Although Campground Road is not posted, there is a state forest campground symbol here. Turn south (left) and the campground entrance is reached in a mile.

Campground: Guernsey Lake has a pair of loops with 12 sites on one and 18 on the other. All sites are situated on a bluff above the lake with stairways and log fences leading down to the water in several places. Forested in oak, maple and red pine, the sites are shaded and well spaced but not totally secluded from each other. A few on the large loop have a glimpse of the lake but none directly overlook the water. Facilities include tables and fire rings, though many are missing, as well as a hand pump for water and vault toilets.

Day-Use Facilities: On a fenced-in bluff overlooking the lake near the boat launch is a pleasant, well-shaded spot that, unfortunately, lacks most of its tables.

Fishing: The campground has an unimproved boat launch directly on Guernsey Lake with additional parking for a handful of vehicles and rigs. Guernsey is stocked annually with rainbow and brown trout but during the summer most anglers end up catching bluegill and, to a much lesser degree, bass. There is a "No Wake" regulation on Guernsey and the lake can easily be fished from a canoe or rowboat.

Nearby are the Little Guernsey Lakes and the one on the west side of Campground Road is the largest and most accessible for those with a hand-carried boat or canoe. Almost directly across from the campground entrance is an unmarked two-track that leads back to another Little Guernsey Lake.

Hiking: Sand Lakes Quiet Area is a 2,500-acre preserve that borders Guernsey Lake to the west with a trailhead in the campground. The foot trail within the quiet area is basically an eight-mile loop with most of the lakes clustered on the west side. It is a 2.6-mile trek to the backcountry campsite on Sand Lake No. 1 if you hike the north half of the loop and 4.4-mile walk along the southern half.

Season: On a July or August weekend this campground could be more than two-thirds full but it is rare to arrive here and not find at least one open site.

74
Power Island
Grand Traverse County Park

Campground: Rustic
County: Grand Traverse **Reservations:** Yes
Sites: 30 **Nearest Community:** Bowers Harbor
Fee: $29.50 for non-county residents
Information: Grand Traverse County Parks ☎ (231) 922-4818

One of the most unusual county parks in Michigan is Power Island and located next to it is one of the most unusual campgrounds in the state, Bassett Island. The unique Grand Traverse County park sits in the heart of Grand Traverse Bay, three miles southwest of the public access site in Bowers Harbor.

The 212-acre Power Island was first called Marion Island after the daughter of a timber baron who bought it in the 1880s, later served as the site of a commercial fishing camp and then in the 1950s was owned by a oil company. In 1975 Eugene and Sadye Power of Traverse City gave the islands to Grand Traverse County to be preserved as a park.

Bassett Island is an islet just north of the much larger Power Island. When the lake level is normal there's a foot of water between them. When it's low you can walk from one to the other without getting your feet wet. Most of the park's users arrive in a motorboat but

A pair of kayakers paddle past Power Island County Park.

not all. In recent years a growing number of kayakers have been paddling out to Bassett Island to spend the night and occasionally even a floatplane arrives for the weekend.

Directions: If you don't have a boat, call Power Island Ferry (☎(231) 929-1004), which makes daily runs to the island during the summer.

Campground: There are five sites at Bassett Island and none offer much in the way of amenities—only fire rings, tables and an outhouse. For drinking water, you have to walk a quarter mile to a hand pump in the day-use area of Power Island. But the setting is well worth the lack of amenities and the extra effort needed to camp here. Every site is along the shoreline and graced with views that include the Leelanau Peninsula to the west, Mission Peninsula to the east and the length of the bay to the north. The sites that face the west allow you to enjoy the spectacular sunsets at night without leaving camp.

Day-Use Facilities: The calmest water and nicest beaches are located on Power Island's leeward side where boaters are protected from the northern winds. This is the day-use area of the park and includes a dock, picnic tables, grills and almost a mile of beach.

Hiking: Departing from near the Power Island dock is the park's trail system. More than five miles of footpaths either skirt the shoreline of Power Island or climb the forested ridge in the middle. The high point of the island is Eagle's Nest Lookout, which rises 142 feet above the bay. From this spot on the ridge you can see all the way to Northport near the tip of the Leelanau Peninsula.

Season: The campground is open from Memorial Day through Labor Day. Because of its limited number of sites, it is filled most summer weekends. Some parties reserve all five sites in advance. By Sunday night Power Island quiets down and in the middle of the week it's considerably easier to get a campsite. Sites can be reserved for the summer beginning in January by calling the County Parks and Recreation Department (☎(231) 922-4818).

75 Whitewater

Whitewater Township Park

Campground: Modern and rustic
County: Antrim
Sites: 55
Fee: $22 to $25
Nearest Community: Williamsburg
Reservations: Yes
Information: Park office ☎ (231) 267-5091

One of the most popular areas to boat in Northern Michigan is Antrim County's Chain of Lakes, a network of 12 lakes and handful of rivers that ends with Elk River flowing into the Grand Traverse Bay at Elk Rapids. What's missing from these lakes are campgrounds. As extensive as the chain is, there is only one public campground along its lakeshore: Whitewater Township Park on the southwest corner of Elk Lake. Thus the nicest features of this 117-acre park is its 2,500 feet of lakeshore and the rare opportunity to camp on a chain of lakes.

Directions: From M-72, turn north on Elk Lake Road, pass through the small town of Williamsburg and continue north for three miles to Park Road. Whitewater Township Park is at the east end of Park Road.

Campground: Whitewater has 55 sites, including 42 with electrical hookups, along with a modern restroom with showers. Although much of the park is surrounded by cherry farms, the campground is in a rolling tract of red pine, providing a forested setting and a bit of privacy between sites not found in most modern facilities. The rustic sites include a handful along the edge of a shoreline bluff, featuring a view of the water through the trees. In fact, there may not be a better campsite in Antrim County than number 13, well isolated and next to an observation deck, where in the evening you can watch the sunset over the shimmering waters of Elk Lake. Modern sites are $25 a night, rustic $22.

Day-Use Facilities: Whitewater also includes a volleyball court, play equipment, bathhouse and swimming area and a picnic grounds with a pavilion.

Hiking: Departing from the campsite is the park's nature trail, a two-mile network of foot paths and benches that wind through the mostly open fields.

Fishing: Elk Lake is the second largest in the chain at 7,730 acres and a popular destination for smallmouth bass. Whitewater Park has an improved boat launch with a parking area for trailers. There is a $5 fee to launch a boat.

Season: The campground is not nearly as popular as the state parks in the area but does fill up on the weekends in July and early August. You can reserve sites beginning April 1 for that summer by calling the Whitewater Township office at ☎ (231) 267-5141, ext. 24.

76 Barnes

Antrim County Park

Campground: Modern and rustic
County: Antrim   **Nearest Community:** Eastport
Sites: 66   **Reservations:** No
Fee: $18 to $22
Information: Park office ☎ (231) 599-2712

The highest speed bumps I've ever driven across are in Barnes County Park. They're so high they're marked on the park map and if you go over one faster than five mph you're likely to leave your trailer behind. But they're simply an indication of the quiet and family-oriented nature of this 120-acre county park.

Barnes Park, half hidden near Eastport, is an extremely clean and well-maintained facility featuring both rustic and modern campgrounds. It lacks boating facilities and opportunities for anglers, but what a beach along scenic Grand Traverse Bay, the reason this campground is filled during the summer.

Directions: The park is 24 miles north of Traverse City along US-31. At the junction of US-31 and M-88, turn west and head a half mile toward the bay.

Campground: Barnes is a single loop of 66 sites and a mixed bag as far as campgrounds are concerned. Half of the sites, 1-35 located along the east side of the loop, are modern with electric and water hookups. The other 31 sites are on the west side and rustic. There is a modern restroom with showers and a dumping station nearby on one half of the loop and vault toilets for the rustic sites on the other half. All sites have a table and either a pedestal grill or a fire ring. Sites range from secluded spots in a hardwood forest to a few near the open day-use area. None of them have a clear view of the bay. Nightly rates for nonresidents of Antrim County are $22 for a modern site and $18 for a rustic one.

Day-Use Facilities: Two shelters, picnic tables and pedestal grills are located in a shady area as you enter the campground. The center of the loop is an open grassy area with play equipment and basketball and volleyball courts. Next to site 66 is parking for a handful of cars and next to site 57 is a change shelter for swimmers. From either one you can access the bay. The beach is wide, sandy and beautiful. To the north you can spot a few cottages but to the south it's nothing but sand and surf as the park includes more than a quarter mile of lakeshore. The bay's sandy bottom makes for excellent swimming.

Season: Barnes is open from mid-May through mid-October. In July through August it's often filled on the weekends even though there are some overflow sites available. No reservations are accepted and generally you can obtain a site Sunday through Wednesday. There is no fee for day-use of the beach.

77 Fisherman's Island State Park

Campground: Rustic
County: Charlevoix
Sites: 81
Fee: $10 plus vehicle entry fee
Information: State park office ☎ (231) 547-6641

Nearest Community: Charlevoix
Reservations: Yes

Half hidden from US-31 south of Charlevoix is Fisherman's Island State Park and those who know about it often associate it with Petoskey stones. The 2,678-acre park is a haven during the summer for lapidaries and others looking for the state stone, a fossil with a honeycomb design.

But the park also features some of the most beautiful stretches of beach in this crowded corner of Lake Michigan. And because of the beach, Fisherman's Island also has some of the nicest rustic sites in the state park system, spots where you can pitch your tent a few feet from the lapping waters of the Great Lake and be so secluded from the rest of the park you practically have a private beach of your own. They're hard to obtain during the summer but thanks to site-specific reservations you can now book them in advance.

Directions: From Charlevoix head five miles south on US-31 and then west on Bell Bay Road. The park is posted on US-31 and its entrance is 2.5 miles along Bell Bay Road.

Campground: The park has 81 rustic sites with tables and fire rings on three separate loops and along Lake Michigan. The loops are well forested in a mix of hardwoods, especially paper birch, and the sites are well secluded from each other. Particularly in the third loop, called South Campground, where there are even a few tent sites tucked up a hill and reached via a short stairway.

But the most popular sites and some of the most scenic in the Lower Peninsula are those along the beach. Fisherman's Island has six sites (No. 9, 30, 34, 37 and 40) right off the park drive where your tent or RV is on a sandy beach and within view of Lake Michigan. They are well spread and for the most part secluded from each other. Some are close to the road but most are tucked away from the asphalt with a beach of their own; such a deal for $10 a night.

Day-Use Facilities: The picnic area is located at the south end of the park drive and includes parking, vault toilets, tables, pedestal grills and access to a beach. A wooden foot

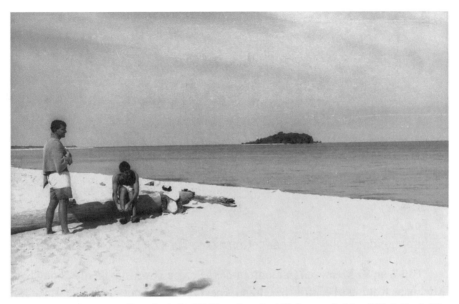

A pair of campers cool off at the Lake Michigan beach at Fisherman's Island State Park. The park's namesake island is on the horizon.

bridge crosses Inwood Creek and from here you can walk over a low dune to more beautiful stretches of sand and surf, totally undeveloped as far as you can see and crowned by Fisherman's Island just offshore. It's a beautiful setting for swimming or sunbathing.

Hiking: The park has a four-mile network of trails that basically forms a path from the contact station to the day-use area with a few spurs, including one to the last loop of sites. There is a parking area near the contact station and from the northern trailhead it's a walk of 3.2 miles to the day-use area and a trek of two miles to the last loop of campsites. The first portion of the trail is a foot path that remains in the woods as you cross McGeach Creek. But eventually it merges into an old farm road and passes through clearings and even an old apple orchard with the trees still bearing fruit. Here you can find some excellent berry patches.

Fishing: There is no boat launch within the park and fishing is limited to river angling for steelhead and salmon near the mouths of McGeach and Whiskey Creek with the best runs taking place in March and May.

Season: Despite being a rustic facility, the campground is full on weekends from the Fourth of July holiday to mid-August, and often daily if the weather is nice during that period. You reserve a site in advance and the beach sites in particular with a site-specific reservations through the state parks Central Reservation System at ☎ (800) 44-PARKS or online at *www.michigan.gov/dnr*. Don't even plan on getting one when you show up. Once in the campground you can also transfer to a beach site if one opens up by being at the contact station at 8 A.M.

78

Bill Wagner

Peaine Township Park

Campground: Rustic
County: Charlevoix   **Nearest Community:** St. James
Sites: 25   **Reservations:** No
Fee: $5
Information: Island Chamber of Commerce ☎ (231) 448-2505

Bill Wagner Memorial Campground is a Peaine Township facility along Lake Michigan, features a beautiful beach and is never crowded, not even on Fourth of July weekend. The catch? It's located on Beaver Island.

A two-hour ferry ride from Charlevoix, Beaver Island is spread over 37,385 acres and has 41 miles of shoreline, making it the third largest island in the Great Lakes. There are two public campgrounds on the island with Bill Wagner being the most pleasant one by far. Despite the cost of getting across, Beaver Island makes for a very unusual weekend camping trip. There are several interesting museums in St. James, lighthouses to view and some scenic mountain biking along the island's two-track roads.

Directions: The round trip fare is $122 to take your car to the island and that's above and beyond the fares for passengers. You also can rent a car in St. James for $60 a day or simply pay a small fare to have the Island Tours and Transit bus drop you off at the campground. For more information call Beaver Island Boat Company (☎(888) 446-4095), Beaver Island Chamber of Commerce (☎(231) 448-2505) or Island Tours & Transit (☎ (231) 448-2500).

Once in St. James, head south on The Kings's Highway, the only paved road outside the town, for six miles and then east on Hannigan's Road. Within 1.5 miles Hannigan's Road comes to an intersection with East Side Drive. The campground entrance is just south on East Side Drive.

Campground: Wagner has 25 rustic sites well scattered in a stand of red pine. None of the sites are directly on Lake Michigan but all are only a short walk away. Facilities include tables, outhouses and a hand pump for water.

Day-Use Facilities: The campground is on Big Sand Bay, a sweeping shoreline of sand where you can stroll for more than three miles. The lake here is shallow enough for swimming while the beach is ideal for falling asleep under the shade of a pine tree.

Hiking: Across from the campground entrance on East Side Drive is the Beaver Island

Nature Trail, a state forest pathway that leads 2.5 miles to Oil Site No. 1 in the interior of the island. Keep in mind that the trails on Beaver Island are poorly marked and maintained.

Season: Bill Wagner Campground rarely fills up. Early October can be a particularly pleasant time to take a trip to Beaver Island. The fall colors can be stunning at this time of year yet most of the tourists have long since departed.

BIKING ON BEAVER ISLAND

In the summer Beaver Island is a place where you come to escape, slow down, lose track of time and, if you bring your mountain bike, ride the island's 100-mile network of dirt roads and trails in search of isolated beaches. Don't even think about bringing your road bike. Except for St. James and four miles of The King's Highway, the roads are dirt and many of them little more than two-tracks. There is some technical mountain biking along state forest pathways in the southern half of the island but most cyclists simply follow the roads that skirt the shoreline.

Unlike Mackinac Island, the other island haven for bikers, there are cars on Beaver Island but not many. Most of the traffic is encountered in the northern tip of the island where most of the summer cottages are located. Here the riding can get dusty at times. The cycling is much more pleasant in the rest of the island, especially along the forested two-tracks in the southern half.

The perimeter of the island is a long 35-mile day on a mountain bike. Many visitors do just a portion of it by arranging a drop-off through Beaver Island Classic Tours. Before you leave St. James, however, stock up on high-energy snacks, fill the water bottle and purchase a map from the Chamber of Commerce office. There is no place to buy junk food outside of the small village and a road sign on Beaver Island is a rarity.

One of the best places to begin is Kelly's Point in the southeast corner. By following South End Road in a clockwise direction you immediately swing into view of the water and in two miles reach Old Beaver Head Lighthouse. The lighthouse is currently being renovated and is a natural spot to take a break. You can check out a few artifacts inside, climb the tower for a better view at the top or walk to the lake.

Beyond the lighthouse, South End Road skirts Iron Ore Bay and turns to sand so soft it's easier to walk your bike than ride it. But you're well rewarded for the struggle through the open dunes. It's hard to imagine a more remote beach anywhere on Lake Michigan. For a half mile all there is you, your bicycle and one picnic table.

From Iron Ore Bay you continue on West End Road, a forest road that ends in 10 miles at the Beaver Island Airport. The last leg of this 20-mile outing is the northern tip of the island, a four-mile ride from McClauley's Point to St. James.

The Straits

 Petoskey

 Camp Pet-O-Se-Ga

 Maple Bay

 Onaway

 Tomahawk Creek

 Ocqueoc Falls

 Twin Lakes

 P.H. Hoeft

 Lakeshore

 Lake Michigan

 Brevoort Lake

 Little Brevoort

 Foley Creek

 DeTour

 Monocle Lake

 Bay View

 Soldier Lake

 Three Lakes

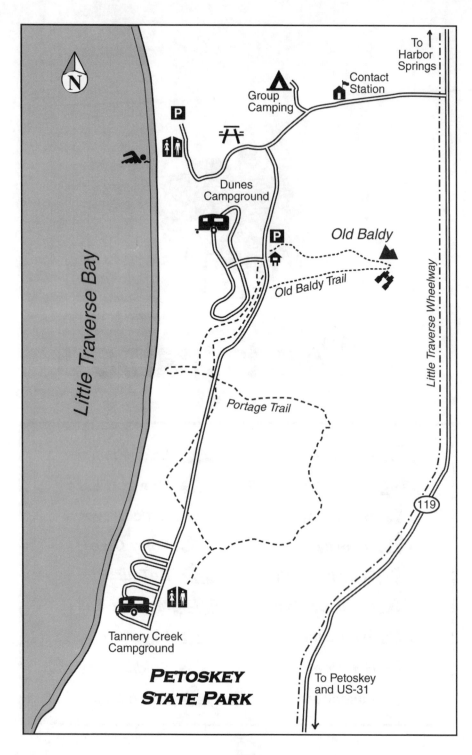

To Harbor Springs

Group Camping

Contact Station

Dunes Campground

Old Baldy

Old Baldy Trail

Little Traverse Bay

Little Traverse Wheelway

Portage Trail

119

Tannery Creek Campground

PETOSKEY STATE PARK

To Petoskey and US-31

79 Petoskey
State Park

Campground: Modern
County: Emmet   **Nearest Community:** Petoskey
Sites: 170   **Reservations:** Yes
Fee: $25 plus vehicle entry fee
Information: State park office ☎ (231) 347-2311

In that commercialized shoreline that is Little Traverse Bay there is one haven from the strip of hotels, marinas and condominiums that begins in Petoskey and doesn't quit until you leave Harbor Springs. That 305-acre sanctuary is Petoskey State Park, which lies between the two tourist towns.

The state park may not be large but it's amazing what it offers: some of the most secluded modern sites in the state, a beautiful beach, good hunting for Petoskey stones, even some short hiking trails. Needless to say, such a facility in a tourist area is going to be filled throughout much of the summer despite its two large campgrounds.

Directions: The park is 4.5 miles north of downtown Petoskey. Follow US-31 to M-119 and then north (left) for 1.5 miles to the posted entrance.

Campgrounds: The park has 170 sites divided between two campground loops. The *Dunes Campground* is the original facility and has 70 modern sites in a forested area of low dunes. For as close as they are to each other, these sites are as secluded as any modern campground you'll find in a state park. The area is heavily forested and the terrain of rolling dunes allows most of the sites to occupy a little nook of their own. Along the backside of the loop, the foredunes are actually pouring into some of the campsites and from here it's only a short walk to the beach. The loop is paved but not the spurs and large RVs might have difficulty with some of the sites.

Tannery Creek Campground is at the south end of the park and consists of four loops of 100 sites in a level, lightly forested area. Tannery Creek lacks that charming seclusion of the Dunes, especially the final loop where many of the sites have no shade at all. Four wooden walkways provide access to Little Traverse Bay and at this end the beach is a mixture of sand and pebbles, dismaying to swimmers but a paradise for Petoskey stone hunters. Both loops have restrooms with showers, sanitation stations, firewood bins and tables and grills at each site.

Day-Use Facilities: At the north end of the park is a shaded picnic area with tables and pedestal grills and the entrance to group campsites. Nearby on the Bay is the beach and a marked swimming area. Here the shoreline is sandy, wide and enclosed by several dunes.

There is a bathhouse/concession store and two parking lots that hold 300 vehicles. The view of the bay is pleasant as you look out over the entire body of water that is often dotted by the colorful spinnakers of sailboats.

Hiking: Old Baldy Trail is a 0.75-mile loop that begins with a staircase across from the camper registration station near Dunes Campground. It's an uphill climb in the first half where at one point you come to a bench and a partial view of Little Traverse Bay at the top of a staircase. That's it for the view as there is none on top unless it's fall. The return is a wild romp down a soft sandy path.

Portage Trail has trailheads near the Tannery Creek restroom and the firewood bin at Dunes campground. Much of it runs parallel to the park drive and is a better ski trail in the winter than a hiker's path during the summer. It does swing east of the road into a forested area of some surprisingly steep hills.

Season: The campgrounds fill daily from Fourth of July weekend to mid-August and are up to 85 percent filled through Labor Day. Reservations (☎ (800) 44-PARKS, *www.michigan.gov/dnr*) are a must here during the summer.

80 Camp Pet-O-Se-Ga
Emmet County Park

Campground: Modern
County: Emmet   **Nearest Community:** Alanson
Sites: 32   **Reservations:** Yes
Fee: $16
Information: Park office ☎ (231) 347-6536

If at Camp Pet-O-Se-Ga you feel like singing Kumbaya around the campfire, go ahead. You won't be the first.

The Emmet County park at the west end of Pickerel Lake started out as a summer camp with boys sleeping in log cabins, eating in a mess hall and spending their days learning archery, canoeing, hiking and swimming. When the County Board of Commissioners purchased the land in 1992 they decided to create a new place to camp during the summer but preserve the history and ambiance of the old summer camp.

Camp Pet-O-Se-Ga dates back to 1934 when Jim Templin, a 23-year-old graduate of University of Kentucky and former Eagle Scout, decided to postpone his business career and open a summer camp on 55 acres of abandoned property where Cedar Creek flows into

CAMP PET-O-SE-GA
EMMET COUNTY PARK

Pickerel Lake. Templin eventually expanded his facility to 300 acres and 19 log buildings, creating a camp that hosted 100 boys.

Templin sold the camp in 1954 but returned after Emmet County purchased the property and organized an alumni group that refurbished the remaining cabins. Today several are available for rent while another serves as a camp museum.

Directions: From US-31 in Alanson head east on M-68 and in less than a mile turn south on Banwell Road. The park entrance is reached within six miles on Banwell Road.

Campground: Camp Pet-O-Se-Ga has 32 sites that are well equipped to handle recreational vehicles. All the sites are wired for electricity and almost half of them feature water as well. Despite being a modern campground, the sites are well spread out in a pine and hardwood forest, where campers can enjoy a wooded and private setting even on a busy weekend.

The county park also has several cabins available for rent. Three of them are small, four-bunk structures called the Honeymoon Cabins that date back to the 1920s when they were rented in Petoskey's Magnus Park.

The two most popular cabins, however, are classic log structures that Templin built for his camp and then refurbished for Emmet County. Both feature electric lights, kitchen areas with refrigerators and stoves, fieldstone fireplaces and a front porch that lets you relax with a full view of Pickerel Lake. The largest one is a two-story cabin that sleeps nine with a bunkroom upstairs where seven beds are lined up side-by-side as if you were at summer camp.

The Honeymoon Cabins are $23 a night for non-county residents and the large log cabin is $70, the smaller one $60. Campsites are $16 per night.

Day-Use Facilities: The most unique part of the park, the area that makes you feel like you're back at summer camp, is Camp Pet-O-Se-Ga's waterfront. It's an open, grassy area bordered on one side by a sandy beach and Pickerel Lake and on the other by a string of cabins and the old mess hall. Flowing through the middle is Cedar Creek. In the back of one of the large cabins is a small museum with historic photos of the summer camp and display cases filled with uniforms, badges and camp song books.

Hiking: The park also has several miles of nature trails. The longest is the *Templin Trail* that follows the lakeshore, climbs up and down a wooded ridge and skirts the north side of Cedar Creek, a cedar-lined trout stream.

Season: Two of the cabins are rented year-round and the rest along with the campground is open from early May to mid-October. The campground can be a popular place on weekends during the summer; it's best to reserve sites in advance if possible by calling the park office at ☎ (231) 347-6536.

81 Maple Bay
Mackinaw State Forest

Campground: Rustic
County: Cheboygan   **Nearest Community:** Brutus
Sites: 36   **Reservations:** No
Fee: $10
Information: Gaylord DNR office ☎ (989) 732-3541

Burt Lake is a busy and heavily developed lake as evident from the line of docks just outside this campground. Still, the 17,120-acre lake is a beautiful body of water, especially on a calm morning when you can sit in the day-use area and enjoy that first cup of coffee while waiting for the sunrise over the east shore. And because of its immense size, there seems to be only minimum conflict between anglers and those zipping across the surface in motorboats or jet skis.

There are two state campgrounds on the lake but my favorite has always been this state forest unit over the modern facility at Burt Lake State Park. Either one has an excellent beach and swimming area and both will be busy through the camping season.

Directions: From I-75, depart at exit 310 at Indian River and head west on M-68 as it curves around the southern end of Burt Lake and the entrance to the state park. In 11 miles you reach the junction with US-31 in the town of Alanson. Head north on US-31 and in three miles head east (right) on Brutus Road. In 3.5 miles you'll reached the posted entrance to Maple Bay.

Campground: Maple Bay is a three-lane loop with 36 sites forested in hardwoods. Six sites on the outside overlook the day-use area and Maple Bay, receiving a nice breeze in the evening. The rest are in a forested area with heavy undergrowth. Though Maple Bay is not as secluded as most state forest campgrounds, it does offer far more privacy than the state park on the southeast corner.

Sites have tables and a fire ring and many feature a pull-through spur, making them ideal for large RVs. Hand pumps and vault toilets are scattered throughout the loop. The two drawbacks of Maple Bay are that the low-lying areas between the sites can get buggy during a wet spell and the raccoons, which are a nuisance here. Every bit of food should be locked in your car.

Day-Use Facilities: Maple Bay features a sandy beach that, while not nearly as wide as the state park, still makes for a pleasant spot to spend a hot summer afternoon. There is a marked swimming area with a soft bottom that is knee-deep shallow for more than 50 yards, perfect for children to splash around. Bordering the beach in a shaded grassy strip are tables and pedestal grills but no playground equipment.

Boating: The campground has an improved boat launch with additional parking for a half dozen vehicles and trailers. Burt Lake is popular with boaters as it is part of the Inland Waterway, an historic 40-mile chain of four lakes and three rivers that was first used by the Indians as a safer and shorter alternative for paddling the Straits of Mackinac from Lake Michigan to Lake Huron. The route actually begins in Conway on Crooked Lake, six miles from Petoskey on Little Traverse Bay, and ends with the Cheboygan River flowing into the Straits. Burt Lake is in the middle of the route.

Fishing: Burt Lake is one of the most heavily fished inland lakes in Michigan. It is regarded as an excellent walleye fishery and anglers are most productive with the gamefish from late May to mid-June and again in the fall. The lake, which is almost 10 miles long, also supports a good perch population as well as bass, rock bass, various panfish species and to a lesser degree northern pike. There are bait and tackle shops in Alanson.

Season: Despite its size, Maple Bay fills up often on the weekends in July and August and during midweek still might have only a handful of sites open.

82 Onaway
State Park

Campground: Modern
County: Presque Isle
Sites: 98
Fee: $16 plus vehicle entry fee
Information: State park office ☎ (989) 733-8279

Nearest Community: Onaway
Reservations: Yes

The perception of state parks by many is a campground where the sites are close together and full for much of the summer. That's true in some units but not Onaway State Park on the south end of Black Lake.

The rolling 158-acre unit is well forested in white pine, maple and oak, attracts an army of morel mushrooms every spring and contains almost a mile of shoreline. But the park's most attractive feature is that it draws fewer than 60,000 visitors a year and a "No Vacancy" sign is rarely seen here.

Directions: From I-75, depart east at exit 310 and follow M-68 to the town of Onaway. Turn north on M-211 and follow it six miles to the park entrance.

Campground: Onaway has 98 sites well scattered on a hillside loop that is lightly forested by towering red and white pine. There are no sites directly on the lake but most of them lie uphill from the shore and have a view of the water. Sites have tables and fire rings while a restroom with showers and a sanitation station is located within the loop.

Day-Use Facilities: There is a picnic area on the east side of the park that includes tables, grills, a shelter that can be rented and parking for 75 cars. But there is no beach and that's the major drawback of Onaway. The only sand is on the west side of the campground and it's a very narrow strip at best. Limited play equipment is located here.

Fishing: Black Lake is the eighth largest in the state, measuring six miles in length, four miles wide and containing 10,130 surface acres. It's a beautiful body of water and regarded by many as one of the finest walleye fisheries in Michigan. The popularity of fishing on Black Lake prompted the Onaway staff to rebuild its boat launch west of the campground.

Black Lake also boasts self-sustaining populations of Great Lakes muskies, northern pike and perch. The rocky shore and points, while not too attractive to swimmers and sunbathers, draws a number of shore anglers to try their luck with long casts.

Season: The campground is open from May through mid-October and generally only fills on Fourth of July and one or two other weekends during summer. You also can reserve sites in advance (☎ (800) 44-PARKS).

83

Tomahawk Creek Flooding
Mackinaw State Forest

Campground: Rustic
County: Presque Isle **Nearest Community:** Onaway
Sites: 39 **Reservations:** No
Fee: $10
Information: Atlanta DNR Office ☎ (989)785-4251

There are three campgrounds in this section of the Mackinaw State Forest and none of them are more than a 10-minute drive from each other. Shoepac Lake offers the best hiking opportunities with the interesting Sink Holes Pathway nearby and the High Country Pathway passing through the area. Tomahawk Lake by far has the best beach and swimming area as well as numerous sites that overlook the undeveloped lake.

But Tomahawk Creek Flooding, at least the east side, has the most scenic views from the sites and the best fishery of the four bodies of water accessible here. Take your pick. I chose the Flooding, but this far north chances are you will find a site in any of them.

Directions: From Atlanta, head north on M-33 for 15 miles then turn east (right) on Tomahawk Lake Highway, which is not highway at all but rather a rough dirt road. The West Unit is posted within a mile, the East Unit follows. Both Tomahawk Lake and Shoepac Lake are posted further east.

Campground: The newest of the three campgrounds in this noted karst (sinkhole) area, Tomahawk Creek Flooding is actually 39 sites split between two units with one on the east side of the lake and the other on the west. The campground was constructed in the early 1980s and its *East Unit* is by far the most scenic. The three loops are lightly forested in hardwoods and on a bluff enclosed by a log fence and overlooking the water. A handful have a spectacular view of not only the lake but the creek beyond and ridges in the distance. Most of the sites have tables and fire rings while vault toilets and a hand pump for water are located within each loop. Long stairways lead down from the edge of the bluff to the water below. The *West Unit* is closer to the shoreline but has no sites directly on it. These loops are heavily forested and the sites are more secluded but the view is not nearly as good.

Day-Use Facilities: Head to Tomahawk Lake where you will find a small but nice beach that is terraced with logs and located in the middle of the campground.

Fishing: Both units of Tomahawk Creek Flooding have an improved boat launch with a cement ramp and additional parking for a handful of vehicles and rigs. Of the four lakes in the area, the Flooding is by far the best with a strong bluegill fishery and other panfish as well as largemouth bass. There is also a pike fishery but the northerns caught are generally undersized. Like most floodings, there is a large number of deadheads, stumps and timber still standing, especially at the south end of the lake. Fishing pressure appears moderate to light through most of the summer.

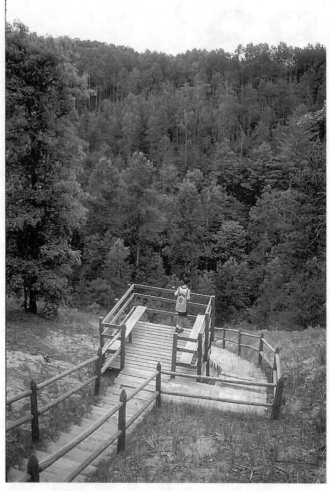

A camper peers into a sinkhole from an observation deck reached from the Sinkhole Pathway near Tomahawk Creek Flooding Campground.

Hiking: Just beyond the entrance to Shoepac Lake Campground is a posted trailhead to *Sinkholes Pathway*. The 2.4-mile loop is an easy to moderate hike around five sinkholes, huge depressions in the ground formed when limestone caves collapsed. The first is the most impressive and is reached only 10 minutes from the trailhead. Also passing through here is the *High Country Pathway*, a 50-mile, five- to seven-day loop that many people begin at Clear Lake State Park to the south on M-33.

Season: All three campgrounds are large and even though some loops are closed due to budget constraints, getting a site in any them is easy midweek or even on the weekend.

84

Ocqueoc Falls
Mackinaw State Forest

Campground: Rustic
County: Presque Isle | **Nearest Community:** Onaway
Sites: 14 | **Reservations:** No
Fee: $10
Information: Atlanta DNR Office ☎ (989)785-4251

Although called Ocqueoc Falls State Forest Campground, the falls, the largest cascade and many say the only true one in the Lower Peninsula, is actually across the street in a day-use area of its own. Even without a view of the small waterfalls, this rustic campground is worth pulling into and can provide you a secluded site among pines and hardwoods overlooking the scenic river.

Directions: The falls and campground are just off M-68 on Ocqueoc Falls Highway, 10 miles northeast of Onaway or 11.5 miles west of Rogers City.

Campground: Ocqueoc Falls is a single loop of 14 sites, all of them near the river, and a half dozen on the edge of the low bluff that towers directly above water. The sites are well separated and secluded from each other in a forest of red pine, paper birch and mixed hardwoods. There are tables and fire rings at most sites, but not all, and vault toilets and a hand pump for water in the campground.

Day-Use Facilities: The posted entrance and paved parking area to Ocqueoc Falls Scenic Site are across the street from the campground. Open from 8 A.M. to 10 P.M., the area has tables, pedestal grills and vault toilets. It's a short walk of 30 yards from the parking area to the river and falls. There is actually another set of falls off the Manistee River in the Lower Peninsula but Ocqueoc is definitely the most impressive. It descends six feet in a series of levels with one drop a particular favorite for children to sit under on a hot summer day.

Fishing: The Ocqueoc River offers a fishery that ranges from warm water species of pike and smallmouth bass in its upper sections where it flows through Barnhart Lake to salmon, brown trout and steelhead in its downstream stretches. Near the campground the river is 15-20 feet wide and can be easily waded in most places. Below the falls it is joined by the Little Ocqueoc River, one of two main tributaries and a noted brook trout stream. During the summer much of the Ocqueoc is not cold enough to hold trout and its heaviest fishing pressure is from steelheaders who arrive in the spring and fall for the annual run.

OCQUEOC FALLS
CAMPGROUND
AND PATHWAY

Ocqueoc River

Loop 3
6 Miles

Loop 2
5 Miles

Loop 1
3 Miles

Two-Track

Ocqueoc Falls

Ocqueoc Falls Rd

68

To Rogers City →

State Forest
Campground

68

Hiking: Ocqueoc Falls Pathway, built in 1976 as a Bicentennial project, begins with a posted trailhead in the parking lot of the day-use area. The trail is designed to be used by both hikers and cross country skiers and consists of three-mile, five-mile and six-mile loops. As far as hiking is concerned, the first loop is not only the shortest but the most scenic of the three.

Canoeing: The Ocqueoc River makes for a 30-mile canoe route that begins at an access site on Lake Emma off County Road 634 and ends at its mouth on Lake Huron's Hammond Bay. You have to portage around the falls and other sections of this river can be challenging. Ocqueoc Falls is the only campground along the river.

Season: This is a lightly used facility that rarely fills up.

85

Twin Lakes
Mackinaw State Forest

Campground: Rustic
County: Cheboygan   **Nearest Community:** Alverno
Sites: 12   **Reservations:** No
Fee: $10
Information: Atlanta DNR office ☎ (989) 785-4251

Twin Lakes is a small, rustic state forest campground on a chain of lakes in the northeast corner of Cheboygan County that provides access to numerous activities, particularly paddling.

Thanks to public access limited to hand-carried boats and strict "No High Speed Boating" regulations by the Twin Lakes Association, this chain of five lakes is a good destination for paddlers during the summer. In the fall, with many of the cottages closed for the season, it is even better. Four of the lakes are sheltered from winds and connected by little passages and channels, making the campground a wonderful place to spend a weekend camping and paddling.

Directions: Twin Lakes State Forest Campground is six miles southeast of Alverno. Head south on Black River Drive for 2.5 miles and then east on Twin Lakes Road for 3.5 miles.

Campground: The campground has 12 sites on a single loop in a heavily wooded setting on a bluff above Twin Lake No. 4. A stairway leads to the shoreline below. All the sites are well separated from each other and isolated from the nearby cottages.

Paddling: The campground leads to a dock on Twin Lake No. 4 but there is no boat launch and that was by design. When the campground was

A kayaker paddling in the Twin Lakes chain.

redesigned in 1974, planners from the Department of Natural Resources wanted to keep this chain of lakes quiet, a concession to the people who had cottages on them. The best way to spend your time at the campground is to arrive with a canoe or kayak and enjoy leisurely paddles. Heading south from the dock you paddle through Twin Lake No. 4 and then squeeze through narrow channels into Twin Lake No. 3 and Twin Lake No. 2. All three lakes are small, under 30 acres in size, and provide calm conditions even when it's windy.

Heading north from the dock you immediately enter Twin Lake No. 5, by far the largest in the chain. In the middle of the lake is a wooded island. Along the shoreline are cottages but many of them are set back away from the water.

Fishing: The chain was originally a wetland complex of old potholes that were flooded to connect them to each other. The water quality is good so the fishing can be very productive at times for a wide range of species.

Twin Lake No. 1, isolated from the rest of the chain by Twin Lakes Road, is a small designated brook trout lake with restrictions on tackle (artificial lures only) and daily possessions. The rest of the chain offers a mixed bag for anglers including largemouth bass, black crappie, bluegill and northern pike.

Hiking: Next to Twin Lake No. 1, a half mile from the campground, is the northern trailhead of the Black Mountain Forest Recreation Area. Spread across this 9,000-acre track of rolling hills and ridges are 30 miles of trails and two shelters open to both hikers and mountain bikers.

Season: This is not a heavily used campground but with only 12 sites can easily be filled on any weekend in the summer.

86 P.H. Hoeft
State Park

Campground: Modern
County: Presque Isle   **Nearest Community:** Rogers City
Sites: 144   **Reservations:** Yes
Fee: $19 plus vehicle entry fee
Information: Park office ☎ (989) 734-2543

In 1922, Paul H. Hoeft, who had spent most of his adult life chopping down trees in Michigan, gave the state 300 timbered acres along Lake Huron. The lumber baron's gift soon became a popular camping area and one of Michigan's original state parks.

Not much has changed since. With few exceptions, the original acreage and boundaries have remained intact. Despite drawing less than 70,000 visitors a year, most of them are campers who can easily fill the 144 sites on any weekend in July and August.

The popularity of Hoeft is easy to understand. The park has a beautiful beach, a series of low dunes for children to climb, a nice network of trails and, if you're an early morning riser, some of the best sunrises in Michigan. Best of all, it rarely seems overrun like so many state parks along Lake Michigan.

Directions: The park is five miles northwest of Rogers City with an entrance on US-23.

Campground: The modern campground has 144 well spread out sites along several loops in a stand of hemlock and pine. There are 15 sites that border the low dunes and provide quick access to the Lake Huron beach. Site 35, though not along the dunes, might be the most secluded modern one in the Lower Peninsula while a few near the road are in a semi-open area.

Along with two shower/restroom buildings, tables and fire rings, the campground features a small store, horseshoe pits, limited play equipment and a firewood bin where timber is sold daily during the summer. There is also a handicapped-accessible site and several mini-cabins that can be rented.

Day-Use Facility: Hoeft's shoreline is a mile of wide sandy beach, ideal for beach-combing or setting up a lawn chair to watch freighters sail by. The day-use area has a classic log and stone shelter, built in 1938 by the Civilian Conservation Corps, that can be rented in advance along with additional play equipment, tables and grills well separated in a stand of pines. There is also a marked swimming area near the campground.

Fishing: Annual plants of salmon, lake and brown trout off Rogers City have resulted

To Cheboygan

23

Park
Office

P

Shelter

Hardwoods Trail

Beach Trail

Nagle Creek Trail

Lake Huron

Birchwood Road

Nagel Creek

To
Rogers
City

**P.H. HOEFT
STATE PARK**

in a strong deepwater fishery within a mile of the Lake Huron shoreline. There is no ramp in the park, but there are launching facilities in both Rogers City and Hammond Bay. The only fishing in the park is at Nagel Creek, which occasionally attracts river anglers in the fall for spawning salmon and steelhead trout.

Hiking: The park has a 4.5-mile network of foot paths that centers around the *Beach Trail*. This 1.2-mile loop begins between sites 21 and 23 and passes through the low dunes before returning through the park's wooded interior. At its east end the *Hardwood Trail* heads south, crosses US-23 and then forms a 1.4-mile loop through a forest of oak, maple and beech. Also extending from the east end of the Beach Trail is *Nagel Creek Trail*, which forms a 0.75-mile loop to the small creek.

Season: Hoeft often fills up on the weekends in July and August and occasionally during the week in mid-August. Contact ☎ (800) 44-PARKS or *www.michigan.gov/dnr* for campsite reservations.

87 Lakeshore
Wilderness State Park

Campground: Modern
County: Emmet   **Nearest Community:** Mackinaw City
Sites: 150   **Reservations:** Yes
Fee: $23 plus vehicle entry fee
Information: State park office ☎ (231) 436-5381

There are two parks in Michigan where you can camp in view of the Mackinac Bridge. One is the Straits State Park in the Upper Peninsula and the other is Wilderness State Park west of Mackinaw City. Of the two…actually there is no comparison between them. Wilderness makes for a far more enjoyable camping trip, offering some of the finest beaches at the Tip, an excellent trail network and fishing opportunities for both children and diehard bass anglers.

The 7,514-acre park has two campgrounds. Pines offers 60 sites in a rolling terrain lightly forested in red pine and oaks. Then there is Lakeshore Campground, a loop of 150 sites with almost a third of them along Big Stone Bay. Quick access to the beach and the beauty of this historical waterway between the Lower and Upper Peninsula make Lakeshore one of the most popular state park facilities.

Directions: The park entrance is eight miles west of Mackinaw City and is reached by following County Road 81 and continuing west on Wilderness Park Drive after crossing Carp Lake River.

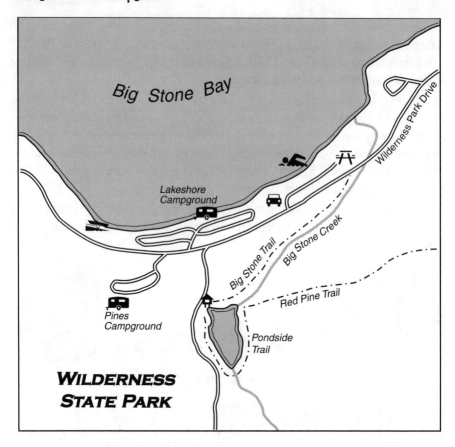

Big Stone Bay

Wilderness Park Drive

Lakeshore
Campground

Big Stone Trail

Big Stone Creek

Red Pine Trail

Pines
Campground

Pondside
Trail

**WILDERNESS
STATE PARK**

Campground: Lakeshore has two loops of 150 sites in a lightly shaded area overlooking the Straits. Forty sites are along the shoreline, many right above the open beach, others are partly shaded and a short walk from the water. Site 38 is a gem, off by itself in a stand of pines. Throughout the loop there is a nice view of the Straits, the Mighty Mac and the Upper Peninsula shoreline. The shoreline along Big Stone Bay is excellent for swimming or just strolling along its sandy beach. Lakeshore has tables, fire rings, two restrooms with showers, a sanitation station and play equipment.

Day-Use Facilities: The park's picnic area is also on Big Stone Bay, just east of the campground. Here you'll find tables overlooking the Straits, pedestal grills, vault toilets and a marked swimming area bordered by a sandy beach.

Fishing: The park has an improved launch just west of Lakeshore Campground. But for Wilderness' most noted fishing opportunity, you don't even need a boat. The rocky inlets and pools along Waugoshance Point are a spawning area for smallmouth bass and when the season opens in May anglers don waders to stalk the beds along the north end of Sturgeon Bay. Drive to the end of the park road and from there it's a half-mile walk to the first pools along the shoreline. Anglers rig up nightcrawlers or use small spinners such as Mepps or Panther Martins to entice the fish.

Children will find fishing opportunities for bluegill and other panfish in Goose Pond. The fish are stunted but plentiful and the most popular spot to toss in bobbers and bait is off the bridge at the south end of the pond.

Hiking: Wilderness has 12 miles of designated foot trails, most of them resembling two-track roads that wander through the backside of the park. But an excellent set of interpretive trails begins at a trailhead on Goose Pond. The *Pondside Trail*, a half-mile walk around the pond, begins here along with *Red Pine Trail,* a 1.25-mile walk east to Mt. Nebo Trail. At this point you can continue on the *Hemlock Trail*, a half-mile walk to the remains of an old lookout tower on Mt. Nebo where there is a partial view of the Straits after the leaves drop. Across from the day-use parking area is the posted trailhead for *Big Stone Trail*, which winds past some interesting beaver activity along the creek.

Season: The campgrounds are open year-round and have electricity but the restrooms are closed from October 30 to May 15. During the off-season vault toilets are installed and water is available from the headquarters. There is an off-season rate of $7 per night. During the summer both campgrounds are filled almost daily from July through mid-August; ☎ (800) 44-PARKS or *www.michigan.gov/dnr* for reservations.

88
Lake Michigan
Hiawatha National Forest

Campground: Rustic
County: Mackinac   **Nearest Community:** St. Ignace
Sites: 35   **Reservations:** No
Fee: $12
Information: St. Ignace Ranger District ☎ (906) 643-7900

Departing from I-75 at the Mackinac Bridge, US-2 heads west the length of the Upper Peninsula before entering Wisconsin and eventually ending at Everett, Washington. It's a beautiful drive but the most scenic section of it might be right at the beginning when it skirts the northern end of Lake Michigan.

From Pointe Aux Chenes until you reach Little Brevort Lake, you enjoy an endless blue panorama of the Great Lake as US-2 is often within skipping stone distance of the water. Most of this shoreline lies in the Hiawatha National Forest and in the middle of eight-mile stretch is the Lake Michigan Campground. Talk about location. This is a beach lover's campground.

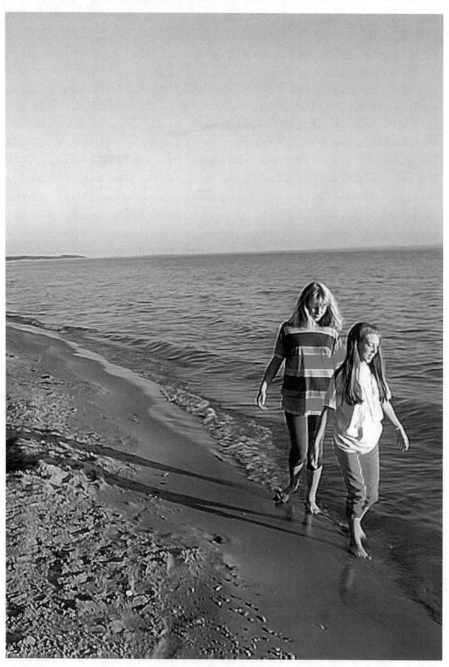

Two campers stroll the Lake Michigan beach from the Lake Michigan National Forest Campground, just a short drive from the Mackinac Bridge.

Directions: From the Mackinac Bridge head west on US-2. Within 11 miles, you cross Point Aux Chenes and from there the highway begins skirting the Lake Michigan shoreline. Lake Michigan Campground is reached in seven miles.

Campground: Lake Michigan Campground is situated on a bluff above the lake with 35 rustic sites separated from each other by towering hardwoods and pines. Half the sites line the bluff above the lake, the other half are closer to US-2. The bad part about this campground is there is no view of Lake Michigan from any site—it's too heavily wooded—and you hear the traffic on US-2 when it's heavy. The good part is you're just footsteps from a beautiful and sandy beach. There are restrooms with flush toilets within the campground but not showers. Other amenities include tables, fire rings and lantern posts.

Day-Use Facilities: The campground has a picnic area with a separate parking lot for day visitors. Tables are on the edge of the bluff above the lake while a stairway leads down to a beach. The sunsets from this spot can be spectacular on a clear summer evening.

Hiking: There are no designated hiking trails at the campground but you can follow the sandy Lake Michigan shoreline several miles in either direction.

Season: The campground is open from mid-May through October. Being right on US-2 and the first facility passed heading west from the Mackinac Bridge, this campground is usually filled on the weekends during the summer and often in the middle of the week as well. If that's the case, keep in mind that nearby there is a large 70-site national forest campground on Brevoort Lake and two smaller state forest campgrounds on Little Brevoort Lake.

89
Brevoort Lake
Hiawatha National Forest

Campground: Rustic
County: Mackinac   **Nearest Community:** Brevort
Sites: 70   **Reservations:** No
Fee: $12-$14
Information: St. Ignace Ranger District ☎ (906) 643-7900

Brevoort Lake is one of the most popular national forest campgrounds in the eastern half of the Upper Peninsula. It offers easy access to great fishing, interesting hiking and the beautiful beaches along the northern shore of Lake Michigan. The sites are large, many are located on the lake and there's even a sanitation station in the campground for recreational vehicles.

The drawback, of course, is that Brevoort Lake is so popular it's filled much of the summer. If there is an open site, grab it. If not, then luckily this is only one of many campgrounds along this stretch of Lake Michigan shoreline.

Directions: Brevoort Lake is located 20 miles west of St. Ignace and is posted along US-2, just past the Lake Michigan National Forest Campground. From US-2, turned north on Brevoort Camp Road and follow the signs into the campground.

Campground: Brevoort Lake is a large facility with 70 rustic sites located along the western end of the lake. The large sites are well separated from each other in a forested setting and 39 of them overlook the lake to provide direct access to the water. Most of them are located along the small peninsula that divides Boedne Bay from the rest of Brevoort Lake. Facilities include fire rings, tables, lantern posts and restrooms with flush toilets but not showers. Sites on the water are $14 a night, inland sites are $12.

Day-Use Facilities: The eastern side of the campground peninsula features a sandy shoreline that is used as a beach and swimming area. Brevoort Lake is also only a five-minute drive from miles of golden beach and sand dunes along the Lake Michigan shoreline. It is a very common practice for people to park along US-2 to spend the day swimming or sunbathing. The sunsets here are spectacular on a clear evening.

Fishing: The campground features an improved boat launch on Boedne Bay with additional parking for trailers and cars. Brevoort is a relatively undeveloped lake that covers 4,233 acres. Its deepest spot is 30 feet but most of the lake is in the 10- to 20-foot range. In the mid-1980s, the U.S. Forest Service built a 2,100-foot-long walleye spawning reef near Black Point in the northeast corner of the lake. Since then walleye fishing has improved along with the lake's smallmouth bass fishery. Other species caught include perch, crappies, panfish and northern pike. Located within the campground is a small store that sells bait and rents boats and canoes.

Hiking: Within the campground is the *Ridge Trail*, a half-mile interpretive loop that rises above Brevoort Lake. Ask the campground host for the accompanying guide to this nature trail. Crossing the entrance drive is the North Country Trail that heads north to cross the Carp River and east toward St. Ignace.

Season: The campground is open from mid-May through October and filled almost daily in July and August. Brevoort Lake is a destination campground with families returning year after year. The average stay is three to four days.

90
Little Brevoort
Lake Superior State Forest

Campground: Rustic
County: Mackinac   **Nearest Community:** Brevort
Sites: 32   **Reservations:** No
Fee: $10
Information: Sault Ste. Marie DNR office ☎ (906) 635-5281

Just west of Brevoort Lake is Little Brevoort Lake, considerably smaller, a little more isolated but with twice as many campgrounds. Lake Superior State Forest maintains two facilities on the lake: Little Brevoort Lake - North Unit and Little Brevoort Lake - South Unit. Of the two campgrounds the South Unit is smaller, more private and closer to the golden beaches of Lake Michigan. Connecting the two campgrounds is *Switchback Ridge Pathway*, an interesting hike through the shoreline sand dunes of Lake Michigan.

Directions: The South Unit is posted along US-2, 1.5 miles before entering the town of Brevort. To the reach the North Unit, turn north on Ozark Road (also known as Carp River Road) in Brevort and then east on Worth Road to the posted entrance of the campground.

Campground: The South Unit is 12 rustic sites well separated on a single loop in a heavily wooded setting. Several are "walk-in" that are reached via a stairway and a few are on a bluff above the lake with a view of the water. The North Unit is a larger facility with 20 sites that are closer together than those in the South Unit. Both campgrounds has fire rings, tables and vault toilets.

Day-Use Facilities: Both campgrounds have a swimming area in Little Brevoort Lake but they are a far cry from Lake Michigan beaches. From the South Unit it's a mile east to the first beaches on Lake Michigan.

Hiking: Within each campground is a trailhead for *Switchback Ridge Pathway*. It's a 1.2-mile walk between the North and South Units or a 3.5-mile loop if the entire pathway is hiked. From the South Unit the trail begins with a steep climb and then traverses the ridge that borders the lake. Along the way to the North Unit you'll enjoy views of Little Brevoort Lake, pass some impressive white pine and hemlock and hike through open sand dunes.

Fishing: There are unimproved boat launches in the campgrounds. Little Brevoort Lake is an undeveloped body of water fished for bass and panfish.

Season: These campgrounds are not nearly as popular as national forest facilities nearby but can still fill up on any weekend summer.

91

Foley Creek
Hiawatha National Forest

Campground: Rustic
County: Mackinac
Sites: 54
Fee: $10
Nearest Community: St Ignace
Reservations: No
Information: St. Ignace Ranger District ☎ (906) 643-7900

The closest campground to St. Ignace is Straits State Park, reached almost soon as you depart the Mackinac Bridge. But a nicer facility is just three miles north of the city: Foley Creek. This national forest facility allows you to escape the summer crowds and the hustle and bustle that St. Ignace attracts as the gateway to the Upper Peninsula and especially Mackinac Island. At Foley Creek you're camping in the woods and are only a short hike away from a federally designated wilderness. Yet hop in your car and you're at Mystery Spot, Castle Rock or any of the other tourist traps that have sprouted at the base of the Mackinac Bridge.

Directions: From I-75 depart at exit 348 and drive first east and then north on Old Mackinac Trail (H-63) to the entrance of the campground.

Campground: Foley Creek has 54 rustic sites that are well spread out on a single loop in a forest of large hardwoods. Only sites No. 2 and No. 4 are actually near Foley Creek. If you want to be near the trail to Horseshoe Bay select a site at the north end of the loop. Foley Creek has tables, fire rings, vault toilets and four sites designated for handicapped campers. There is usually a camp host at the facility throughout the summer.

Hiking: The *Horseshoe Bay Hiking Trail* departs from near site No. 42 and winds for 1.2 miles through to Horseshoe Bay on Lake Huron. This small, 3,790-acre federally designated wilderness was created in 1987 but has changed little since loggers passed through at the turn of the century. For the most part the tract is a series of low forested ridges separated by narrow, shallow swamps, whose dense cedar stands are especially attractive to deer.

The outstanding feature of this wilderness is seven miles of undeveloped shoreline in Lake Huron's St. Martin Bay. The northern two-thirds of the shore includes Grosse Point and ranges from stretches of cobblestone to marsh. But Horseshoe Bay itself is a beautiful beach, where the sand is smooth and the water is a tropical turquoise in color. Best of all, more times than not, there's nobody around.

Fishing: Seven miles north of Foley Creek is a public access site on the mouth of Carp River. The boat launch is reached via Old Mackinac Trail (H-63) and Forest Road 3127 and the river is fished for steelhead, salmon, brook trout and brown trout depending the time of the year.

Season: Due to its close proximity to St. Ignace and Mackinac Island, Foley Creek is often full most weekends in July and August and often in the middle of the week as well.

92

DeTour
Lake Superior State Forest

Campground: Rustic
County: Chippewa
Sites: 21
Fee: $10
Nearest Community: DeTour Village
Reservations: No
Information: Newberry DNR office ☎ (906) 293-5131

As small as it is, this rustic campground on St. Vital Point was at one time a state park. Today DeTour is part of the Lake Superior State Forest and is the only public campground along M-134, a beautiful road that skirts the northern end of Lake Huron.

Directions: DeTour is near the end of M-134, just five miles from the Village of DeTour or a 50-mile drive from the Mackinac Bridge.

Campground: DeTour has 21 sites that are well spread out on a single loop. Many of them are on St. Vital Bay or have a good view of the water. Facilities include hand pumps for water, tables, fire rings and vault toilets.

DeTour
STATE FOREST CAMPGROUND

Day-Use Facilities: Past the Les Cheneaux Islands, M-134 skirts numerous Lake Huron beaches that are not as large as those along Lake Michigan and US-2 but not nearly as popular either. Here you can find a stretch of sand and surf you can call your own for an afternoon.

There are three beaches along St. Vital Point. One is at the end of the campground loop and the largest is in the next cove to the south. Both these beaches face St. Vital Bay and usually have calmer water. The third beach faces Lake Huron on the east side of the point.

Hiking: There is a half-mile foot trail that departs the campground road and swings back to M-134.

Fishing: DeTour also has a public access site where anglers can launch their boats for an afternoon of fishing in Lake Huron. The Les Cheneaux area is a popular destination for anglers to fish for perch.

Season: This is a lightly used facility that only fills up on an occasional weekend in the summer.

93

Monocle Lake
Hiawatha National Forest

Campground: Rustic
County: Chippewa   **Nearest Community:** Brimley
Sites: 39   **Reservations:** No
Fee: $10
Information: Sault Ste. Marie Ranger District ☎ (906) 635-5398

Handicapped campers are still a rare sight at most public campgrounds but not at Monocle Lake, a Hiawatha National Forest facility that in 1994 became one of the first totally accessible rustic campgrounds in Michigan. Monocle Lake was built in the 1960s on the east shore of the 172-acre lake but had deteriorated to the point that in the early 1990s the U.S. Forest Service decided to renovate the entire facility. The Americans With Disabilities Act mandated that any improvement in the campground meet its guidelines, thus every site, every toilet, every pathway was made handicapped-accessible.

Whether you're handicapped or not, this is a first-class facility in a scenic area that can serve as a base while visiting many of the nearby sites, including Point Iroquois Lighthouse and Spectacle Lake Overlook.

An angler casts off the fishing pier at Monocle Lake Campground.

Directions: Monocle Lake is 21 miles from Sault Ste. Marie. From Brimley head northwest on Lake Shore Drive and in seven miles turn west on Forest Road 3699 to quickly reach the entrance of the campground.

Campground: Monocle Lake has 39 sites well spread out in a forest of northern hardwoods and white birch. None are directly on the water but all are a short walk to the shoreline. There are 36 drive-in sites with a hard-packed surface; these are equipped with specially designed picnic tables, fire rings and lantern posts that can be easily used by wheelchair-bound campers. The campground also includes three walk-in sites for tent campers, barrier-free flush bathrooms and a pressurized water system that replaced hand pumps.

Day-Use Facilities: At the west end of the campground is a picnic area with a small swimming beach.

Fishing: The most impressive feature of the campground is a fishing pier that extends 20 yards out into the lake. At the end of the day the pier attracts not only anglers but also any camper who wants to watch the sun set behind the forested ridges that form the west shore. With the exception of a few cottages at the north end, Monocle Lake is an undeveloped body of water with a healthy bass, perch and bluegill fishery. There is a walleye spawning reef near the boat launch and the lake is stocked annually with walleye.

Hiking: Departing from the day-use area is a nature trail that begins with a boardwalk across a beaver dam where at times it's possible to the see the resident engineer at work. From the pond the trail skirts Monocle Lake for a quarter mile and then begins climbing the high bluff on the west shore. Within two miles of the campground the trail reaches an overlook with benches that allows hikers to view St. Mary's River and the rugged hills on the Canadian side.

Season: Monocle Lake is open from late May to mid-October and features a campground host most of the summer. The campground is occasionally full on the weekends but usually has open sites from Sunday through Thursday.

94

Bay View
Hiawatha National Forest

Campground: Rustic
County: Chippewa
Sites: 24
Fee: $10

Nearest Community: Raco
Reservations: No

Information: Sault Ste. Marie Ranger District ☎ (906) 635-5398

Bay View Campground is located on the shores of Lake Superior, only six miles north of M-28 at Raco and 24 miles from I-75. Its two dozen sites have the usual amenities of any national forest campground. But more than half of the sites face the Great Lake, where it's a short walk from your tent to one of the most beautiful beaches in the Upper Peninsula.

Okay, so maybe you can't swim except for those three days in August when the temperature actually breaks 90 degrees. But you can walk for miles in either direction and wonder about the lake they call *Gitche Gumme* and look out where the freighter, the *Edmund Fitzgerald*, sank.

Directions: Depart I-75 at exit 386 (six miles south of Sault Ste. Marie) and head west on M-28. Within 18 miles turn north on Ranger Road to Lake Shore Drive. Bay View Campground is two miles west on Lake Shore Drive.

Campground: Bay View Lake Campground has 24 rustic sites with 14 of them bordering Lake Superior. The facility is forested in white pine, oak, maple and white birch and the sites are well spread out and include picnic tables, fire rings with a sliding grate and lantern posts.

Day-Use Facilities: The campground borders a wide sandy beach, excellent for beachcombing. A mile east of the campground with a separate entrance and parking area is Big Pine Picnic Area with tables and grills. At either the campground of the picnic area, the sunsets are spectacular in the evening.

Interpretive Center: Six miles east of the campground on Lake Shore Drive is the Point Iroquois Lighthouse. Listed on the National Register of Historic Places, the lighthouse was built in 1870 and today contains a small museum dedicated to the lightkeepers who spent their lives saving ships. Even better is the sweeping view of Lake Superior from the top of the 65-foot tower. The lighthouse is open daily from Memorial Day through Labor Day.

Season: Bay View is open from mid-May through October and managed during the summer by a campground host. Other than an occasional summer weekend, this campground is rarely filled.

95

Soldier Lake
Hiawatha National Forest

Campground: Rustic
County: Chippewa   **Nearest Community:** Strongs
Sites: 44   **Reservations:** No
Fee: $9
Information: Sault Ste. Marie Ranger District ☎ (906) 635-5398

Soldier Lake Campground in the Hiawatha National Forest is just south of M-28 and only 23 miles west of I-75 in Chippewa County. Yet it retains a quiet, remote atmosphere and in the middle of the week often less than a third of the 44 sites are occupied. Even on weekends you can usually count on getting a spot to pitch the tent.

Log shelter at Soldier Lake

Directions: Six miles south of Sault Ste. Marie, depart I-75 at exit 386 and head west on M-28. The campground is posted along M-28, four miles before you pass through the village of Strongs.

Campground: The campground surrounds Soldier Lake and 19 of the 44 sites line the lakeshore. All the sites are well spread out in a forest of jack pine, aspen and maple.

Day-Use Facilities: There are two large picnic areas at the northwest corner of the lake. The picnic areas are in an open grassy meadow and overlook an excellent beach and swimming area. Near the beach is a large log shelter with a stone fireplace built in the 1930s by the Civilian Conservation Corps.

Hiking: A short foot trail winds around the lake. For a longer hike, there is a trail that departs from site No. 38 as a two-track and within a quarter mile leads you to the *North Country Trail.*

Fishing: The 15-acre lake is non-motorized and fished for perch. There is no ramp in the campground but boats can be easily hand-launched from many sites and the picnic area.

Season: The campground is from late May to mid-October. Usage is light and it is rarely filled.

SOLDIER LAKE
HIAWATHA
NATIONAL FOREST

To M-28

P

Picnic Area

Shelter

Soldier Lake

Spur to
North Country
Trail

96

Three Lakes
Hiawatha National Forest

Campground: Rustic
County: Chippewa   **Nearest Community:** Strongs Corner
Sites: 28   **Reservations:** No
Fee: $9
Information: Sault Ste. Marie Ranger District ☎ (906) 635-5398

Nestled among three small lakes is Three Lakes Campground, a quiet and scenic spot to pitch a tent or park a trailer. The National Forest facility overlooks Walker Lake and is farther away from M-28 than Soldier Campground, making it not as busy and likely to have an open site even on the weekends. Two of the three lakes offer fishing opportunities while nearby bogs can be explored to view the abundance of insect-eating pitcher plants.

Directions: Three Lakes is 38 miles from Sault Ste. Marie. From Strongs Corner on M-28 head south on Strongs Road (Forest Road 3142) to the posted campground entrance.

Campground: Three Lakes is a single loop of 28 sites along the north shore of Walker Lake. Most of the sites are right off the lake but do not have a clear view of the water. The campground is situated in an impressive stand of white pines and mixed hardwoods and the sites are well spread out and very secluded from each other. Facilities include tables, fire rings, vault toilets and hand pumps.

Day-Use Facilities: There is a picnic area on the east end of the lake that is separate from the campground. A trail connects the two areas.

Hiking: A mile-long loop winds around Walker Lake beginning in the picnic area and passes through the campground. The trail is easy and stays fairly close to the lake in the beginning. At one point you climb a ridge and descend to a view of the small, unnamed lake to the north.

Fishing: There are no boat ramps on the lakes but near the picnic area is a place to hand-launch boats into Walker Lake. It is also easy to launch boats from many of the lakeside sites in the campground. A small pull-out on Strongs Road (FR 3142) allows you to do the same on Whitemarsh Lake. The lakes receive very light fishing pressure. Whitemarsh is reputed to be the best of the three with anglers targeting northern pike, bass and crappie. Walker Lake is the largest at 19 acres and is fished for panfish and bass.

Season: The campground is open from late May to mid-October. Usage is light, even on most summer weekends.

To M-28

N

Brown Lake

Whitemore Lake

National Forest Campground

Walker Lake

Strongs Road (Forest Road 3142)

Walker Lake Trail

THREE LAKES
HIAWATHA NATIONAL FOREST

To M-123

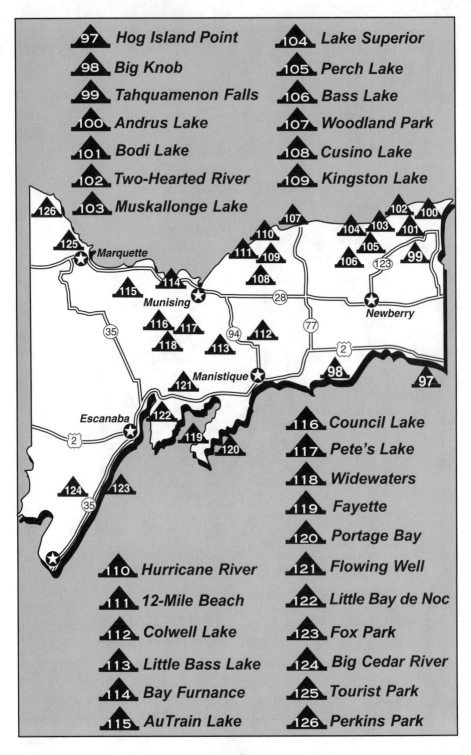

97 Hog Island Point
98 Big Knob
99 Tahquamenon Falls
100 Andrus Lake
101 Bodi Lake
102 Two-Hearted River
103 Muskallonge Lake

104 Lake Superior
105 Perch Lake
106 Bass Lake
107 Woodland Park
108 Cusino Lake
109 Kingston Lake

116 Council Lake
117 Pete's Lake
118 Widewaters
119 Fayette
120 Portage Bay
121 Flowing Well
122 Little Bay de Noc
123 Fox Park
124 Big Cedar River
125 Tourist Park
126 Perkins Park

110 Hurricane River
111 12-Mile Beach
112 Colwell Lake
113 Little Bass Lake
114 Bay Furnace
115 AuTrain Lake

Central
Upper Peninsula

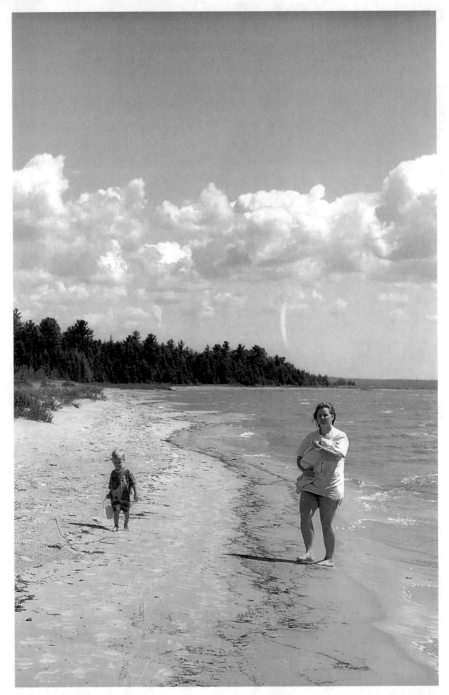

A mother and her son enjoy a morning walk on the Lake Michigan shoreline. Great beaches are a special feature of several campgrounds in this region of the state including Hog Island Point, Big Knob and Fox Park.

97

Hog Island Point
Lake Superior State Forest

Campground: Rustic
County: Mackinac   **Nearest Community:** Naubinway
Sites: 59   **Reservations:** No
Fee: $10
Information: Sault Ste. Marie DNR office ☎ (906) 635-5281

Only a 30-minute drive west of the Mackinac Bridge, Hog Island Point is another in the series of Lake Michigan campgrounds along US-2. The state forest campground occupies a small peninsula seven miles east of Naubinway, providing a scenic setting to spend a night or two.

The east side of the point is formed by a picturesque bay where rocky islets smooth out the surf rolling in from Lake Michigan. The west side is a stretch of shoreline that you can follow almost to Naubinway.

Directions: From the Mackinac Bridge head west; you'll reach the posted entrance of the campgrounds in 35 miles.

Campground: There are 59 rustic sites in two loops on the point with most of them along the shoreline. The sites are well spread out in a moderately heavy forest for a bit of privacy and 17 of them have an open view of Lake Michigan. Facilities include vault toilets, hand pumps for water, tables and a handful of handicapped-accessible sites.

Day-Use Facilities: A small picnic area with a separate parking lot is on the east side of the point, where the best beach is located. Here the shoreline is sandy and a rocky islet in the mouth of the bay protects it from the Lake Michigan surf. The water is shallow but swimmers need to be aware of the undertow. The shoreline on the west side is not nearly as sandy.

Season: Being right on US-2, this campground is often filled on the weekends and can be more than half full during the week. If that is the case, try Big Knob State Forest Campgrounds (see page 210), which is more secluded from US-2 and thus more likely to have an open site. There is also Black River State Forest Campground, which is seven miles northeast of Naubinway via US-2 and Balc River Road, a relatively short drive away. Overlooking the Black River, this campground has only 12 sites but is not filled nearly as often as Hog Island Point.

98

Big Knob
Lake Superior State Forest

Campground: Rustic
County: Mackinac   **Nearest Community:** Naubinway
Sites: 18   **Reservations:** No
Fee: $10
Information: Sault Ste. Marie DNR office ☎ (906) 635-5281

If for some reason Hog Island Point is full, continue west on US-2 for another nine miles and then head south at the sign for Big Knob State Forest Campground. This dirt road winds and weaves its way through the woods and ends at one of the most remote beaches on Lake Michigan.

The campground is located in a mature pine forest just off a beautiful stretch of Lake Michigan. You can stroll the beach for more than a mile in either direction and not encounter a single hot dog stand or cottage. With three interesting hiking trails nearby, this is a campground where you can stay put for a few days.

Directions: From the Mackinac Bridge head west on US-2 for 44 miles and then turn south on Big Knob Road and follow it for six miles to the campground at the end. Big Knob is posted along US-2 but it's easy to miss the sign.

Campground: Big Knob is a single loop of 18 rustic sites that are well spread out in an older pine forest. Seven of the sites face Lake Michigan and have short paths leading through the trees right to the beach. Facilities include tables, fire rings and vault toilets.

Day-Use Facilities: The beach at Big Knob is stunning. It extends as far as the eye can see and is completely undeveloped. You can beachcomb for miles here and the shallow water offshore makes for ideal swimming conditions. The campground has a small picnic area with a separate parking lot and a few tables.

Hiking: Near the campground are three short trails. Departing from the day-use parking area is the *Marsh Lake Trail*, a 1.5-mile loop that begins in the forest but within a half mile begins to skirt several bogs and marshes. Eventually you come to a viewing area of Marsh Lake, a great place to spot wildlife in the early evening.

The other two trails have trailheads across from each other on Big Knob Road 2.5 miles from the campground. On the west side of the road is *Crow Lake Pathway*, 2.5-mile hike

BIG KNOB & CROW LAKE FOOT TRAILS

To US-2

Big Knob Road

Crow Lake

Knob Lake

Big Knob Trail

Crow Lake Trail

Beaver Pond and Dam

McNeil Creek

To Big Knob Campground

Lake Michigan

that swings past views of Crow Lake. On the east side is *Big Knob Trail*, a delightful quarter-mile walk to an overview of Knob Lake. All three trails pass through extensive blueberry patches.

Season: Because of its distance from US-2, Big Knob is not filled as often during the summer as other campgrounds right on the highway. You can usually count on getting a site on the weekends and almost always in the middle of the week.

99

Lower Falls

Tahquamenon Falls State Park

Campground: Modern and rustic
County: Chippewa   **Nearest Community:** Paradise
Sites: 176   **Reservations:** Yes
Fee: $10 to $21 plus vehicle entry fee
Information: State park office ☎ (906) 492-3415

The Upper Falls at Tahquamenon Falls State Park is the most impressive cascade in the Upper Peninsula and very possibly the most beloved natural attraction in the state. The falls, nearly 200 feet across with a 50-foot drop, are often cited as the third largest east of the Mississippi River as only Niagara Falls and Cumberland Falls in Kentucky have longer drops. So spectacular are the falls and its wooded setting, especially during fall colors, that it easily makes this unit the most popular park in the Upper Peninsula with more than 500,000 visitors annually.

The park contains 38,496 acres and stretches 13 miles from Whitefish Bay in Chippewa County into Luce County. There are three developed areas and two of them contain four campgrounds with a total of 319 sites. The most popular campground in the park is Riverbend Campground near the Lower Falls. There are no camping facilities anywhere near the Upper Falls. The other developed area with camping is the Rivermouth Unit on Whitefish Bay

Directions: The Rivermouth Unit is four miles south of Paradise on M-123, while the Lower Falls Unit is 12 miles from the small town where the state highway swings to the west. The Upper Falls unit is 21 miles from Newberry on M-123 or two miles west of the Lower Falls

Campground: The park has four separate campgrounds with two in each of its Lower Falls and Rivermouth units. At the Lower Falls there are 176 modern sites with 81 of them in the Riverbend Campground, including a handful along the river itself. The rest are located in the Overlook Campground, and both areas are well wooded. At the Rivermouth Unit there is a modern campground of 75 sites and a rustic campground of 55 sites.

Modern sites at Tahquamenon Falls are $19 to $21 per night, rustic sites at the Rivermouth Campground are $10 per night. You also need either a daily $6 vehicle entry permit or a $24 annual state park pass.

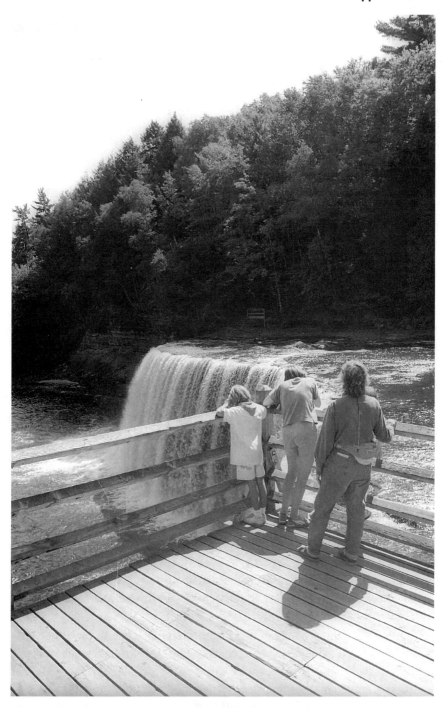

Visitors stand at the observation deck above the Upper Falls at Tahquamenon Falls State Park, the most impressive cascade in Michigan.

Day-Use Facilities: The Upper Falls is a day-use area, and from its huge parking lot there is a paved path that winds a quarter mile through a stately beech-maple forest to an impressive overview of the cascades. In contrast, the Lower Falls lack the overwhelming power of those upstream, but they possess a charm of their own. The Lower Falls are actually a series of seven cascades on both sides of a 25-acre island with a total drop of 30 feet. Access to the falls from the parking area is via a barrier-free, half-mile path. The best way to view the Lower Falls, however, is to rent a rowboat or canoe from a park concessionaire and paddle or row across the river to the island where there is a dock. You can then follow a mile-long foot trail around the island, stopping along the way for a close view of the falls or even to cool off by stepping into the smaller falls.

Other facilities at the Lower Falls include a picnic area along the banks of the Tahquamenon and a concessionaire that rents rowboats and canoes daily during the summer.

Hiking: The park has 40 miles of hiking trails, including several interconnecting loops in the Tahquamenon Natural Area north of M-123 that provide an escape from the crowds around the falls. The *Giant Pines Loop* is one of those trails, a 3.7-mile hike that begins and ends at the Upper Falls parking area and includes a giant stand of pines. The most interesting hike south of M-123 and the most popular one in the park is the *Tahquamenon River Trail*, a one-way hike of four miles from the Upper Falls to the Lower Falls. This moderately difficult trail skirts the river most of the way, allowing hikers to pass through old growth forests of beech maple and hemlock or view stretches of rapids. Beginning at the east loop of the Overlook Campground is the *Overlook Nature Trail*, a two-mile walk with interpretive displays that skirts a 90-foot ridge to the Lower Falls and then loops back along a small tributary of the Tahquamenon River. The *North Country Trail* also passes through the park.

Fishing: The best fishing in the park is found in the Tahquamenon River. Anglers below the Lower Falls, often in canoes or waders, cast for northern pike, muskies and walleye that measure up to 28 inches in length. Walleye and brown trout are caught in the river between the two falls, while farther up, above the Upper Falls, there are good populations of perch. There is also a run of steelhead in the Tahquamenon up to the Lower Falls in late October and after ice-out in the spring. Most anglers fish for the trout either from boats in the lower portions of the river or by surf casting spoons and spawn near the mouth in Whitefish Bay. The park maintains a boat access site at the Rivermouth Unit, while canoes can be launched in the Lower Falls Unit.

Season: The campgrounds are open May through October. Because the park is a vacation destination, the modern sites are occasionally filled Monday through Wednesday from July through mid-August but available on the weekends. Often there are open semi-modern sites throughout the summer in the Rivermouth section of the park. Sites can be reserved in advance by calling the state park Central Reservation system at ☎ (800) 44-PARKS or by going online at *www.michigan.gov/dnr*.

100

Andrus Lake
Lake Superior State Forest

Campground: Rustic
County: Chippewa   **Nearest Community:** Paradise
Sites: 28   **Reservations:** No
Fee: $10
Information: Newberry DNR office ☎ (906) 293-3293

North of the town of Paradise in an isolated section of the Upper Peninsula is a pair of state forest campgrounds, Andrus Lake and Shelldrake Dam. Andrus Lake is the more pleasant of the two facilities, providing shoreline campsites, a good swimming beach and fishing opportunities.

It also has an ideal location, especially if you can't get a site at Tahquamenon Falls State Park. The famous cascades are only a 20-minute drive away while a short drive to the north is the intriguing Great Lakes Shipwreck Museum (☎ (906) 635-1742). For a very unusual outing, spend an afternoon driving out to Crisp Point Lighthouse on the shores of Lake Superior.

Directions: From Paradise head north on Whitefish Point Road for five miles and then turn left on Vermillion Road. Within a quarter mile Vermillion Road passes the campground entrance.

Campground: Andrus Lake has 28 sites on two loops. The sites are well spread out in a stand of red pine and 10 of them are right along the shoreline of the scenic lake. The campground has tables, fire rings, vault toilets, hand pumps for water and handicapped-accessible sites. The only drawback of this campground is that just to north of it is a vast clear cut.

Day-Use Facilities: The campground also has a picnic area that leads to a sandy beach and a nice swimming area on the lake. The swimming is excellent in the clear water of this spring-fed lake.

Fishing: Andrus is a 33-acre lake with an undeveloped shoreline. It reaches depths of up to 30 feet almost due west of the campground and is fished for bass, northern pike and bluegill. The campground has an unimproved boat launch and a fishing pier. Shore anglers can also follow trails to fish much of the east shoreline.

Season: Like many state forest campgrounds in this region of the Upper Peninsula, this is a lightly used facility.

LOOKING FOR CRISP POINT LIGHTHOUSE

Our drive to the Crisp Point Lighthouse turned into an unexpected hike. We were trying to reach the remote Lake Superior light from Paradise when the rutted two-track we were bumping along at 10 mph became a quagmire of loose sand and large rocks.

The washout forced us to abandoned the vehicle, lace up our hiking boots and grab the county map. Two miles later we emerged at the Great Lake and there, a half mile down the beach, was the light.

The 58-foot tall, rounded brick tower was picturesque; the setting was stunning. Like a beacon in the wilderness, the light was the only structure along a sweeping shoreline where we were the only souls.

The washout, we decided, was necessary. The best way to appreciate the desolation and loneliness that most lighthouse keepers faced at the turn of the century is to reach one of the historical structures today on foot.

Today Crisp Point Lighthouse is much easier to reach along a route that is much better marked. But the lighthouse is still Michigan's most remote lighthouse. From M-123, five miles west of the Upper Falls of Tahquamenon Falls State Park, head north on County Road 500 for eight miles and after it passes Little Lake and continue east on County Road 412 for six miles following signs to the lighthouse.

Keep in mind that these are mostly dirt roads beyond M-123 that curve and wind through the woods with few posted road signs. Keep alert! Once at the lighthouse you'll find a boardwalk around the structure and interpretive displays erected by the Crisp Point Light Historical Society, which was formed to try to save the light.

For a map to the lighthouse call the Newberry Area Tourism Association at ☎(906) 293-5562 or go online at *www.crispppointlight.org*.

101

Bodi Lake
Lake Superior State Forest

Campground: Rustic
County: Luce   **Nearest Community:** Newberry
Sites: 16   **Reservations:** No
Fee: $10
Information: : Newberry DNR office ☎ (906) 293-5131

There aren't many places to park a trailer farther north in Michigan than the area many refer to as Superior Country. Nor is there any place in the state with a greater concentration of campsites than in the northern half of Luce County.

Lake Superior State Forest stretches from Munising to the east tip of Drummond Island to comprise of 1,026,058 acres, by far the largest of any of the six state forests. Yet clustered around the Two-Hearted River, along the Lake Superior shoreline and on many of the hundreds of inland lakes north of Newberry, are almost half of its 43 rustic campgrounds. All of them are traditional camping spots, frequented by families and fishermen almost as soon as the first Model Ts began to appear in the U.P. in the 1920s. Today in Superior County you have a camper's paradise: great scenery, lots of water and always an open site. One of the many campgrounds on inland lakes is Bodi Lake. This state forest facility combines scenic sites on the water, good fishing opportunities and even a short pathway into the surrounding the woods.

Directions: From Newberry head northeast on M-123 and in 17 miles turn north on County Road 500. Follow the dirt road for 13 miles and after the entrance of Culhane Lake State Forest Campground head east on County Road 437. The posted entrance to Bodi Lake is reached in 1.5 miles on CR-437. The nearest food, supplies and gas is at Pike Lake, seven miles away on County Road 414.

Campground: Bodi Lake has 16 sites on a single loop with 10 of them overlooking the lake. All the sites are well spread out in a forest of hardwoods and large red pines for a very scenic setting. Facilities include vault toilet and tables.

Fishing: Bodi Lake can be a productive fishery for anglers. The 200-acre lake reaches depths of 40 feet in several spots and is targeted mostly for walleye, perch and northern pike. Next to the campground is an improved boat launch. The nearest bait shop is at Pike Lake.

Hiking: Within the campground is the trailhead for the *Bodi Lake Pathway*, a 1.25-mile long trail into the pine and hardwood uplands that surround the lake.

Season: This is a lightly used facility.

102

Two-Hearted River
Lake Superior State Forest

Campground: Rustic
County: Luce   **Nearest Community:** Newberry
Sites: 45   **Reservations:** No
Fee: $10
Information: : Newberry DNR office ☎ (906) 293-3293

The mouth of Two-Hearted River is the third largest campground in Lake Superior State Forest, the most remote and in my mind the most scenic. It's hard to imagine a campground with a more scenic location than this rustic facility located at the end of the river that Ernest Hemingway immortalized.

The campground is perched on the spot where the Two-Hearted River empties into the Great Lake. From the first loop a large swing bridge crosses the river to the low dunes along Lake Superior that give way to the shoreline itself. This is a rare stretch of undeveloped Great Lake shoreline where to the west you can beachcomb for miles and the sunsets are spectacular anywhere along the dunes.

Directions: Driving to this campground is an adventure. The facility is 35 miles northeast of Newberry and is best reached from M-123 where it is posted at County Road 500. Head north and then follow the signs to the Rainbow Lodge. From CR-500 you turn northwest on CR-414, continue on CR-412 and finally CR-423. It ends at Rainbow Lodge, a small store and gas station at the entrance to the campground.

Campground: There are two loops at the mouth of the Two-Hearted River with 25 sites on the first one. These sites are in an area of birch, aspen and other woods and a few of them are along the river. The second loop has 20 sites, including four walk-in sites a short stairway above the campground. Most of this loop is situated in a stand of red pine with moderate undergrowth. Sites at the second loop are more spread out and thus a little more private than the first loop.

An impressive swingbridge crosses the Two-Hearted River and provides access to the Lake Superior shoreline at the mouth of the Two-Hearted River State Forest Campground.

Rainbow Lodge (☎(906) 658-3357) just outside the campground has a café and motel rooms and sells gas, limited groceries, bait, and camping supplies.

Day-Use Facilities: From the first loop you can cross an impressive swing bridge to Lake Superior and hike the shoreline for miles. The scenery here is spectacular as you can stand on the low dunes and gaze at a watery horizon. Also located on this sandy spit is a state historical marker detailing the lifesaving station that was here in 1876. The stone foundations of the lighthouse can still be seen. Even more interesting to many campers is the pebbles at the waterline. The shoreline attracts agate hunters and others interested in taking home a Lake Superior gem.

Hiking: The *North Country Trail* passes right through the campground and is posted in the second loop near site No. 19. Also in the second loop is a trail that winds 50 yards uphill to a bench and a scenic overlook.

Canoeing: The big Two-Hearted River is designated wilderness upstream from the weir and motors are not allowed. A parking area with a cement boat launch is provided near the first loop for entry into the river. Rainbow Lodge rents canoes and will provide drop-off and pick-up service along the river.

Season: Despite its remote location, or maybe because of it, the campground is often half to three-quarters filled from July through mid-August. Not finding any open sites on a weekend, however, would be rare.

103

Muskallonge Lake
State Park

Campground: Modern
County: Luce   **Nearest Community:** Newberry
Sites: 175   **Reservations:** Yes
Fee: $16 plus vehicle entry fee
Information: State park office ☎ (906) 482-0278

The narrow, quarter-mile wide strip of land between Lake Superior and Muskallonge Lake was the site of the original village of Deer Park, a lumbering town in the 1800s that included a hotel, store, doctor's office and, of course, the sawmill. Other than a few of the original dock pilings on Lake Superior, it's hard to imagine Muskallonge Lake State Park as a bustling lumbering town.

Located in northern Luce County, the 217-acre park is split by County Road H-37 (also labeled County Road 497). To the south you can set up at a lakeshore camp, go fishing or take a dip in the warm waters of Muskallonge Lake. Cross the gravel road and you can descend the shoreline bluffs to a sandy and pebbled beach along Lake Superior where rockhounds search for colorful agates. The two lakes combine to give the park an exceptionally moderate climate year-round, rarely hot in the summer, not as cold as the rest of the Upper Peninsula during the winter.

Directions: Muskallonge Lake is 28 miles from Newberry and 18 miles east of Grand Marais. From Newberry head north on M-123 for four miles then turn west on H-37 and follow it 14 miles to the park entrance.

Campground: The park has 175 modern sites on five loops along the shores of Muskallonge Lake. The area is well shaded and a number of sites overlook the lake, while others are near a small beach for the campers. Site 155 is a gem, secluded in a heavy-forested corner of the loop with a picnic table overlooking the water. Facilities include modern rest rooms with showers, a sanitation station for RVers and horseshoe courts. In the evening a concessionaire sells firewood in the campground.

Day-Use Facilities: The park has a day-use area on a small bay of Muskallonge Lake east of the campground. The lake is shallow enough so that the water warms up quickly for swimming during the summer. There is parking for 20 vehicles and an adjacent picnic area.

Located right off County Road H-37 is a parking-picnic area for Lake Superior. From

Lake Superior

North Country Trail

County Road H-37

MUSKALLONGE LAKE
STATE PARK

Muskallonge Lake

here visitors can descend a wooden staircase to reach the beautiful lakeshore and views of the Great Lake. The lake is generally too cold to swim but is a popular destination for agate hunters. The best time to search is after a storm or a heavy north wind, which will push a layer of new rocks onto the beach. The most sought-after rock is the Lake Superior agate, which can be seen in both its rough and polished state at the two stores located near the park.

Hiking: Following the Lake Superior shoreline is a portion of the *North Country Trail.* There are about 1.5 miles of this national trail in the park, and backpackers can follow it west five miles to Lake Superior State Forest Campground or even further to hook into the *Lakeshore Trail* in Pictured Rocks National Lakeshore. Ten miles of hiking to the east is the Two-Hearted River State Forest Campground on the mouth of the famous river. The DNR staff has also added a spur that combines with a portion of the *North Country Trail* to form a 1.5-mile loop from the Lake Superior parking area to the west end of the park.

Fishing: The 780-acre Muskallonge Lake is known best by anglers for northern pike, perch and smallmouth bass. In recent years the DNR Fisheries Division has begun stocking the lake with walleye. The park maintains an improved boat launch with a cement ramp and a dock on the inland lake at the west end of the campground. There are no launching facilities on Lake Superior. Three resorts, located just outside the park, rent boats and motors and allow campers to tie them up at the park.

Season: Most of the summer a site is easily obtained, but from the Fourth of July to mid-August, the facility is vulnerable to filling up on weekends. Sites can be reserved by calling ☎(800) 44-PARKS or online at *www.michigan.gov/dnr.*

104

Lake Superior

Lake Superior State Forest

Campground: Rustic
County: Luce **Nearest Community:** Newberry
Sites: 18 **Reservations:** No
Fee: $10
Information: Newberry DNR office ☎ (906) 293-3293

Lake Superior State Forest Campground is another remote and scenic gem in Luce County. This is one of the few places in the Upper Peninsula where you can camp along the Lake Superior shoreline.

When the Great Lake is kicking up, the surf here is an awesome sight with the rollers crashing onto the beach and the roar of the waves filling the air. On such evenings, the power of Lake Superior stays with you long after you have fallen asleep at your campsite.

Directions: The campground is on County Road H-58, west of Muskallonge Lake State Park or 15 miles east of Grand Marais.

Campground: Lake Superior is a single loop of 18 sites that lies between CR-H58 and Lake Superior. All but one site is located just inside the treeline on a low bluff overlooking the Great Lake and many have a partial view of the water. Sites are well spread out in the predominately hardwood-birch forest and the moderate undergrowth provides a bit of seclusion from your neighbors. Facilities include tables, fire rings, vault toilets and a hand pump for water.

Day-Use Facilities: From the campground a low sandy bluff with patches of dune grass descends to a pebbled shoreline that is well known for its agates. Usually there is a rockhound at the campground who will be searching the beach for the colorful and waxy stones. A few times in August after a high-pressure system settles in, temperatures soar above 80 degrees and some hardy swimmers take a dip in the lake, but most of the time Lake Superior is too cold for people to handle.

Hiking: Passing through the campground is a portion of the *North Country Trail.* To the east the NCT winds along the edge of the trees in the campground and is marked by faded blue blazes. After it passes the vault toilets at the east end it dips down to the open beach and follows it for quarter mile until it arrives at a large trailside map for Blind Sucker. To the west the NCT skirts the edge of the shoreline bluff for some nice views as it rises steadily above the beach below.

Blind Sucker Pathway is a six-mile loop that passes the large impoundment to the south before circling back. Within 0.7 miles of the campground you arrive at the stream and in another half mile you arrive at Blind Sucker No. 1 State Forest Campground. Here a path goes over the dam to Blind Sucker No. 2 Campground while another trail, clearly marked with a trailside map, heads west back to Lake Superior. This is great blueberry country, especially where Blind Sucker Pathway passes through open areas that have been logged.

Season: Lake Superior is very popular and despite its remote location will often fill up on the weekends and midweek as well. This campground tends to be a destination spot and sometimes you may have to wait a day or two get in. The nearest state forest campground is Blind Sucker No. 2 Unit.

105
Perch Lake
Lake Superior State Forest

Campground: Rustic
County: Luce   **Nearest Community:** Newberry
Sites: 35   **Reservations:** No
Fee: $10
Information: Newberry DNR office ☎ (906) 293-3293

Perch Lake Campground is 20 minutes north of Newberry and right off paved County Road H-37, making it considerably easier to reach than many of the state forest facilities to the east and west. Yet on the Sunday I was there setting up a tent, only three other sites were occupied. The state forest campground provides access to good fishing opportunities while its location makes it ideal as a base camp to explore this unique region of the Upper Peninsula.

Directions: Perch Lake is 25 miles north of Newberry via M-123 and CR-H-57. The entrance is at the corner of CR-H37 and County Road 410.

Campground: Perch Lake has two loops of 35 sites with most of them situated in a stand of red pines. There is little to no undergrowth here but the sites are well spread out for some privacy. More than a dozen sites are situated along the edge of a bluff overlooking the lake. They make for an especially nice spot to pitch a tent as you can sit at your table and view the entire lake. Facilities include tables, fire rings, vault toilets and hand pumps for water.

Fishing: An improved boat launch with a cement ramp is located just outside the campground. Parking for a dozen cars and rigs is provided, indicating the popularity of the lake among anglers. Fishing pressure is moderate on the large and mostly undeveloped lake that is known more for bass than perch.

Season: Perch Lake receives moderate use.

106
Bass Lake
Lake Superior State Forest

Campground: Rustic
County: Luce   **Nearest Community:** Newberry
Sites: 18   **Reservations:** No
Fee: $10
Information: Newberry DNR office ☎ (906) 293-3293

If you like the drive to a campground to be as adventurous as the camping, when you finally arrive you want that miles-from-civilization feeling complete with mud on the headlights, bugs on windshield and branches clinging to the roof, then head to Bass Lake.

The Superior State Forest facility is 15 miles northwest of Newberry in the remote heart of Luce Country and reached via to County Road-455. The dirt road plunges into a thick hardwood forest and for seven miles there are usually more deer along the side of road than signs indicating where you could possibly be. If you don't get lost, you'll end up at a scenic and very isolated campground where you never have to worry about getting a site.

Directions: From Newberry head north on M-123 but veer off on CR-H37 within four miles. In another four miles head west onto CR-455. The campground is reached in seven miles.

Campground: The 18-site campground is a typical state forest facility—small and rustic with lots of space between you and your neighbors. Half of the sites are in a grassy clearing that in the early 1900s was the site of a logging camp. The rest of them are scattered in thick hardwood forest. None of the sites are directly on Bass Lake.

Fishing: On the other side of CR-455 from the campground is an improved boat launch with a small parking area. Bass Lake is a good-sized body of water, 143 acres on the surface and reaching a depth of 74 feet at one point. Its shoreline is totally uncluttered with cottages and littered with downed trees and half-submerged deadheads, making it perfect habitat for smallmouth bass. The lake also supports a trout fishery.

Season: Bass Lake is a lightly used state forest facility. Being so remote, it's hard to imagine this campground ever filling up.

107

Woodland Park
Grand Marais Township

Campground: Modern and rustic
County: Alger   **Nearest Community:** Grand Marais
Sites: 114   **Reservations:** No
Fee: $13 to $18
Information: Park office ☎ (906) 494-2613

Located at the eastern end of Pictured Rocks National Lakeshore is Grand Marais, a sleepy little town with one of the most scenic ports along Lake Superior, a well-protected harbor with a sandy beach, a lighthouse and usually a sailboat or two anchored in the middle.

Just three blocks from the harbor and downtown area is Woodland Park, a municipally-operated campground that puts you within easy walking distance of the town's museums and restaurants. Park the trailer and then stroll over to the Lake Superior Brewing Company for a cold beer or a whitefish sandwich.

Directions: From Seney on M-28, head north on M-77 for 25 miles. The state highway leads you right into the heart of Grand Marais. From the downtown area head west on Brazel Street to reach the campground.

Campground: Woodland Park is a pleasant, modern campground with 114 sites on a shady bluff overlooking the blue horizon of Lake Superior. There are 35 sites near the edge of the bluff with a partial view of the lake and a higher nightly rate. Most sites have electric hookups, water and even cable TV service. A few sites have electricity only or no hookups at all. There is also a secluded primitive area with 20 walk-in sites, mostly designed for backpackers who plan to hike the *Lakeshore Trail* from Grand Marais to Munising.

The campground also has two bathhouses with coin-operated showers, a dump station for RVers and fire rings at most sites. Lakefront sites with electricity and water are $18 per night (cable TV is an additional charge), electricity-only are $17 and nonelectric and walk-in sites are $13.

Day-Use Facilities: Three stairways descend the bluff from the campground to a wide sandy beach along Lake Superior. The shore is great for beachcombing or agate hunting but the swimming can be chilly for much of the summer. Other facilities include a picnic area, two play areas for children, horseshoe pits, tennis courts, a basketball court and a softball diamond.

Hiking: By heading west for two miles along the Lake Superior Shoreline you will enter Pictured Rocks National Lakeshore and reach the *Sable Falls Trail*. The trail heads inland along Sable Creek to this beautiful cascade. An entire afternoon can be spent hiking to the falls and nearby Grand Sable Dunes.

Season: Arrive early at Woodland Park. The campground can be occasionally filled from July through mid-August and does not accept reservations.

SABLE FALLS: A WALK IN THE DUNES

Within minutes of lacing up our boots, we arrived at a fork in the trail and were faced with our first decision of the hike: dunes or waterfalls? To the right, the trail sign said, is Sable Falls. To the left is Grand Sable Dunes.

There are dozens of trails in the Lower Peninsula that will lead you to sand dunes and there are probably an equal number in the Upper Peninsula that wind past waterfalls. But the Dunes and Falls Trails in Pictured Rocks National Lakeshore is the only one we know of that gives you the option to view falling water or climb steep sandy slopes.

We decided to do both and use a stretch of Lake Superior beach, known for its abundance of agates, to turn this hike into a 2.6-mile loop.

We headed left for the dunes, descended to a bridge across Sable Creek and on the other side began the long climb to the top of the dunes. The transition was amazing. We began climbing in a shady, serene jack pine forest and then suddenly, in three steps or less, were in the hot, sandy and unsettled world of the Grand Sable Dunes. We crossed the open dunes to a high point where stretched out before us was Lake Superior, blue and endless.

We descended to the shoreline, headed east and within a mile were at the mouth of the Sable Creek. On its east bank was *Sable Falls Trail,* which entered a narrow canyon that the creek has carved and within a 0.3 mile arrived at Sable Falls. Sable Creek descends 140 feet on its way to Lake Superior, with a good bit of it occurring as a series of drops that is Sable Falls. The waterfall makes for a quiet, shady spot where you can sit for a spell and listen to the water splash past you. And you should. The final leg of this loop is a stairway of a 125 steps.

To reach the Sable Falls trailhead from Grand Marais, head a mile west on County Road H-58. Just beyond the trail is the Pictured Rocks' Grand Sable Visitor Center, ☎(906) 494-2660.

108

Cusino Lake
Lake Superior State Forest

Campground: Rustic
County: Schoolcraft **Nearest Community:** Seney
Sites: 6 **Reservations:** No
Fee: $10
Information: Seney DNR office ☎ (906) 499-3346

M-28 between Seney and Shingleton is a road so straight that if your wheels are properly alined you may never have to turn the steering wheel. The scenery is so blase, at least for the U.P., that many people never stop between the two towns. So the next time you're up there skip M-28 and traveled from Seney to Munising via Forest Road 450. What is usually a 40-minute drive can be turned into a three-day adventure.

That's because FR-450 heads north into Lake Superior State Forest where it skirts the Fox River and provides access to both this noted trout stream and the Fox River Pathway. Then it swings west and stays in the state forest until it emerges at H-52 on the underside of Pictured Rocks National Lakeshore.

What you will find along the way are eight state forest campgrounds, small facilities where there might be only four or five sites, not 40 or 50. The Forest Management Division calls it "small campsites in wild settings." That pretty much describes Cusino Lake Campground, one of the eight facilities in this area.

Directions: From M-28 in Seney, follow FR-450 for 22 miles to Cusino Lake Campground signs. From Munising head east along H-58 to the hamlet of Melstrand. Cusino Lake is 11 miles from Melstrand via HR-52 and FR-450.

Campground: Cusino Lake has six sites, all of them along the shoreline in a stand of impressive hemlock pines on the east side of the lake. Facilities, like any state forest campground, are basic: fire pit, picnic table, a pair of outhouses that may or may not be stocked with toilet paper. But you don't come to this campground for the facilities, you're here for the remoteness.

Day-Use Facilities: Cusino Lake has a small beach and swimming area.

Fishing: The 160-acre lake is totally undeveloped and fished for northern pike, panfish and bass. There is no boat launch in the campground but it is easy to hand-launch canoes and small boats from most of the campsites.

Season: Usage of Cusino Lake is light and you can usually secure a spot. But with only six sites the campground can be unexpectedly filled anytime during the summer.

109

Kingston Lake
Lake Superior State Forest

Campground: Rustic
County: Alger
Sites: 16
Fee: $10
Nearest Community: Grand Marias
Reservations: No
Information: Seney DNR office ☎ (906) 499-3346

Kingston Lake is a spectacular place to pitch the tent because of both its location and setting. The state forest facility was already established when Pictured Rocks National Lakeshore was created in 1966. The campground is still managed by the state but now it's surrounded by the crown jewels of a national park.

A 10-minute drive from your site is the sweeping Lake Superior shoreline at Twelvemile Beach. Within 15 minutes you can be checking out shipwrecks near Hurricane River or hiking to the restored Au Sable Light Station. In 30 minutes you're frolicking in the Grand Sable Dunes.

As good as the location is, the campground's setting is even better as almost every site overlooks Kingston Lake. The lake lies on the northern edge of the Kingston Plains, the result of loggers clearing thousands of acres of pines in the 1880s and the slash fires that followed. The plains are now a mix of second growth forest and open meadows that provide ample opportunities to pick wild berries as well as observe wildlife, the reason for the "Beware of Bears" warning in the campground.

Directions: From M-28 in Seney head north 25 miles on M-77 to Grand Marais and then west on County Road H-58. Kingston Lake is posted along H-58 and is a 22-mile drive from Grand Marais.

Campground: The campground's 16 sites are on a peninsula that stretches into the middle of the 123-acre lake and all but two face the water. Site No. 3 is the charmer, a private spot isolated on a small knob and surrounded on three sides by the lake.

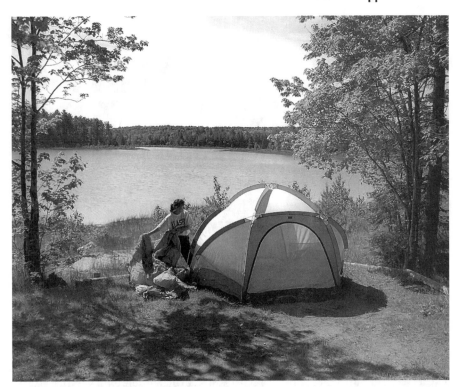

A camper sets up her tent at Kingston Lake State Forest Campground located south of Pictured Rocks National Lakeshore.

Day-Use Facilities: Before entering the campground you pass a small picnic area with a handful of tables near the shoreline. It's possible to go swimming in this section of the lake.

Fishing: A boat launch in the picnic area allows anglers to spend their days fishing Kingston Lake for muskellunge, smallmouth bass, walleye and panfish.

Hiking: Passing through the campground is the *Fox River Pathway*, the 27.5-mile trail that stretches from Pictured Rocks to the town of Seney. Head south and within a couple of miles you'll be hiking through an area of Kingston Plains dubbed the "stump museum" due to the sea of giant white pine stumps that surround you.

Head north from the campground on the pathway and within four miles you'll be standing on a remote stretch of Lake Superior shoreline. Even if your party is not up for a long hike to the Great Lake, the first half mile north is interesting. The trail skirts the shore of Kingston Lake and then breaks out into an open, sandy area so thick with blueberries you could pick a quart in 10 minutes or less.

Season: Due to its close proximity to Pictured Rocks, Kingston Lake can be filled on the weekends in July and August or even in the middle of the week.

110

Hurricane River
Pictured Rocks National Lakeshore

Campground: Rustic
County: Alger   **Nearest Community:** Grand Marias
Sites: 21   **Reservations:** No
Fee: $10
Information: NPS Information Center ☎ (906) 387-3700

There are three drive-in campgrounds within Pictured Rocks National Lakeshore. Twelvemile Beach is the largest with 37 sites, Little Beaver Lake (eight sites) is the farthest from Lake Superior and—in my opinion—Hurricane River is by far the most scenic.

This National Park Service facility is located where the Hurricane River rushes into the Great Lake under a natural archway of cedars. None of the sites are directly on the lake but all are close enough so at night you can hear the waves pounding the shoreline. Passing through the campground is the Lakeshore Trail where you can spend hours or even the entire day exploring.

Directions: From Grand Marias head west on County Road H-58, past Grand Sable Lake to reach the entrance of the campground in nine miles. Three miles farther east along H-58 is Twelvemile Campground.

Campground: Hurricane River has 21 sites with 11 on a lower loop and 10 on an upper loop near the mouth of the river. None of the sites are directly on the water but all are only a short walk from the Lake Superior shoreline. Facilities include tables, fire grate and a tent pad while nearby are vault toilets and hand pumps for water. Volunteer campground hosts usually staff the lakeshore campgrounds in Pictured Rocks.

Day-Use Facilities: The shoreline here is a sandy beach but Lake Superior is usually too cold for most people to do anything but stick a toe into it.

Hiking: Passing through the campground is the park's *Lakeshore Trail*, a popular backpacking route that stretches almost 43 miles from Grand Marias to Munising. Even if you're not up for hauling a pack around, the Lakeshore Trail makes for very interesting dayhiking. Just 1.5 miles east of the campground is the AuSable Lightstation, which is reached by hiking along a stretch commonly known as the Shipwreck Trail. A gate in the campground's lower loop marks the Lakeshore Trail but a "Shipwreck" sign next to it has most people scrambling immediately to the beach. The first wreck, the *Mary Jareck*, lies

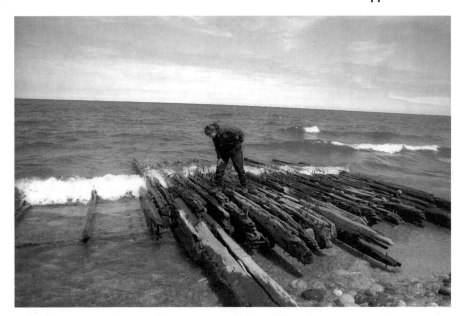

A hiker studies the shipwreck ruins near Hurricane River Campground in Pictured Rocks National Lakeshore.

20 yards off the beach and can be hard to see clearly when there is a chop on the water. The wooden bulk freighter was carrying iron ore and grounded on the AuSable Reef in July 1883. After being pulled off the reef, the ship was left to be battered by Lake Superior.

The Lakeshore Trail departs from the campground as an old two-track and skirts the shoreline from above. Within a mile you arrive at the second shipwreck sign. After descending to the beach, head east (right) 1,500 feet to the first remains. These lie on the beach and the timbers and ironwork indicates it's the ships' hulls that are half buried in the sand. The first wreck is the *Sitka*; a wooden freighter that grounded October 4, 1904 and the next day broke in half. The second is the *Gale Staples*—another wooden freighter built in 1881 that was loaded with coal when she beached herself on the sandy reef on October 1. From these shipwrecks it is only a short walk to the AuSable Lighthouse.

Interpretive Center: The wrecks are so popular that every Sunday, Thursday and Saturday at 3 P.M. from July through Labor Day, a park ranger leads a "Shipwrecks and Lighthouses" hike that begins in the campground. After visiting the wrecks, the ranger continues to the AuSable Lightstation, which has been restored by the National Park Service and includes interpretive displays outside. The tour includes climbing to the top of the lighthouse for a view of the shoreline.

Season: Pictured Rocks campgrounds are popular during the summer and often filled both weekend and weekdays from July through mid-August. Sites are handed out on a first-come, first-served basis so it is wise to plan a mid-morning arrival and have a backup campground in mind in case there are no openings.

111

Twelvemile Beach
Pictured Rocks National Lakeshore

Campground: Rustic
County: Alger   **Nearest Community:** Grand Marias
Sites: 37   **Reservations:** No
Fee: $10
Information: NPS Information Center ☎ (906) 387-3700

If Hurricane Campground is filled, head three miles west along County Road H-58 to Twelvemile Beach Campground, the other National Park Service facility along Lake Superior. This is the park's largest campground but is also very popular during the summer and often filled in July and August.

Directions: From Grand Marias head west on County Road H-58, past Grand Sable Lake to reach the entrance of the campground in 12 miles.

Campground: Twelvemile Beach has 37 sites along two loops with many of the sites on a sandy bluff above its namesake Lake Superior beach. Both the entrance road and many of the sites lie in a picturesque stand of white birch. Facilities include tables, fire grate and a tent pad while nearby are hand pumps for water, a pavilion and vault toilets.

Day-Use Facilities: Near the campground is a small picnic area. Lake Superior is too cold for most people to swim in but Twelvemile Beach is a great place to beachcomb or to take in a sunset on a clear evening.

Hiking: Passing through the campground is the park's *Lakeshore Trail*, a popular backpacking route that stretches almost 43 miles from Grand Marias to Munising. It is roughly a five-mile hike from the campground east to the AuSable Lightstation. To the west the backcountry campsites at Seven Mile Creek are reached in three miles.

Also at the campground is the *White Birch Trail*. This two-mile loop is an interpretive trail that explores the ancient Lake Nipissing beach and the upland plants and trees. There is usually a supply of trail brochures at the trailhead.

Season: Like Hurricane River, Twelvemile Beach can also be filled both weekend and week days from July through mid-August. Sites are only handed out on a first-come, first-served basis so it is wise to plan a mid-morning arrival and have a backup campground in mind in case there are no openings.

TWELVEMILE BEACH CAMPGROUND
PICTURED ROCKS NATIONAL LAKESHORE

112

Colwell Lake
Hiawatha National Forest

Campground: Rustic
County: Schoolcraft   **Nearest Community:** Shingleton
Sites: 35   **Reservations:** Yes
Fee: $7 to $12
Information: Manistique District Office ☎ (906) 341-5666

Located just off M-94 is Colwell Lake, one of the few national forest campgrounds in the Upper Peninsula where a site can be reserved in advance through the National Recreational Reservation Service. Colwell is a large facility with a great beach, a nature trail and access to a diverse fishery in the lake.

Directions: From Shingleton, a small town 10 miles east of Munising, head south on M-94 to reach Colwell in 10 miles. From Manistique, Colwell is 25 miles north on M-94.

Campground: Colwell has 35 sites on a single loop. The sites are well secluded and spread out in a maple and beech forest and more than half of them are along the lake with a partial view of the water. At Sites No. 31, 33 and 34 it's possible to tie up a small boat or canoe at your camp. One end of the campground loop provides access to M-94. Amenities include tables, fire rings, hand pumps for water, vault toilets and a dump station.

Day-Use Facilities: Between Sites No. 6 and 8 is a sandy beach surrounded by an open grassy area and parking for a few additional vehicles. Colwell is an excellent lake for swimming. The campground maintains a marked swimming area that features a sandy and gently sloping bottom.

Fishing: At the north end of the loop is an improved boat launch with cement ramp and a parking area for vehicles and trailers. At 158 acres, Colwell is a large lake but reaches depths of only 20 feet. The lake is totally undeveloped and attracts moderate fishing pressure from anglers casting for largemouth bass, black crappies, bluegills and other panfish and northern pike.

Hiking: Near the boat launch is the trailhead for the *Stutts Creek Nature Trail*, a two-mile walk through the forest along the east side of the lake.

Season: Colwell is open from mid-May to October and receives a moderate number of campers though it rarely fills up even on the weekends. Still you can reserve a site in advance through the National Recreational Reserve Service by calling ☎ (877) 444-6777 or through its web site at *www.reserveusa.com*.

113

Little Bass Lake
Hiawatha National Forest

Campground: Rustic
County: Schoolcraft
Sites: 10
Fee: $7
Nearest Community: Steuben
Reservations: No

Information: Manistique District Office ☎ (906) 341-5666

Little Bass Lake is a scenic facility located in an isolated area of the Hiawatha National Forest near Steuben. There are only 10 sites at Little Bass Lake but it is rare for this campground to be filled. The limited number of sites on a totally undeveloped lake makes for a quiet evening in a wilderness-like setting.

Directions: Little Bass Lake is 23 miles northwest of Manistique and 25 miles southwest of Munising. From Shingleton, a small town 10 miles east of Munising, head south on M-94 for 12 miles to Forest Road 437. The forest road is posted along M-24 by a "Steuben" sign. Turn west on FR 437, head two miles into the hamlet of Steuben and then turn south on Bass Lake Road. The campground is two miles south on Bass Lake Road.

Campground: Little Bass Lake is a single paved loop of 10 sites. Situated in a predominately maple-beech forest, four of the sites are on a high bank with a partial view of the lake. The entire facility is well wooded with moderate undergrowth but the sites are not totally secluded from each other. Amenities include tables, fire rings with sliding grills, lantern posts and vault toilets.

Fishing: The campground has a dirt, unimproved boat launch for hand-carried boats; a post blocks you from driving a trailer into the water. There is parking here for four vehicles and rigs. Bait and limited fishing supplies are available in a Steuben, two miles away.

At 84 acres, Little Bass Lake is small enough to be easily covered in a canoe or small rowboat with electric motor. It is a horseshoe-shaped body of water with the northern end reached from a path next to the boat launch, obviously a favorite stretch for shore anglers. The lake is undeveloped, only 18 feet deep, and features a shoreline of many small bays with pencil weeds and lily pad patches, which attract the attention of anglers. Perch is the main species caught but anglers also land largemouth bass, northern pike, bluegill and black crappies.

Season: Little Bass Lake is a lightly used facility that is open from mid-May through October.

114

Bay Furnace
Hiawatha National Forest

Campground: Rustic
County: Alger
Sites: 50
Fee: $10

Nearest Community: Christmas
Reservations: No

Information: Munising District Office ☎ (906) 387-3700

Situated on Lake Superior and near the bizarre little town of Christmas, Bay Furnace has the distinction of being the most popular campground in the Hiawatha National Forest. Part of its popularity is due to its location. It's a funnel during the summer for campers traveling from Pictured Rocks to their next stop in the Keweenaw Peninsula.

And part of it is its setting. In the 19th century, this was the site of the town of Onoto, a prosperous little iron-smelting town of 500 people until it burned down in 1877. Today all that remains of the past is an iron kiln in the picnic area. The rest of the rustic campground is a pleasant mix of open and secluded wooded sites, many with a view of Lake Superior and Grand Island only two miles away.

Directions: From Munising, head west on M-28 for five miles to reach the campground in the town of Christmas.

Campground: Bay Furnace Campground has 50 sites along two loops. A few of the sites overlook Lake Superior and a row of them are near Furnace Creek, which is crossed when entering. The sites are well spread out in the trees and feature fire pits, tables and lantern posts. There is also a sanitation station for trailers and recreational vehicles.

Day-Use Facilities: An open picnic area with tables and grills overlooks Lake Superior. The shoreline here is sandy and occasionally in August the water warms up enough that people go swimming. Nearby is one of the remaining iron smelting furnaces from the town of Onoto along with historical displays.

Season: The campground is open mid-May to October. Bay Furnace has an occupation rate of more than 75 percent from June through September and in July and August it's filled nearly every night.

115

AuTrain Lake
Hiawatha National Forest

Campground: Rustic
County: Alger   **Nearest Community:** AuTrain
Sites: 37   **Reservations:** No
Fee: $9
Information: Munising District Office ☎ (906) 387-3700

The national forest campground at the southeast corner of AuTrain Lake in Alger County is called a "recreation area" because it offers more than just fire rings and pit toilets. By far the most interesting aspect of the AuTrain Recreation Area is its *Songbird Trail*. On this nature trail hikers first rent a tape recorder then listen to a narrative tape while walking to learn about the more than 40 species of songbirds that commonly frequent the area.

The recreation area also boosts a wildlife observation deck, a sandy beach, a large campground, good fishing on the lake and a popular canoe route that ends in Lake Superior. Being only 10 miles from Munising, this is delightful place to set up camp for a few days while you're exploring Pictured Rocks National Lakeshore.

Directions: From Munising head west on M-28 for 10 miles and then at the town of AuTrain turn south on County Road H-03 for four miles. Turn east on Forest Road 2276 for a mile and then north on Forest Road 2596 for two miles to reach the campground.

Campground: AuTrain has 37 rustic sites that are well spread out in a hardwood forest of maple and beech. Ten of them overlook the lake's Buck Bay and these are always the first filled. Facilities include tables, fire pits, vault toilets and hand pumps for water.

Day-Use Facilities: The campground has a picnic area that includes a bathhouse and a sandy beach. The swimming in AuTrain Lake is only fair. More spectacular is AuTrain Beach on Lake Superior near the M-28 and CR H-03 intersection. Lake Superior, however, can be a cold place to swim throughout most of the summer. AuTrain also has a wildlife-viewing platform on the lake where birders have sighted bald eagles, ospreys, wood ducks and shorebirds.

Fishing: Within the campground is an improved boat launch with parking for vehicles and trailers. AuTrain is the largest inland lake in Alger County at 830 acres. It has a depth of up to 30 feet and an average depth of 12 feet. Fishing is considered good for walleye, northern pike and yellow perch. There are several bait shops and boat liveries along CR H-03 on the west shore of the lake.

CALLING THE SONGBIRDS AT AUTRAIN

From the little boombox we were instructed to carry down the trail, a taped narrator discussed the life of a common yellow throat warbler and gave a sample of the bird's call.

"Witchery-witchery-witchery."

My children and I were just casually hiking along when we suddenly stopped dead in our tracks. From out of the trees, high above us, came a resounding "Witchery! Witchery! Witchery!" Was it real or was it Memorex?

Well, we had the tape so it had to be a real. A common yellow throat was calling back to our boombox, rather angrily I thought, making the AuTrain Songbird Trail as realistic a nature trail as we've ever hiked.

It was Lon Emerick, a retired Northern Michigan University professor, who realized that the woods, wetlands and water around Buck Bay Creek were the perfect habitat for songbirds. In 1989 he convinced the U.S. Forest Service to build the unusual nature trail that includes renting a songbird kit with a tape recording. The 28-minute tape is keyed to 20 color plaques posted along the two-mile trail, each one devoted to a different songbird.

You learn that the black-throated green warbler actually has a yellow face and is often seen in conifers, that the white-breasted nuthatch descends trees head first and the ovenbird, unlike most other warblers, walks on the ground rather than hops.

Then there are the calls at every stop, often prompting the birds to call back and once so infuriating a red-eyed vireo that it flew down and attacked Emerick's tape recorder.

Hiking: The *AuTrain Songbird Trail* begins next to site number 12 and is a two-mile loop. Before the hike head into the town of AuTrain where you rent a songbird kit for a small fee at AuTrain Grocery and A & L Grocery on County Road H-03. Each kit contains a tape recorder, binoculars and a bird identification guide. The 28-minute tape is keyed to 20 color plaques posted along the trail, each one devoted to a different songbird. Biologists estimate that the area around Buck Bay Creek attracts more than 40 species of songbirds. From the campground, the trail swings past Grass Pink Bog and then Buck Bay Creek and a posted junction with the North Country Trail. Plan on at least 90 minutes to walk the trail and stop at each interpretive plaque to listen to the tape. To spot the most birds, hike either at dawn or dusk.

From a longer day of hiking there is the *North Country Trail*, the 3,200-mile national pathway that swings near the recreation area.

Canoeing: AuTrain Lake is the beginning of an easy but scenic canoe route that ends

10 miles to the north on the shores of Lake Superior. The route includes the AuTrain River; the slow-moving and meandering nature of the waterway is due to the heavy logging activity that took place in 1800s. The result is an absence of rapids and portages, the perfect conditions for a relaxing five-hour paddle that usually includes a number of encounters with waterfowl, great blue herons, turtles and other wildlife. Canoes are available for rent from many of the resorts along AuTrain Lake and can be put in at the recreation area or at one of two bridges where County Road H-03 crosses AuTrain River.

Season: AuTrain is open from mid-May to October and can be a popular campground at times. Sites are usually available except on holidays and an occasional weekend during the summer.

116

Council Lake
Hiawatha National Forest

Campground: Rustic
County: Alger
Sites: 6
Fee: $10 for one to three nights
Nearest Community: Munising
Reservations: No
Information: Munising District Office ☎ (906) 387-3700

County Road H-13 that heads south of Munising is an avenue to seven national forest campgrounds and several chains of lakes. The most obscure chain, so obscured there isn't even a name for this collection of small lakes, is located just north of Widewaters. Anchoring the chain are Council Lake and Halfmoon Lake while lying between them are five smaller ones, all connected by a series of channels and unmarked portages.

Council Lake Dispersed Camping Area is the main access point to the chain and makes for a great place to set up for a weekend of camping, fishing and paddling.

Directions: From M-28, just east of Munising, you head south on H-13 for 10 miles and then turn west on Forest Road 2661. It's a dirt road that is poorly marked but within 1.5 miles ends at Council Lake.

Campground: Council Lake has six sites, with three of them along the shoreline, along with pit toilets and fire rings. But there is no source of drinking water—bring a filter or boil water from the lake—and more important, no toilet paper. Bring your own.

Just before you reach Council Lake, Forest Road 2216A is marked and veers off to the northwest and in a quarter mile reaches Red Jack Lake, the other access point. Red Jack

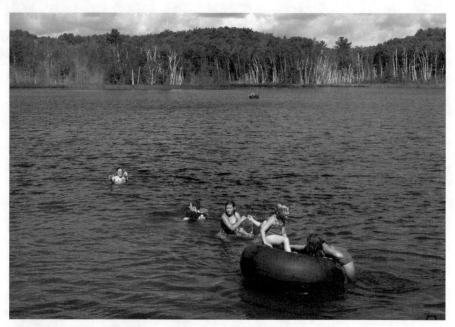

Children play in the Council Lake at the national forest campground.

Lake is connected to Council Lake by a small channel and has a single dispersed camping site and a dirt launch that can handle trailers.

Camping at Council Lake is by permit only and costs $10 for one to three nights and $20 for four to seven nights. For a permit call the Hiawatha National Forest Visitor Center at ☎ (906) 387-3700.

Day-Use Facilities: At Council Lake there is a stretch of sandy beach that is used by the campers as a swimming beach.

Fishing: You can launch hand-carried boats at Council Lake and trailer boats in at Red Jack Lake. Council Lake is 14 acres in size, has a depth of 20 feet and produces bluegill, perch, black crappie, northern pike and largemouth bass. At the north end of the lake a channel leads east to Red Jack Lake, 12 acres in size, while another leads north to even smaller Scout Lake. It's an easy paddle north from Scout Lake into Lion Lake, which is as far as anybody can go who trailered their boat in.

Paddling: Lion Lake is bordered on the west side by a 60-foot-high forested bluff. Climb that with a canoe or kayak and you can reach two more lakes, Rock and Hike Lake. There are no marked trails but it's hard to miss them. The portage to either is less than 100 feet long. Hike Lake is the most interesting. It's only 11 acres in size but more than 34 feet deep in places, enabling it to support a brook trout fishery.

At the north end of Lion Lake is another small channel, the smallest one of all, that leads into Halfmoon Lake, the largest of the chain at 31 acres. A single kayaker or a canoeist in an empty boat can squeeze through the marsh area that separates the two lakes without getting wet feet. Halfmoon is a quiet lake, free of any cabins, framed by hardwoods that are beautiful in the fall.

Hiking: Departing from the Council Lakes campsites is *Red Buck Trail* that winds two miles south to end at *Bruno's Run Trail* (see Pete's Lake Campground) near Fish Lake. Along the way you pass three walk-in campsites.

Season: Council Lake is lightly used but with only six sites it can easily become filled on a weekend.

117

Pete's Lake
Hiawatha National Forest

Campground: Rustic
County: Alger   **Nearest Community:** Munising
Sites: 41   **Reservations:** No
Fee: $8 to $13
Information: Munising District Office ☎ (906) 387-3700

More than any other Forest Service campground along County Road H-13, Pete's Lake Recreation Area is a destination rather than just a place to park the trailer or pitch the tent. This rustic campground offers so much to do, it's best to plan on staying for a few days.

There's a day-use area with a bathhouse and a swimmer's beach bordered by an open grassy area where you can lie out in the sun if it's not black fly season in the U.P. Passing through the campground is Bruno's Run Hiking Trail while the 190-acre lake offers anglers a mixed warm water fishery.

Directions: From M-24/94, three miles east of Munising, head south on County Road H-13. Pete's Lake is posted 12 miles south and is a third of a mile east of H-13 on Forest Road 2173. It is best to stock up on supplies in Munising. There are very few services available along CR H-13.

Campground: Pete's Lake has 41 sites that are well spread out and secluded in a stand of mixed hardwoods. A couple of the sites overlook the lake but the rest are well away from the shoreline. Pete's Lake has five handicapped-accessible sites with paved spurs, special tables and stand-up grills. There are also two walk-in sites, reached after a short walk from the east end of the campground. If you don't mind carrying in the tent, both are a charming place to spend a night or two. Site No. 7A is right on the lakeshore while Site No. 8A is another quarter mile to east and set in an impressive stand of pines. Both are within view of the water and like all the other sites have fire rings and picnic tables.

PETE'S LAKE CAMPGROUND

Day-Use Facilities: Pete's Lake has a large day-use area with a separate parking area. Picnic tables and grills are set under large hardwood trees with a view of the lake. A grassy area surrounds the beach and the swimming area features clear water with a sandy bottom.

Also nearby are changing rooms for day visitors. A paved path connects the beach area to the campground.

Fishing: Pete's Lake has an improved boat ramp with a large parking area for vehicles and trailers. The 190-acre lake reaches depths of up to 40 feet and is mainly targeted by anglers for northern pike, smallmouth bass and bluegill. Other warm water species caught include yellow perch and black crappie. Just south of the campground on CR H-13 is a small store with tackle and bait.

Hiking: Passing through the campground is *Bruno's Run Trail*, a 9.7-mile loop that winds around eight other lakes and near Widewaters National Forest Campground on the west side of CR H-13. An excellent dayhike is to head west from Pete's Lake to a stand of towering pines known as the Hemlock Cathedral. These 300-year-old white pines tower above you and are reached after a 2.6-mile one-way hike. A quarter mile beyond the stand of old-growth pines is Widewaters Campground, an excellent place to have lunch before turning around.

Season: Pete's Lake is open from mid-May to October and occasionally is filled on summer weekends.

118

Widewaters
Hiawatha National Forest

Campground: Rustic
County: Alger   **Nearest Community:** Munising
Sites: 34   **Reservations:** No
Fee: $9
Information: Munising Ranger District ☎ (906) 387-3700

On the west side of Country Road H-13 and within a mile of Pete's Lake is Widewaters Campground, a scenic spot that lies between Irwin Lake and the Indian River. Widewaters not only offers you a secluded setting in the woods but also access to some quiet lakes for fishing or wildlife watching.

A canoe would be excellent to have while camping at Widewaters. From the campground you can paddle the Indian River into a chain of six small lakes and ponds for a wilderness-like fishing adventure.

Directions: From M-24/94, three miles east of Munising, head south on County Road H-13. Widewaters is posted 13 miles south and is a half of a mile west of H-13 on Forest Road 2262.

Campground: Widewaters has 34 sites well spaced out on a single loop. On the west side of the loop the sites are near the Indian River where there are benches along the banks. On the east side Forest Road 2262 lies between the sites and Irwin Lake. Sites are well secluded from each other and have fire pits with sliding grills and tables. There is a small store just north of the campground on CR H-13 but it is best to stock up on supplies either in Munising or Manistique.

Fishing: Within the campground is an improved boat launch on the Indian River. Widewaters gets its name from this stretch of the Indian River, which heads north into a series of three wide ponds. From there it is easy to continue into Fish Lake or even farther into Bar Lake. In all, the campground provides access to six ponds and lakes that can be reached without portaging your canoe. There is also a boat access site to Irwin Lake passed on Forest Road 2262 just before reaching the campground entrance.

Fish Lake is the largest at 60 acres and reaches depths of 40 feet. Anglers fish it for bluegill, largemouth bass and northern pike. Occasionally somebody even catches a walleye. Bar Lake is smaller but slightly deeper in spots at 50 feet. It is also fished for panfish, largemouth bass and northern pike but not walleyes. Both 10-acre Irwin Lake and the Indian River are fished for brook trout.

Hiking: Like Pete's Lake, *Bruno's Run Trail* also passes through Widewaters Campground. This 9.7-mile loop winds around eight other lakes and crosses CR H-13 twice. Just a quarter mile north of Widewaters, Bruno's Run passes through an impressive stand of towering pines known as the Hemlock Cathedral.

Season: Widewaters is open from mid-May to October and occasionally is filled on summer weekends.

119

Fayette
State Park

Campground: Semi-modern
County: Delta
Sites: 61
Fee: $13 plus vehicle entry fee
Nearest Community: Garden
Reservations: Yes
Information: State park office ☎ (906) 644-2603

In the mid-1800s iron ore was shipped from the Upper Peninsula to the foundries in the lower Great Lakes at a tremendous cost the companies. Fayette Brown, general manager of the Jackson Iron Company, studied the problem and decided to build a company-owned furnace far from the mine, where the ore could be smelted into pig iron before it was shipped to the steelmaking centers. In 1866 Brown chose a spot on the Garden Peninsula overlooking Big Bay De Noc because it possessed a natural harbor for shipping and limestone and hardwood forests needed to smelt the ore. When he built a company town and gave it his first name, Fayette was born.

In 1891 the company closed down the furnaces, and within a few years Fayette was a ghost town of more than 20 buildings and structures. Today the area is preserved as Fayette State Park, a 711-acre unit in Delta County. The state park contains not only a fascinating interpretive area but also a scenic campground, a swimming beach and an interesting trail system. Fayette requires a little out-of-the-way driving to reach but this state park is worth it. Plan on spending at least two or three nights here.

Directions: From US-2, head south on Country Road 483 for 15 miles on the Garden Peninsula. The park entrance is eight miles beyond the town of Garden.

Campground: Fayette has a semi-modern campground that lacks modern restrooms and showers but provides electricity at all 61 sites. The sites are located on three loops in a wooded area near Lake Michigan but not directly on it. Foot trails provide access to both the historic town to the north and the park's swimming beach to the south.

Day-Use Facilities: Fayette features a beautiful beach on Sand Bay at the south. The facility includes parking, tables and a bathhouse and has a separate entrance just south of the park's main entrance on County Road 483.

Interpretive Center: At its height, some 500 people lived, worked and enjoyed a good life in Fayette. The town featured not only a furnace complex and numerous charcoal kilns but also baseball fields, a hotel, even an opera house. A walking tour of the area begins in the Visitor Center. The centerpiece of the museum is a scale model of Fayette as it was in the late 1880s. The tour continues in the ghost town, where there are 22 buildings and structures, including the kilns and furnaces needed to produce pig iron. Many have been renovated and feature displays inside including the Company Office, Opera House and Machine Shop. Although you can visit the town any time of the year, the museum and buildings are open from mid-May to mid-October daily from 9 A.M. to 7 P.M. Visitors can cover the ghost town on their own with a walking tour brochure or join a guided tour staged from mid-June through Labor Day.

Hiking: Fayette has seven miles of hiking trails with the longest loop being a two-mile path that begins in the campground and swings through the wooded interior south of the park road before returning. Of the four loops, however, the most scenic is the 1.5-mile *Overlook Trail*. The trail begins just up a hill from the parking lot to the townsite passes three overlooks from the edge of the limestone bluffs above Snail Shell Harbor.

Fishing: Big Bay De Noc is a fishery well known for perch, smallmouth bass and northern pike. In recent years walleye have been planted annually as well as salmon and trout. The park maintains an improved boat launch located in its day-use area. Often during July and August, schools of perch move into Snail Shell Harbor and attract the interest of anglers who fish for them from anchored boats or off a dock located in the small bay.

Season: Fayette rarely fills up during the summer with the exception of Fourth of July weekend. You can reserve a site at ☎ (800) 44-PARKS or *www.michigan.gov.dnr*.

120

Portage Bay
Lake Superior State Forest

Campground: Rustic
County: Delta
Sites: 23
Fee: $10

Nearest Community: Garden
Reservations: No

Information: Gladstone DNR office ☎ (906) 786-2351

One of Michigan's most secluded shoreline campgrounds accessible by car is located on the east side of Garden Peninsula, not far from Fayette State Park. Portage Bay State Forest Campground features 23 sites that are well hidden among the towering red pines and border its namesake bay. No matter where you camp you're only three steps from a beautiful sandy beach and the clear waters of Lake Michigan.

For those campers that take to time to find this charming little campground, it often turns out to be a personal paradise. For only $10 a night they enjoy a beach they can call their own in a setting that is almost tropical in the middle of the summer.

Directions: Just reaching this campground is an adventure. From the town of Garden, head south on County Road 483 for two miles to the junction known as Devil's Corner. Curve to the west and you'll head for Fayette State Park. To reach Portage Bay Continue straight on the gravel road posted with a *State Forest Campground* sign. Turn left on Lane 12.75 and then hang on. The rugged dirt road bumps for five miles on its way to the east shore and the campground entrance.

Campground: Portage Bay has 23 sites that line this quiet bay on the east side of Garden Peninsula. Each site faces Lake Michigan and is well separated from the others. You end up with not only a place to pitch the tent but your own private stretch of beach. The rustic facilities include vault toilets, a hand pump for water, and fire rings and picnic tables.

Day-Use Facilities: Portage Bay is a crescent moon beach, lined by pines and enclosed by a pair of rocky points at each end. The water in this part of Lake Michigan warms up nicely by mid-July and the swimming here is excellent.

Hiking: Departing from the campground is the *Ninga Aki Pathway*, a 2.2-mile interpretive trail of several loops, including the 1.5-mile Lake Michigan Loop marked by a display sign at the north end of the campground. Ninga Aki is an Ojibway word that means

"Mother Earth," and posts along the trail point out the staples of Indian life here when they lived off the land. Though many of the posts are missing, trail guides can still be obtained by stopping at the DNR Regional Office (☎ (906) 786-2351) at the corner of US-2 and M-41/M-35 in Gladstone.

Season: Portage Bay is a lightly used facility though people tend to spend a longer time camping here due to its incredible setting. Subsequently the campground can be filled occasionally during the summer.

121

Flowing Well

Hiawatha National Forest

Campground: Rustic
County: Delta   **Nearest Community:** Rapid River
Sites: 10   **Reservations:** Yes
Fee: $7
Information: Rapid River Ranger District ☎ (906) 474-6442

Flowing Well Campground is only three miles north of US-2, a road that is beset with travelers during the summer, but might as well be a hundred miles from anywhere. Tucked away on the banks of the Sturgeon River, this small facility provides a quiet and serene setting, unlike most campgrounds along US-2.

The campground's name is from the well in the picnic area that was the result of oil exploration in 1929. Prospectors drilled 1,160 feet into the ground only to watch water, not crude, bubble up. They abandoned the test drill but left the well flowing and today it produces 100 gallons a minute from the same strata of sandstone that forms the Pictured Rocks 30 miles due north on Lake Superior.

Directions: Flowing Well is right off H-13, three miles north of US-2 and 25 miles west of Manistique.

Campground: Flowing Well has 10 sites that are well spread out and isolated from each other. Six of the sites are on the edge of the Sturgeon River with a view of this scenic waterway. Each site is equipped with tables and fire rings. The only source of water in the campground is the flowing well in the picnic area, which is safe to drink, but has a heavy iron and sulfur content. To many people it tastes like somebody's been boiling eggs all morning.

Day-Use Facilities: The campground also has a small picnic area with tables and grills on a grassy point that is surrounded by the Sturgeon River on three sides. The flowing well is located here.

Fishing: The Sturgeon River is fished for brook trout during the summer and steelhead and salmon in the spring and fall. There are bait and tackle shops in Rapid River, 14 miles to the west on US-2.

Canoeing: Short paddling trips are possible both north and south of the campground on the Sturgeon River if you have a canoe. You can put in at the campground and then paddle south for an easy three-mile trip down the gentle flowing Sturgeon before pulling out at County Road 497, just beyond US-2.

You can experience Tenmile Rapids. Driving north two miles on H-13 and put in at 14 Mile Bridge. It is a four-mile paddle back to the campground.

Season: Flowing Well is open from mid-May to October and is a lightly used facility. You can reserve a site in advance, however, through the National Recreational Reservation Service by calling ☎(877) 444-6777 or through the NRRS web site at *www.reserveusa.com.*

122

Little Bay de Noc
Hiawatha National Forest

Campground: Rustic
County: Delta
Sites: 38
Fee: $9 to $10

Nearest Community: Rapid River
Reservations: Yes

Information: Rapid River District office ☎ (906) 474-6442

The Hemlock Cathedral in the Little Bay de Noc Recreation Area is a stand of hemlocks that somehow survived the logging era Michigan experienced at the turn of the century. In Escanaba, residents could see the giant trees on the other side of Little Bay de Noc and by the late 1800s the spot was a popular weekend retreat known as Maywood. When a small resort hotel was built there in 1904, this pocket of old growth was preserved from the loggers advancing down the Stonington Peninsula.

Today the Hemlock Cathedral is as quiet and impressive as it was a century ago and is where you go to see what a 300-year-old tree looks like. These giant pines are just one reason why Little Bay de Noc is a popular stop for campers and natural lovers crossing the Upper Peninsula.

Directions: Little Bay de Noc is on the west shore of the Stonington Peninsula. From US-2, east of Rapid River, head south on County Road 513, to reach the campground in seven miles.

Campground: Little Bay de Noc has 38 individual sites along three loops. The sites in the North Maywood (No. 1-14) and Oaks Loop (No. 17-29) are scattered in a hemlock/hardwood forest and offer a bit privacy from your neighbors. Twin Springs Loop (No. 30-38) is an open grassy area and the sites here provide the best views of the bay and Gladstone on the other side. All sites face Little Bay de Noc, which allows campers to enjoy a cooling breeze during the summer, but other than Two Springs Loop, most do not have a clear view of the water. Facilities include fire rings, tables, vault toilets and drinking water.

Day-Use Facilities: A picnic area is located between the campground and Hunter's Point Boat Launch. Picnic tables and grills are scattered in a large grassy area that overlooks a sandy beach and designated swimming area on the bay. From the picnic area or anywhere along the shoreline, the sunsets on a clear evening are spectacular. If you're not camping at the recreation area, there is a daily fee to use the beach and picnic grounds.

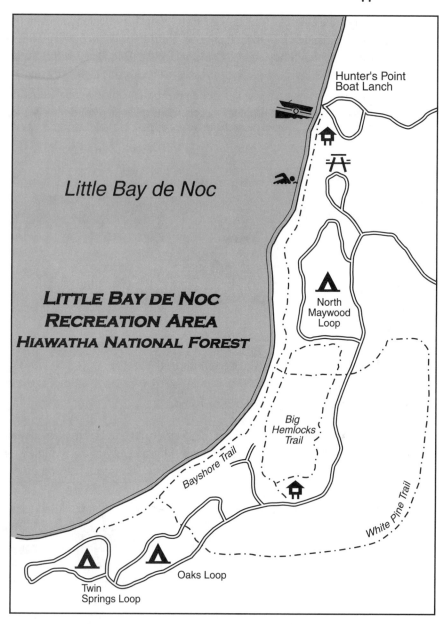

Fishing: Hunter's Point is an improved boat launch with a separate entrance a half mile north of the campground entrance on County Road 513. Little Bay de Noc is generally regarded as one of the finest walleyes fisheries in Michigan as well as a place to go for yellow perch and smallmouth bass. There are bait and tackle shops in Rapid River and Gladstone.

Hiking: The recreation area has four trails that total 3.5 miles. To view the Hemlock Cathedral hike the half-mile *Maywood History Trail,* a paved, interpretive path that departs from near the Maywood Groups sites. The *Bayshore Trail* is 1.2 miles long and skirts the shoreline from the boat launch to Twin Springs Loop. The *Big Hemlocks Trail* is a 0.8-mile loop that also wanders through the Hemlock Cathedral and the *White Pine Trail* is 1.3 miles long. It departs from the Bayshore Trail and crosses to the east side of the park road.

Season: Little Bay de Noc is a popular facility in the Hiawatha National Forest but large enough that it is usually not a problem securing a site other than holiday weekends. You can reserve a site through NRRS (☎ (877) 444-6777).

123

Fox Park
Cedarville Township

Campground: Rustic
County: Menominee   **Nearest Community:** Cedar River
Sites: 20   **Reservations:** Yes
Fee: $10
Information: Park supervisor ☎ (906) 753-6911

Fox Park is beach campground along Lake Michigan operated by Cedarville Township and located only 30 miles north of the Wisconsin border. If you can stand all the Cheddarheads that will be camping around you then this nice place to set up camp and a very affordable one. The fee is only $10 a night.

Directions: From Escanaba, head south on M-35 and the campground will be reached in 25 miles.

Campground: The park has 20 rustic sites with 11 of them right along Lake Michigan. Sand and surf will be less than three steps from your trailer. Site No. 12 on the beach is surrounded by brush for a bit of privacy. In all the rest you'll know your neighbor by the end of the weekend. If you're not camping along the beach, then you're near M-35 and the traffic noise might get tiresome on a busy weekend. Otherwise there is a campground host that enforces quiet hours from 11 P.M. to 6 A.M. Facilities include tables, fire pits and vault toilets.

Day-Use Facilities: The park has a nice picnic area with tables, grills and playground equipment. The beach here is beautiful, wide and sandy. There are no lifeguards.

Season: The campground is open from Memorial Day to Labor Day. The beach sites fill up fast but there is usually an opening in this small county park for another tent or trailer. Sites can be reserved by calling ☎ (906) 753-6911.

124

Big Cedar River

Escanaba State Forest

Campground: Rustic
County: Menominee   **Nearest Community:** Cedar River
Sites: 17   **Reservations:** No
Fee: $10
Information: Gladstone DNR office ☎ (906) 786-2351

The water from the well at the Big Cedar River State Campground is not to be missed. It's so cold, pure and sweet that locals come to the remote campground from miles around to fill up large bottles and take it home with them.

It tastes best, however, on a warm summer evening just after you finish pitching your tent or setting up the trailer in this state forest campground. This is a pleasant place to set up camp. There always seems to be a site open and you can spend a day or two hiking, mountain biking, trout fishing or relaxing without leaving the campground.

Directions: From M-35, just north of the town of Cedar River, turn west onto River Road, where there is state forest campground sign. Follow River Road in a northwest direction for six miles to the posted campground entrance.

Campground: Big Cedar River has 17 rustic sites in a wooded setting. Four of the sites are right on the banks of the river where you can pitch your tent in the shade of towering pines and spend the evening watching trout rise. The rest of the sites are away from the river. Unfortunately many of the sites are missing a table or fire ring.

Fishing: The Big Cedar River flows 80 miles from northern Menominee County to Lake Michigan. It is stocked with brook, rainbow and brown trout and also hosts a steelhead run in the spring.

Hiking: Near the campground is the *Cedar River Pathway*. This state forest pathway totals 8.5 miles and has three crossover spurs that form four different loops. Loop 1 (two miles in length), Loop 2 (3.5 miles) and Loop 3 (five miles) are predominantly in mature stands of hardwoods and pines and twice break out at the Cedar River. Loop 4 is the longest at seven miles and crosses over River Road to wind through an area that was actively logged in 1994. The main trailhead is in a parking lot, reached before you enter the campground itself.

Season: Big Cedar River Campground is a lightly used facility. There are usually few problems getting a site even on the weekends.

125

Tourist Park
City of Marquette

Campground: Modern
County: Marquette   **Nearest Community:** Marquette
Sites: 110   **Reservations:** Yes
Fee: $12 to $22
Information: Park office ☎ (906) 228-0465

A half century ago the trend in northern Michigan was for communities to build "tourist parks," public campgrounds located in town. The idea was to attract more tourists to the area by offering them an inexpensive place to stay near all the sights they wanted to see.

The tradition lingers on in the Upper Peninsula where a handful of towns still maintain tourist parks with the best one located in Marquette. Built in 1951, Marquette Tourist Park is a campground on 40 acres along the Dead River minutes from the Northern Michigan University campus. It location allows you to spend the day exploring the museums and sights surrounding the largest city in the Upper Peninsula while enjoying a campfire at night.

Directions: From US-41/M-28, on the west side of the city near the Wal-Mart store, turn north on County Road 492. Continue on CR-492 as it swings east and becomes Wright Street and then turn north on Sugarloaf Avenue. The campground entrance will be a half mile on the left.

Campground: Tourist Park has 110 campsites, including 54 with the electric hookups and 46 with full hookups—electricity, water and sewer. All hookups were upgraded in 2002 to 30 amps. Some sites are open but most are shaded by towering red pines, birch and hardwoods.

The most interesting sites are 10 designated for tents. The rustic sites have a view of the water and three of them are on the edge of the shoreline where the Dead River is less than 15 feet from your picnic table.

Tent sites are $12 a night, electric sites are $20 and full hookups $22. There is also a dump station ($4) and restrooms with showers ($3).

Day-Use Facilities: Other park amenities include three picnic areas with tables and grills, a children's play area, a softball field and a sandy beach that is split in the middle by a grayish rock so flat and large three people could sunbathe on top of it. The water of the Dead River is much more suitable for swimming than the nearby Lake Superior beaches.

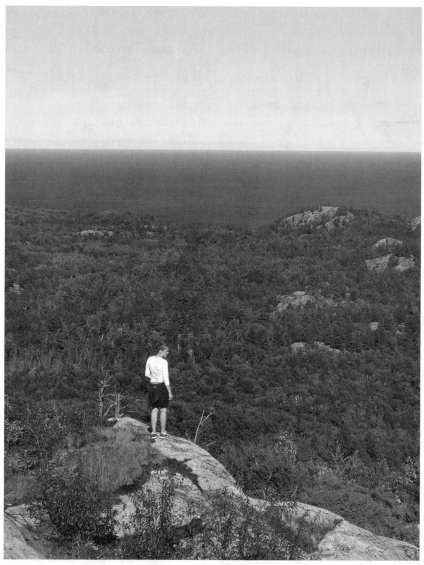

A short drive north of Tourist Park on County Road 550 is Little Presque Isle State Forest Recreation Area that offers some of the most scenic hiking in Marquette, including sweeping vistas from Hogback Mountain.

Fishing: A small dam has turned this stretch of the Dead River into a reservoir, an undeveloped body of water with only the campground at its east end. In the summer the Dead River Basin attracts paddlers in canoes and kayaks and anglers casting for northern pike and panfish. Near its entrance on County Road 550, just below the power dam, is a handicapped-accessible fishing pier on the Dead River where salmon and trout are caught. There is no boat ramp at the park but hand-carried boats can be launched.

Cycling: At the park's entrance on Sugar Loaf Road is *Marquette Bike Path*, six miles of paved trail that loops around the city. Cycling is such a popular way for campers to reach Marquette's museums and other attractions that bicycles are rented at Tourist Park for $10 an hour.

Next to the fishing pier is a trailhead for the *Noquemanon Ski Trail* that heads west toward Ishpeming and in the summer is used by mountain bikers.

Hiking: A five-minute drive north on CR-550 is Little Presque Isle State Forest Recreation Area, a 3,040-acre tract offering some of the finest hiking in the area. *SugarLoaf Trail* is a 1.2-mile climb to the top of the granite knob for a panoramic view of the Lake Superior shoreline. *Wetmore Pond* is an interpretive trail with an extensive boardwalk through bogs and wetlands. *Hogback Mountain Trail* is a 3.2-mile trek with a steep climb to its rocky peak for an even more expansive view than Sugarloaf.

Season: Tourist Park campground is open from mid-May to mid-October. You can reserve sites in advance by calling the Parks and Recreation Department at ☎ (906) 228-0465 or online at *www.mqtcty.org*. In the off-season call ☎ (906) 228-0460.

126

Perkins
Marquette County Park

Campground: Modern
County: Marquette   **Nearest Community:** Big Bay
Sites: 72   **Reservations:** Yes
Fee: $10 to $18
Information: Park office ☎ (906) 345-9353

Country Road 550 heads north from Marquette and in 26 miles ends at Big Bay, a delightful village overlooking Lake Independence and nestled in the foothills of the Huron Mountains.

Established in 1904, Big Bay was a bustling lumber town and the site of one of Henry Ford's many factories in the Upper Peninsula. It's best known as the place where scenes from the 1959 film *Anatomy of a Murder*, starring Jimmy Stewart and Lee Remick, were shot. The story is true and today you can still belly up to the bar for a beer at the Lumberjack Tavern where the famous murder occurred.

On the edge of town is Perkins Park, a Marquette County campground with 72 campsites on the west shore of Lake Independence. Perkins Park is a pleasant campground that is an easy walk to "downtown Big Bay" and well worth spending a couple of nights at to explore the area.

Directions: From Marquette head north on County Road 550 and in 25 miles, just before entering Big Bay, is the entrance to Perkins Park.

Campground: Perkins Park has 72 sites; 30 with full hookups, nine electric-only and 33 rustic. The park also maintains a rental-tent at one site. The sites are scattered along two loops in a well-shaded area. Only three modern sites (No. 37, 38 and 39) and one tent site (No. 65) have a clear view of the lake.

Perkins Park installed new restroom and shower buildings in 2002 and maintains a dump station for recreational vehicles. Full hookup is $18 a night or $74 for five nights. Electric-only is $14 a night or $58 for five nights and tent sites are $10 a night or $42 for five nights. The rental platform tent is $20 a night.

Day-Use Facilities: The campground has a small sandy beach and marked swimming area on Lake Independence along with a bathhouse. Nearby is play equipment for children, a picnic area with a pavilion, and a basketball court.

Fishing: Lake Independence is spread across 1,860 acres and reaches depths of 30 feet in places. It is regarded as a good fishery for northern pike, walleye and smallmouth bass. Many anglers also fish it for yellow perch.

In recent years Perkins Park has rebuilt its boat ramp and added a fish cleaning house and a wonderful fishing pier for campers without a vessel. Within Big Bay is a sports and bait shop that sells tackle, minnows and crawlers.

Season: Perkins Park is open Memorial Day to mid-October and does occasionally fill on weekends. You can reserve sites in advance by mailing the dates, one night's fee and $1 reservation fee to Perkins Park, P.O. Box 31, Big Bay, MI 49808.

Copper Harbor

138

139

41

Houghton

26

Ontonagon

147

148

149

45

140

150

28

Ironwood

28

146

2

141

136

135

127

144

145

143

128

142

Iron River

134

131

133

132

130

129

Iron Mountain

2

127 Horseshoe Lake

128 Squaw Lake

129 Carney Lake

130 Gene's Pond

131 Glidden Lake

132 Bewabic

133 Pentoga

134 Lake Ottawa

135 Lake Ste. Kathryn

136 Norway Lake

137 Big Eric's Bridge

138 Fort Wilkins

139 McLain

140 Bob Lake

141 Bonds Falls

142 Clark Lake

143 Moosehead Lake

144 Henry Lake

145 Pomeroy Lake

146 Lake Gogebic

147 Union Bay

148 Presque Isle

149 Black River Harbor

150 Little Girl's Point

Western Upper Peninsula

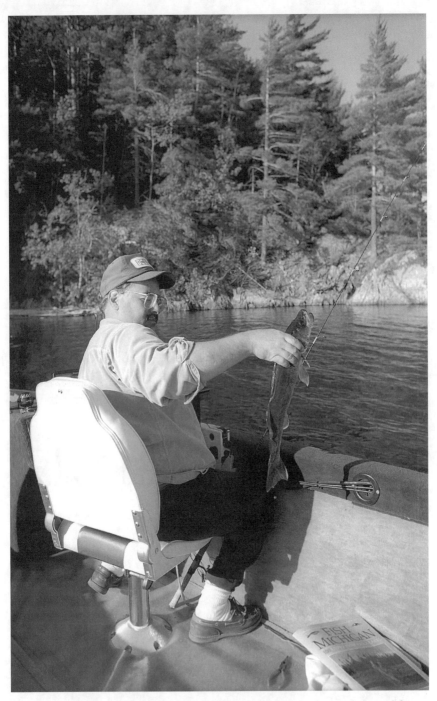

Many state forest campgrounds in the Western U.P., such as Carney Lake and Squaw Lake, offer outstanding fishing for walleye, bass and bluegills.

127

Horseshoe Lake
Escanaba River State Forest

Campground: Rustic
County: Marquette   **Nearest Community:** Witch Lake
Sites: 11   **Reservations:** No
Fee: $10
Information: Gwinn DNR office ☎ (906) 346-9201

Horseshoe Lake is the first of two small state forest campgrounds in the remote southwest corner of Marquette County. It takes a little effort to drive out to either one but in doing so you are ensuring yourself a quiet evening in the middle of the Upper Peninsula in a campground that is rarely filled.

What price is solitude these days?

Directions: From US-41/M-28, head south on M-95 for 18 miles to Witch Lake and then turn west on Fence River Road, a paved road. Within 1.25 miles is the marked turnoff for Horseshoe Lake, a dirt road that heads north to reach the lake within a mile.

Campground: The campground is located on one of several small peninsulas that protrude into the lake, thus its name. Horseshoe Lake has 11 sites in a well forested setting with most of them either directly on the water or within view of it through the trees. The usual state forest campground amenities—picnic tables, fire rings and vault toilets—are provided as well.

The most charming aspect of Horseshoe Lake is its three walk-in sites. They are at the end of the loop perched out at the tip of the peninsula and provide a view of both sides of the lake. It's only a short climb from the parking area but a world away from the rest of the campground.

Fishing: Within the campground is a spot to launch hand-carried boats while located on the opposite peninsula is an improved boat launch with a cement ramp and parking for eight vehicles and trailers. Near the boat launch is a loop that used to be South Horseshoe Lake Campground but was closed to state budget cutbacks in 1990s. Too bad. Here all 13 sites sit high above the water with a beautiful view of the lake below.

Horseshoe Lake is 126 acres in size and supports a warm water fishery. It is generally regarded as a good bass lake but anglers also target northern pike and panfish.

Season: This is a very lightly used campground.

128

Squaw Lake

Escanaba River State Forest

Campground: Rustic
County: Marquette
Sites: 15
Fee: $10
Information: Gwinn DNR office ☎ (906) 346-9201

Nearest Community: Witch Lake
Reservations: No

Farther along, Fence River Road will lead you down the road to Squaw Lake, the site of the second state forest campground in the southwest corner of Marquette County.

The campground is not nearly as scenic a place as Horseshoe Lake to pitch a tent or set up your trailer. But for those who camp here that's unimportant. Squaw Lake's trophy fishing is the reason they seek out this small, obscure campground.

Directions: In Marquette, stock up on your favorite lures and bait—there is little in Witch Lake—and then head west on US-41/M-28 for 27 miles and south on M-95 for 18 miles. At Witch Lake turn west on Fence River Road and follow it past the posted entrance road to Horseshoe Lake. In another two miles head north on Squaw Lake Road, a narrow road that winds through the woods and leads to the campground in two miles.

Campground: Squaw Lake has 15 rustic sites on two loops on the west side of the lake. None of them are directly on the water or even in view of it but all are well spread in very private settings. One pleasant aspect of the campground is that Squaw Lake is home to nesting loons and often the birds can be heard and seen in the evenings.

Fishing: The boat launch is separate from the campground and features a cement ramp and parking for seven vehicles and trailers. The lake covers 247 acres and reaches depths of 80 feet, the reason for its long history of being stocked with rainbow trout and splake.

But most anglers do better fishing for bluegill and smallmouth bass. Since 1995 Squaw Lake has produced seven Master Angler fishing awards. Five of them were for bluegills that ranged from 10.5 to 12 inches in length. Another was for a 21-inch long smallmouth bass. One of the best spots to fish for bluegills is near the campground at the south end of the lake where there are some remnants of fish shelters in 10 to 20 feet of water.

Season: Like Horseshoe Lake, this campground is not heavily used.

129

Carney Lake
Copper Country State Forest

Campground: Rustic
County: Dickinson
Sites: 16
Fee: $10
Information: Crystal Falls DNR office ☎ (906) 875-6622

Nearest Community: Iron Mountain
Reservations: No

The road to Carney Lake is a rough ride of flying gravel and rising dust. But if its washboard surface doesn't slow you down, the scenery will. Along the way you pass towering rock outcroppings, rolling wooded ridges on the horizon and possibly even some wildlife ranging from flocks of wild turkeys to whitetail deer.

By the time you arrive at this isolated spot in Dickinson County, you're ready to kick back and relax for a few days. This is an excellent place to do it. Often called one of the most scenic state forest campgrounds in the Upper Peninsula, Carney Lake offers not only a spectacular setting but also good fishing.

Directions: Carney Lake is 16 miles northeast of Iron Mountain. Just before US-2 swings west to cross the Michigan/Wisconsin border, continue north on M-95 for four miles to Merriman, the site of a small store and restaurant. Turn east on Merriman Truck Trail. The first two miles are paved and then the road becomes gravel. At an intersection posted with a State Forest Campground sign, turn south and follow the dirt road for five miles to Carney Lake. Along the way you pass the public access site for Rock Lake.

Campground: Carney Lake has 16 sites that are well spread out on single loop in an area forested in primarily birch. Eight sites are right on the lake with a good view of the shoreline. The rest are only a short walk away from the water. Facilities include vault toilets, tables, fire rings and a hand pump for water.

Day-Use Facilities: The campground has a picnic table in an open grassy area along the lake. There is no beach here but the sandy bottom of the lake provides some opportunities for swimming.

Fishing: Carney Lake is a beautiful body of water. There are a few cabins on the lake but for the most part they are set away from the water and hidden in the large birches that ring the shoreline. The campground has an improved boat launch with a separate parking area large enough to handle a half dozen vehicles and trailers. The lake is primarily fished for walleye and smallmouth bass. Pick up tackle and bait in Iron Mountain before arriving at the campground.

Season: This is a lightly used campground.

130

Gene's Pond
Copper Country State Forest

Campground: Rustic
County: Dickinson **Nearest Community:** Felch Mountain
Sites: 14 **Reservations:** No
Fee: $10
Information: Crystal Falls DNR office ☎ (906) 875-6622

We were in the land of misnomers. We couldn't find any mountains in Felch Mountain, Gene's Pond, where we camped that evening, is no pond and Labor Day, one of the busiest holidays for campgrounds, was a quiet weekend in northern Dickinson County. Gotta love the Upper Peninsula, where a hill is a mountain, a lake is a pond and a crowded campground is when there is another family two sites away.

Part of the Copper Country State Forest, this rustic campground is what we expect to find in the U.P.: small, out-of-the-way, wooded sites that are well spread out. A quiet place where you can spend an evening observing wildlife.

Directions: Gene's Pond is 6.5 miles northwest of Felch Mountain. From M-69 turn north onto Country Road G-67 and then west on Country Road 422 where the campground is posted.

Campground: Gene's Pond has 14 sites well spread out in a mature hardwood forest on two loops. None of the sites are directly on the water but all are a short walk away from this undeveloped lake. Facilities include fire rings, vault toilets, tables and a hand pump for water.

Hiking: Technically a flooded portion of the Sturgeon River's East Branch, Gene's Pond is surrounded on its south side by marshes. The wetlands and the open water makes this a crossroads for wildlife, the reason the campground is designated as a Wildlife Viewing Area by the Department of Natural Resources. The best way to spot wildlife is to be on the lake at dusk or to hike *Gene's Pond Pathway.*

This trail is a 2.3-mile loop that departs from near the boat launch and heads east through the rolling woods. It begins on an old two-track, switches to an overgrown trail and within a half mile leads to the top of a rocky bluff where you can view most of Gene's Pond and the scenic wetlands that surround it. The other interesting stop along the pathway is Old Hans Mine. In the 19th century it was a small iron mining operation; today all that remains is a large pit, a few rotting timbers and a small hill of tailings that have long since been covered by moss and ferns.

Fishing: There is an unimproved boat launch at the campground. Gene's Pond is reputed to be a good fishing hole with catches of smallmouth bass, crappie, bluegill and perch possible.

Season: This is a lightly used facility.

131

Glidden Lake
Copper Country State Forest

Campground: Rustic
County: Iron   **Nearest Community:** Crystal Falls
Sites: 23   **Reservations:** No
Fee: $10
Information: Crystal Falls DNR office ☎ (906) 875-6622

Located southwest of Crystal Falls in the corner of Iron County is Glidden Lake, a pleasant state forest campground on a small, remote body of water. Demand for spots in this campground is not heavy during most of the summer and its lakeshore sites are often available. Departing from the campground is the *Lake Mary Plains Pathway*, a trail system that can provide hiking opportunities for those who want to walk for an hour or all day.

Directions: From Crystal Falls, head east on M-69 for four miles and then south on Lake Mary Plains Road to Glidden Lake Campground.

Campground: Glidden Lake has 23 sites that are well spread out on two loops in a heavily forested area. Ten sites are close enough to the shoreline for a view of the lake through the trees. The campground has vault toilets, a hand pump for water and tables and fire rings at every site.

Day-Use Facilities: The campground has a picnic area with a small sandy beach where you can quickly cool down on a hot summer afternoon.

Hiking: Since being partially destroyed by a forest fire in 1983, *Lake Mary Plains*

Loop 1
3.4 Miles

To M-69

Glidden Lake

State Forest
Campground

7

1

2 Two-Track

Lake Mary Plains Road

Loop 2
4.5 Miles

3

6

4

Loop 3
3.9 Miles

Two-Track

5

GLIDDEN CAMPGROUND
AND LAKE MARY
PLAINS PATHWAY

Pathway has been restored as one of the finest trail systems in Iron County. A portion of its first loop has also been upgraded into a handicapped-accessible nature trail that includes a long boardwalk through the swamp at the north end of Glidden Lake.

The pathway contains three loops that total more than nine miles, with the perimeter being a 7.3-mile walk. Designed primarily as a cross country ski trail, Loop 3 has a tendency to be wet and sandy in spots and, having been recently logged, is not nearly as interesting. But the first two loops can be combined into a 4.5-mile hike that is hilly in stretches and very scenic at the end. The entire system is extremely well marked with trail maps at almost every junction and is accessed through trailheads in the campground and the parking area for the beach.

Fishing: There is an unimproved boat launch in the day-use area of the campground. Glidden Lake is an undeveloped body of water that is fished for walleye and perch.

Season: This is a light to moderately used facility.

132

Bewabic
State Park

Campground: Modern
County: Iron
Sites: 144
Fee: $16 plus a vehicle entry fee
Information: State park office ☎ (906) 875-3324

Nearest Community: Crystal Falls
Reservations: Yes

Bewabic State Park is located on the corner of the first Fortune Lake. Head south in a canoe or boat and you'll enter the Second Lake, the Third Lake and finally the Fourth Lake. This chain of small lakes extends south of US-2 and is the most attractive feature of this 315-acre park in Iron County. The other attractive feature is a modern campground with sites that offer both hookups and a bit of privacy from your neighbors.

Directions: The park is located four miles west of Crystal Falls on US-2.

Campground: Bewabic has 144 modern sites, four semi-modern ones (no electric hookups) and a Rent-A-Tent in a campground located on a hill above the lake. The sites are located along three loops and range from many in an open grassy setting to No. 88 to 144, which are in a wooded area. These sites are well spread out and offer a surprising amount of privacy for a modern campground.

Day-Use Facilities: Bewabic's beach on Fortune Lake is limited, but the rest of the day-use facility is a lightly shaded, grassy area that features tables, play equipment and a shelter. Most unusual are the tennis courts. Built in the 1940s when the area was a county park, the courts remained when the state acquired the land in 1966, and now Bewabic is the only unit in the state park system where visitors can pack their racket along with their fishing pole.

Fishing: A small boat with a motor can reach all four Fortune Lakes in a day, and anglers often do in their search for perch, largemouth and smallmouth bass, walleye and bluegill. Most anglers concentrate in First Lake, the largest one at 192 acres with a depth of 72 feet. Bewabic maintains an improved boat launch near the day-use area with parking for 12 vehicles and rigs. Additional parking is allowed along the park drive. Shore fishermen can also wet a line and perhaps the best spot is off the island at the north end of the park. There is a steep drop-off on the far side of the island where it's possible to catch perch and bluegill.

Hiking: Bewabic has a pleasant two-mile foot trail with benches along the way that begins at Site No. 144 in the campground and drops through the wooded section in the south end of the park before circling back to the day-use area. There is also a very short trail that follows the shoreline of the island just off the day-use area. Visitors use a footbridge to reach the trail.

Canoeing: The chain of lakes makes for an ideal day trip, departing from the state park and returning through the four lakes, connected by small channels. Keep in mind that there are many cabins on the first two and no public land, other than the state park, on any of the lakes where paddlers could camp overnight.

Season: The campground fills up only for Fourth of July weekend during the summer. Call the Central Reservation System at ☎ (800) 44-PARKS or go online at *www.michigan.gov/dnr* to make reservations.

133

Pentoga
County Park

Campground: Modern
County: Iron   **Nearest Community:** Crystal Falls
Sites: 100   **Reservations:** No
Fee: $15
Information: Park office ☎ (906) 265-3979

There is usually a difference of opinion as to why Pentoga County Park is such a great place to camp. Ask any kid there and it's the water slides that make this place so special. Located on the south end of Chicagon Lake near the Wisconsin border in Iron County, Pentoga features two slides that can only be reached after getting your feet wet. You splash your way 20 yards into the lake's swimming area, climb up either slide and swish! You're flying down the metal ramp into the cool, clear waters of Chicagon Lake.

Good old-fashioned fun on a hot day in August. But many adults enjoy Pentoga County Park for another reason. This place is loaded with Indian history, legend and lore. Where else in Michigan can you camp next to an Ojibway burial grounds complete with spirit houses?

Several interpretive displays cover the significance of this spot, including a huge stone monument that was erected in 1934 denoting the park as the last home of the Ojibway Indians in Iron County and honoring their chief, Mush-Quo-No-Na-Bi, and his wife, Pen-To-ga, whom the park is named after.

The area was discovered in 1851 when Guy H. Carleton, a government surveyor, stumbled onto a little known Indian village. The lake and its trout fishery was such a favorite gathering spot for the tribes that the small trees along the shore today are due to, not loggers, but Indians clearing the area for their tepees.

The tribe dwindled in numbers until 1891 when the chief and his wife sold the land and moved away. By 1903 only a few burial houses and a brush fence remained from the ancient village. But along came Iron County engineer Herbert Larson who convinced local officials to preserve the area and restore the grounds for its historical significance and in 1922 Pentoga became one of the first county parks in the state.

Directions: From Iron Mountain, follow US-2 through Wisconsin and back into Michigan. Three miles south of Crystal Falls turn west onto County Road 424 through the town of Alpha and past Indian Lake to the posted entrance of the park.

Campground: Pentoga Park has 100 sites with electric hookups on two loops. Sites are close together with little privacy but well shaded by large maples and oaks. Also within the campground are showers, a fish cleaning station and wood shed where firewood is sold nightly.

Day-Use Facilities: Pentoga's picnic grounds are a grassy area that leads down to the lakeshore. There is no beach here but the lake has a sandy bottom that makes it ideal for

Indian spirit houses are one of the features of Pentoga County Park.

wading and splashing around. Within the day-use area is a stone bathhouse, picnic shelter, playground equipment, horseshoe pits, volleyball courts and tennis courts.

Fishing: Pentoga does not have a boat launch but there is an access site nearby on the south end of the lake. Chicagon Lake is a large body of water at 1,075 surface acres and a length of three miles. It's also a deep one with one spot 115 feet deep. The spring-fed lake is best known for its northern muskellunge and often yields muskies more than 20 pounds. Most anglers, however, fish for walleye and smallmouth bass.

Hiking: The south end of the *Pentoga Trail* is located in the campground and from here the foot path winds through paper birches until it reached its northern trailhead on US-2, a walk of two miles.

Season: From July through mid-August this campground is often filled on the weekends and occasionally Wednesday and Thursday as well.

134

Lake Ottawa
Ottawa National Forest

Campground: Rustic
County: Iron   **Nearest Community:** Iron River
Sites: 32   **Reservations:** No
Fee: $7 to $12
Information: Iron River Ranger District ☎ (906) 265-5139

The most popular campground in Ottawa National Forest is Lake Ottawa, located west of Iron River. Despite also being one of the largest with 32 sites, this facility is filled almost daily during July. Its popularity comes from the great swimming and scenic beauty of Lake Ottawa, a large body of water that is crystal clear and free of cottages, cabins or any other development.

Directions: From Iron River head west on US-2 and in two miles turn south on M-73. Within a mile turn west on Lake Ottawa Road (also known as Forest Road 101) and follow the signs to the entrance of the park.

Campground: Lake Ottawa has 32 sites that are well spread out and isolated from each other in a maple forest. None of the sites are directly on the lake but a short trail leads from the campground to the day-use beach area. Facilities include paved access roads and sites, pressurized water systems and restrooms with flush toilets. There are no showers.

Day-Use Facilities: Next to the campground is a grassy picnic area that leads to a sandy beach on Lake Ottawa. The swimming is excellent here.

Fishing: There is a fishing pier in the day-use area and an improved boat launch reached from a separate entrance next to the campground. Lake Ottawa covers 550 acres and reaches depths of 90 feet. The main species targeted is walleye but anglers also catch northern pike, bass and yellow perch.

Hiking: The *Ge-Che Trail* is an 11-mile system that extends between Lake Ottawa, Hagerman Lake to the south and Brennan Lake to the east. You can pick up the trail in the boat launch and then head east on the Breenan Lake Loop, a three-mile hike, or south on the Ge-Che Loop, a five-mile outing.

Season: Lake Ottawa is open mid-May to mid-September. This is a popular facility and often filled five out of seven days in July and most weekends in August.

135

Lake Sainte Kathryn
Ottawa National Forest

Campground: Rustic
County: Iron
Sites: 26
Fee: $7 to $9
Nearest Community: Sidnaw
Reservations: No
Information: Kenton Ranger District ☎ (906) 852-3501

Lake Sainte Kathryn is located in the Kenton Ranger District of the Ottawa National Forest and features opportunities for both fishing and hiking. It is also a fairly large campground by national forest standards in a semi-remote location. Chances are good that a site will be available no matter when you arrive.

Directions: From Sidnaw on M-28, head south on South Sidnaw Road. Within seven miles is the intersection with Marten Lake Road (Forest Road 2125) where the northern trailhead of Deer Marsh Trail is located. Continue another mile south on South Sidnaw Road to reach Lake Sainte Kathryn.

Campground: Lake Sainte Kathryn has 26 sites that are well spread out in a forested setting. Six sites are on the water with a nice view of the entire lake. The rest have a partial view of the water or are a short walk away. The campground includes tables, fire rings, hand pumps for water and vault toilets.

Day-Use Facilities: The campground has a small picnic area with tables and grills adjacent to the boat launch.

Fishing: Sainte Kathryn is a 150-acre lake that reaches depths of up to 20 feet. It has been planted with fish cribs and today anglers target northern pike, walleye and smallmouth bass. Along with a boat launch and parking for trailers and vehicles, the campground is equipped with a fishing cleaning area.

Hiking: The *Deer Marsh Interpretive Trail* is a 2.5-mile loop that includes a series of interpretive displays. The trail winds around a large marsh but for the most part offers dry footing. Early in the morning and at dusk the marsh is an excellent place to spot deer, beavers and other wildlife. The main trailhead is a mile north of campground at the corner of South Sidnaw Road and Marten Lake Road, but a spur extends from the boat launch to west side of the loop.

Season: Lake Sainte Kathryn is open from May through the firearm deer season in November. In the summer this is lightly to moderately used campground where obtaining a site is rarely a problem.

136

Norway Lake

Ottawa National Forest

Campground: Rustic
County: Iron
Sites: 28
Fee: $7 to $9
Information: Kenton District Office ☎ (906) 852-3501

Nearest Community: Sidnaw
Reservations: No

Norway Lake is a delightful campground in a remote section of the Ottawa National Forest. But in case you want to put even more distance between you and civilization, there are also a pair of walk-in campsites reached from *Norway Lake Trail*. Haul a tent and sleeping bag a half mile to the first one and you are guaranteed a quiet evening alone on your own corner of the lake.

Directions: From M-28 in Sidnaw, head south on Sidnaw Road for six miles and then west on Forest Road 2400 where Norway Lake Campground is posted on the corner. You reach the campground in two miles.

Campground: Norway Lake has 26 drive-in sites on two loops on a bluff above the water. The first loop has 18 sites with half of them featuring an incredible view of the lake. Site No. 4 is the best of them all, a secluded spot in the pines with a panorama of this undeveloped lake. There are eight more sites on the second loop but most are not within view of the lake. Campground facilities include a log shelter that makes for a nice place if it's raining. There is also a payphone in the picnic area.

Day-Use Facilities: There is a pleasant picnic area in the campground with tables overlooking the lake from the bluff. Norway Lake also has a small sandy beach, a designated swimming area and bathhouse. A better beach is nearby in the day-use area of Nesbit Lake.

Fishing: There is an improved boat launch in the campground. Norway Lake has depths up to 20 feet and was planted with five fish cribs in 1988 and a few more in 1995 to provide more structure and improve the fishing. Still the action is reportedly slow for walleye and bass, the main species anglers target.

Hiking: *Norway Lake Trail* is a 1.2-mile loop that departs the boat launch and winds along the narrow strip of land that separates its namesake lake from Nesbit Lake to the west. It features 15 interpretive posts that examine everything from deer tails to where you can look for pitcher plants. But the charming aspect of this short trail is its pair of walk-in campsites, one on each lake.

The first is less than half mile from the trailhead. There are absolutely no facilities here but the site is a level spot in a stand of red pine. At this point the trail swings away from Norway Lake and cuts over to Nesbit Lake. Heading north you reach the second campsite 0.7 mile from the boat launch trailhead. This one is delightful. It's situated on a small peninsula on the east side of the lake and usually catches enough wind to keep the bugs at bay. The spot is not very big and it's not very level but there is more than enough room for a small tent that can be pitched only a few feet from the water. If there is no group at the youth camp, you'll virtually have the lake to yourself.

Season: Norway Lake is a lightly to moderately used campground.

137

Big Eric's Bridge
Copper Country State Forest

Campground: Rustic
County: Iron **Nearest Community:** Skanee
Sites: 20 **Reservations:** No
Fee: $10
Information: Bargara DNR office ☎ (906) 353-6651

There are popular campgrounds that are usually overrun with trailers and families. There are rustic, hidden-in-the-woods campgrounds where only a handful of people spend the night. Then there is Big Eric's Bridge Campground. When we arrived one weekend in July nobody was there.

This remote facility, located on the edge of the Huron Mountains in the Upper Peninsula, does attract a crowd in April and May when anglers line the banks of the Huron River in an effort to catch a steelhead or two. But for much of the summer Big Eric's Bridge Campground is a very lightly used facility. And sometimes it's just plain empty.

The state forest campground is located off by itself in upper Baraga County in a spot that's not on the way to anywhere. But in an area of the state that is blessed with many scenic places to pitch a tent, this is one of the best in the U.P.

Directions: From L'Anse on US-41, head north out of town on Skanee Road. In 18 miles you'll pass through the town of Skanee and then reach the posted entrance of the campground in another six miles.

Campground: Big Eric's Bridge is a single loop of 20 rustic sites, well spread out and secluded in a hardwood forest with moderate undergrowth. Most of them are on the edge of bluff above the Huron River. It is tough to see the river from your campsite. The gorge is so steep and the foliage so thick you barely get a glimpse of the water through the trees. But you can clearly hear what lies below. The cascading rumble of Big Eric Falls is the most charming aspect of the campground.

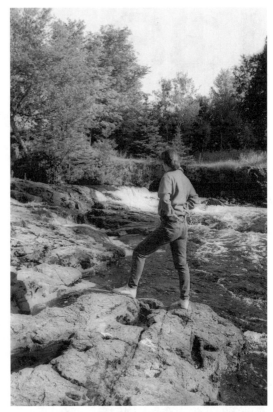

A camper enjoys Big Eric's Falls just below Big Eric's Bridge State Forest Campground northeast of L'Anse.

Waterfalls: Big Eric Falls begins just downstream from the Huron River bridge and is actually a series of small cascades, drops and swirls that form a stretch of whitewater the length of the campground. There are three main cascades, the largest is a five-foot drop over an embankment of smooth stone. In between the patches of whitewater are deep pools, the attention of anglers in the spring and overheated campers in the summer. All around are slaps of bronze-colored boulders.

You can spend a spare day searching and exploring three other nearby waterfalls along the Huron River that are accessed from Black Creek Road, passed just before reaching the campground. They include West Branch Falls, Eric's Falls and Big Falls and all are upstream from the bridge. Pick up *Baraga County Guide To Waterfalls* brochure at the Baraga County Tourist Center in L'Anse on US-41 for directions and descriptions of all the cascades in the area.

Season: The campground is open year-round but roads are not plowed beyond Skanee during the winter. Other than during the spring and fall steelhead runs, this is a lightly used facility.

138

Fort Wilkins
State Park

Campground: Modern
County: Keweenaw   **Nearest Community:** Copper Harbor
Sites: 165   **Reservations:** Yes
Fee: $19 plus vehicle entry fee
Information: State park office ☎ (906) 289-4215

Sometimes you have to learn your history. Sometimes a lesson is inevitable. At Fort Wilkins State Park a history lesson is inevitable but enjoyable, even to children on summer vacation. This 203-acre park, which lies on the narrow band of land between Lake Fanny Hooe and Lake Superior, is where the U.S. Army chose to build a military post in 1844 during the height of the Keweenaw Peninsula copper stampede.

The copper rush began in 1843, and quickly Copper Harbor became the center of exploration parties, newly-formed mining companies and "a rough population" of enterprising prospectors, miners and speculators. Due to the seedy nature of the miners and the constant threat of Chippewa tribes wanting to reclaim their lost land, Secretary of War William Wilkins dispatched two companies of infantry to the remote region of Michigan. They arrived in late May of 1844, and by November Fort Wilkins was built.

The appearance of the fort has changed little since that boom-and-bust period and today is the main reason why the state park attracts 180,000 visitors a year. The majority of them arrive in the summer when this far north the area is so scenic and pleasant you're ready to enlist at the fort.

Directions: Fort Wilkins is 49 miles northeast of Houghton near the tip of the Keweenaw Peninsula. The main entrance to the park, including the fort, East Campground and the day-use area, is a mile east of Copper Harbor on US-41.

Campground: Fort Wilkins has 165 modern sites and a Mini-cabin divided between the East Campground and the West Campground. Both are in wooded areas with a row of sites near the shoreline of Lake Fanny Hooe and a trail to the historic fort. Each has its own entrance off US-41. Sites are equipped with tables, fire rings and electric hookups. Within the campgrounds are restrooms with flush toilets and showers, sanitation stations and pressurized water systems.

Day-Use Facilities: Just east of the fort, there is a pleasant wooded picnic area that

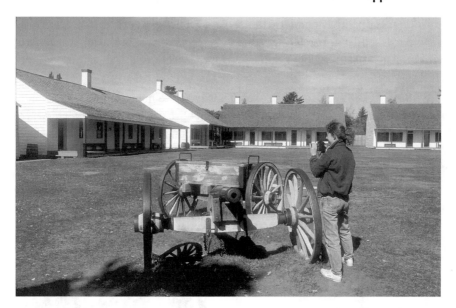

Fort Wilkins State Park includes a modern campground and a military fort that dates back to 1844.

includes a shelter. Also in the area is a park store but there is no beach or designated swimming area on Lake Fanny Hooe.

Interpretive Centers: The centerpiece of the state park is the restored Fort Wilkins. When built, the stockade was the northernmost post in a chain of forts that stretched from the Gulf of Mexico to the tip of the Keweenaw Peninsula in forming a western perimeter of national defense. In reality, however, the fort was of little military importance as the threat of Indian hostilities never materialized and the troops quickly discovered the Upper Peninsula winters were long and cold. In 1846, less than two years after it was built, Fort Wilkins was abandoned.

Although insignificant militarily, the fort is an outstanding example of a mid-19th century frontier outpost as 12 of its 19 buildings are from the original structure. The individual buildings are open mid-May through mid-October from 8 A.M. to dusk. Ranging from kitchen and mess room to the bakery, company barracks and hospital, many contain restored furnishings and artifacts depicting the rough life troops endured here. From mid-June to Labor Day interpreters in period dress give tours daily and add a touch of realism to the fort.

Also part of the state park is the Copper Harbor Lighthouse. The structure was built in 1866 and was occupied until 1919. Today the interior is restored as a lighthouse museum and can be visited through a boat tour operator that leaves the Copper City Harbor hourly during the summer from 10 A.M. to 5 P.M. There is a fee for the boat tour to the lighthouse but none for viewing the fort other than a vehicle entry permit.

Hiking: The park has almost two miles of trail, much of it connects the fort with the campgrounds and day-use area. The *Lake Superior Nature Trail* begins in the picnic area and forms a circuit that runs along Lake Fanny Hooe, Copper Harbor and Fanny Hooe Creek before passing the fort.

Fishing: Lake Fanny Hooe is stocked annually with rainbow trout and splake and in the past with walleye. Anglers also catch smallmouth bass. The park maintains a boat launch on Lake Fanny Hooe near the West Campground. There is no ramp on the Lake Superior side of the state park, but the DNR Waterways Division maintains a large public marina in Copper Harbor.

Season: Fort Wilkins is a popular tourist attraction so the campgrounds tend to fill a handful of weekends in July and early August. For reservations go online at *www.michigan.gov/dnr* or call ☎(800) 44-PARKS.

139

F.J. McLain
State Park

Campground: Modern
County: Houghton   **Nearest Community:** Hancock
Sites: 103   **Reservations:** Yes
Fee: $22
Information: State park office ☎ (906) 482-0278

One of only four state parks overlooking Lake Superior, F.J. McLain State Park is a 443-acre unit located northwest of the Houghton-Hancock area in the heart of Michigan's Copper Country.

Its best feature is two miles of Lake Superior shoreline and the bluff that rises above it. The sun melting into the shimmering horizon of Lake Superior on a clear evening in the summer makes for a spectacular sunset.

Directions: The park entrance is on M-203, eight miles north of Hancock.

Campground: At one time McLain featured more than 20 sites on the edge of the shoreline bluff with great views of the Great Lake, but most have since been removed due to erosion. The park now has 103 modern sites on a single loop in an area lightly forested in red pine and oaks.

McLain also features some of the finest mini-cabins in the state park system. The six mini-cabins, perfect for a family of four, are along the park road that skirts the Lake

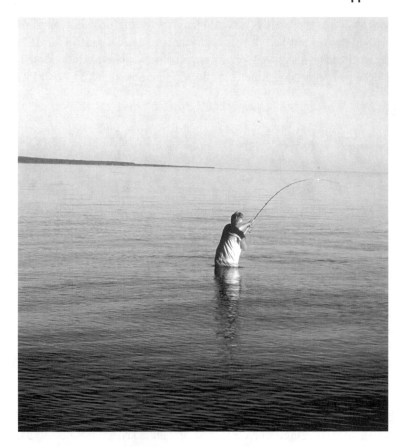

A surf angler fishes in Lake Superior at McLain State Park.

Superior bluff, well away from the bustling campground. Three of the cabins are tucked back into the trees and three of them are just off the road with a clear view of the water. Mini-cabins are $32 a night.

Day-Use Facilities: The park has a small, sandy beach and a bathhouse located where Portage Lake Ship Canal flows into Lake Superior. The sand is protected from the ravages of the Great Lake by a long breakwall and the walk out to the Keweenaw Upper Entry Light makes for an interesting stroll. The park also has a picnic area with a shelter.

Hiking: Bear Lake Trail is a three-mile loop that crosses M-203 and then follows the shoreline of Bear Lake to an old fishing pier before returning. The trail is a pleasant hike any time of the year and spectacular in late September when autumn colors are peaking.

Fishing: There is little fishing activity in Bear Lake. Shore anglers, however, gather along the breakwall where in the spring and fall they cast spoons and spawn for steelhead and coho salmon and in the summer fish for whitefish.

Season: McLain is a popular destination for campers and from mid-July to mid-August can be filled any day of the week but particularly the weekends. It is usually also filled on Labor Day weekend. Reservations for campsites or mini-cabins can be made online at *www.michigan.gov/dnr* or through the Central Reservation System at ☎ (800) 44-PARKS.

140

Bob Lake
Ottawa National Forest

Campground: Rustic
County: Houghton   **Nearest Community:** Mass City
Sites: 17   **Reservations:** No
Fee: $5
Information: Ontonagon District Office ☎ (906) 884-2085

Bob Lake is one of those wonderfully remote campgrounds in the Ottawa National Forest that is hard to find and even harder to leave. It features lakeshore sites, an interesting nature trail, a small sandy beach and even the opportunity to see some wildlife. If you love secluded, rustic campgrounds seemingly in the middle of nowhere, you'll love Bob Lake and should plan on spending at least a couple of nights here.

Directions: From M-38, 30 miles west of L'Anse, turn south on Forest Highway 16 for five miles and then west on Pori Road for two miles. Turn south on Forest Highway 1470 to reach the campground in two miles.

Campground: Bob Lake has 17 rustic sites well spread out in a heavily forested area. Six of them are right on the shoreline where at night you can sit at your picnic table and watch a pair of loons.

Day-Use Facilities: Next to the campground is a day-use area with a small sandy beach, changing rooms and a few picnic tables.

Fishing: Bob Lake is a totally undeveloped lake that is accessed via a boat launch in the campground. The lake is spread over 133 acres with an average depth of 15 feet. Most anglers fish it for walleye and perch.

Hiking: Originally built in the late 1960s, *Beaver Lodge Nature Trail* was renovated in the early 1990s, which included installing walkways, bridges and 24 interpretive plaques. In 1995, the loop was designated a Watchable Wildlife Trail by the U.S. Forest Service.

The trailhead for the 1.25-mile loop is near the day-use area with the trail beginning and ending on a former railroad bed that still features a few of the original ties. In between you skirt a small pothole lake, past a spur that leads to the *North Country Trail* and a beaver pond with an active lodge and a huge dam. A second pond is just down the trail and at either you can sit quietly and often spot a variety of wildlife, ranging from waterfowl and bald eagles to whitetail deer, fox, a fisher and, of course, beavers.

Season: Bob Lake is open from mid-May to mid-November and is a lightly used campground.

141

Bonds Falls
Upper Peninsula Power Company

Campground: Rustic
County: Gogebic   **Nearest Community:** Pauling
Sites: 48   **Reservations:** No
Fee: $8
Information: Bonds Falls Outpost ☎ (906) 827-3753

The camp sites along Bond Falls Flowage are not modern sites with electric hookups, heated restrooms and showers, where campers are so close together they're "on display" whenever somebody drives through the campground. Nor are they considered rustic or even primitive (fire ring in the middle of the woods).

At this huge recreational facility, owned and operated by the Upper Peninsula Power Company (UPPCO) in southern Ontonagon County, you pitch your tent or park your trailer in what is described as "wilderness campsites." While UPPCO's idea of a wilderness site and mine are two totally different concepts, the campground at Bond Falls Flowage is unique because the sites are so far apart. You're definitely not on display here. You're lucky if you can even find your site, much less see your neighbors.

The fishing is excellent in the Flowage but the high point for most campers is Bond Falls, one of the most impressive cascades in the Upper Peninsula.

Directions: From US-45 in Paulding, turn east onto Bond Falls Road and in 3.2 miles you'll come to the trailhead and the cascade, parking area and park office where you can obtain a campground map and register a site.

Campground: Bond Falls Flowage features 48 sites that are situated, not on a single

Bond Falls, a stunning cascade, is reached from the day-use area of the Bond Falls Flowage Campground.

loop but rather around the shoreline of a 2,200-acre lake. Rugged dirt roads lead away from Bond Falls Road to sites on both sides down of the Flowage. There are 10 sites scattered around the north end and 20 more on its west side. The most isolated ones, however, are the 18 on the east side. Many are on small peninsulas, overlooking the water and offering campers their own secluded corner of the lake. Amenities include fire grills, tables and vault toilets.

Day-Use Facilities: At the north end of the lake is a picnic area with tables, grills, play equipment for children and a small store.

Fishing: After loggers took out the pine along the Middle Branch of the Ontonagon River at the turn of the century, a plan was proposed to dam up the river and divert the water to a hydroelectric station near Victoria. The dam and a two-mile-long canal was constructed in 1937 and what was the Middle Branch and three feeder streams became a lake…a very big lake. Bond Falls Flowage covers 2,200 acres and has a depth of more than 55 feet. This is a fishing hot spot—northern pike up to 33 pounds and muskie as large as 41 pounds have been taken from the flooded timber below and many anglers jig for walleye and bass. There is a boat launch on a small bay between Site No. 10 and Site No. 11.

Hiking: The trailhead for Bond Falls is on the north side of Bond Falls Road across from the picnic area. Many consider Bond Falls second only to Upper Tahquamenon in terms of spectacular beauty. The cascade descends almost 50 feet in a series of step-like drops. The trail to the falls is only a half mile long but includes numerous stairways.

Season: The campground is open year-round but the Bond Falls Outpost is open from June 1 through Labor Day from 8:30-11:30 A.M. and 1:30-4:30 P.M.

142

Clark Lake
Sylvania Recreation Area

Campground: Rustic
County: Gogebic **Nearest Community:** Watersmeet
Sites: 48 **Reservations:** No
Fee: $8
Information: Park office ☎ (906) 644-2603

Sylvania Wilderness is an 18,327-acre tract that includes 36 named lakes connected to one another by portages and footpaths. This non-motorized area is renowned among paddlers looking for a wilderness adventure, good fishing and the possibility of spotting a variety of wildlife from black bears to bald eagles.

At the north end of the wilderness, overlooking Clark Lake, is Sylvania Recreation Area. Even if you have no desire to haul a canoe between lakes, you can enjoy this pristine slice of the Ottawa National Forest by staying at this drive-in campground within the recreation area. But bring a canoe if you can. The only way to enjoy the beauty or outstanding fishing in Clark Lake is by paddling.

Directions: Near the corner of US-2 and US-45, just south of Watersmeet, is the Watersmeet Visitor Center that has maps, books and displays about the area and the Ottawa National Forest. From the center head west on US-2 for four miles and then south on County Road 535, which passes the posted entrance to the Clark Lake Campground.

Campground: Clark Lake has 48 sites on four loops spread out between Clark Lake and Katherine Lake. The campground lies just beyond the wilderness area but is well wooded by old growth hemlocks and other towering trees. None of the sites are within view of the lakes but are well isolated from each other for a good bit of privacy. The campground has flush toilets, tables, fire rings and a pressurized water system. Showers are available in the day-use area.

Day-Use Facilities: A developed beach and picnic area is at the north end of Clark Lake, a mile west of the campground. The swimming is excellent and facilities include a bathhouse with hot showers.

Fishing: Within Sylvania are 36 named lakes with six lakes larger than 250 acres in size. Clark Lake is one of the largest at 820 acres and depths up to 75 feet. From the south end of Clark Lake, portages extend to three more: Hay Lake, Loon Lake and Crooked Lake.

What makes these lakes so precious is their clarity. They sit on the divide between the

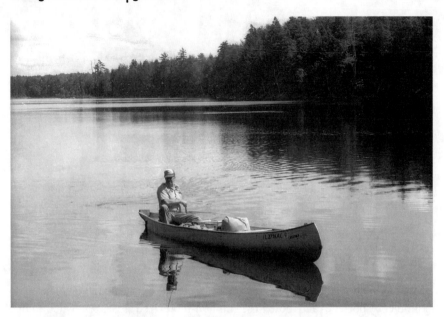

Clark Lake is part of the Sylvania Wilderness, a 18,327-acre tract that includes 36 named lakes connected to one another by portages. The lakes are non-motorized, making a canoe the best form of transportation for campers.

Lake Superior and the Mississippi River drainages but have no surface outlet to either one. Nor do they have any rivers or streams pouring nutrient matter into them. They are landlocked lakes fed by springs, bogs and rain. They are, for all practical purposes, rain barrels with water so clear that you can lean over the side of your canoe and see the bottom...30 or 40 feet down.

A trophy fishery, especially for smallmouth bass, has developed over the years due to inaccessibility of the lakes and the special regulations to protect them. Only artificial lures are allowed, no worms or other live bait can be used to entice the fish. You can't fish before the last Saturday in April or after October and you couldn't keep a bass regardless of its size.

Clark Lake is non-motorized and there is a boat launch near the day-use area with additional parking for vehicles and trailers. The lake is fished primarily for smallmouth bass and trout. Other lakes can be fished for northern pike and panfish as well.

Hiking: Within the wilderness are 30 miles of foot trails for those who want nothing to do with canoeing. These paths traverse the old growth forests and pass the shores of many lakes. One of the best hikes is the eight-mile loop that departs the day-use area and skirts Clark Lake. For much of the way the trail skirts the shoreline and at times passes through stands of old growth hemlocks.

Season: Clark Lake is open from the last week of May through November. It's not unusual for the campground to be filled any time in July and the first half of August. There is a 14-day limit on camping.

143

Moosehead Lake
Ottawa National Forest

Campground: Rustic
County: Gogebic   **Nearest Community:** Marenisco
Sites: 13   **Reservations:** No
Fee: $6
Information: Bessemer Ranger District ☎ (906) 667-0261

Even if you have been to Wisconsin before, the attraction of camping on Moosehead Lake is being able to paddle to Wisconsin. Several times a day if you wish. Moosehead is a pleasant, rustic campground on the state border that is connected to Little Presque Isle Lake, just to the south and outside of Ottawa National Forest. Here you can camp and visit two states, fish two states and never once get in your car.

Directions: From US-2, east of Marenisco, head south on Forest Road 7300 for eight miles. Turn right on County Road 530 (also called Pomeroy Lake Road) and in a mile veer left onto Forest Road 6860. Within 1.5 miles veer left at Forest Road 6862 and the campground is two miles at the end of the road.

Campground: Moosehead Lake has 13 sites on the edge of a shoreline bluff forested in red pine. The sites are well spread out and from half of them you have a view of the lake, which on a topographical map really does look like the head of a moose. The campground has the usual U.S. Forest Service amenities: tables, fire rings, lantern posts, a hand pump for water and pit toilets.

Fishing: Moosehead is a 43-acre lake with a depth up to 35 feet and an undeveloped shoreline. There is a boat launch in the campground and anglers fish the lake for northern pike, largemouth bass and even a muskie. It's also possible to catch bluegills and perch.

Even better, Moosehead is surrounded by other lakes. This is canoe country. Just north of the campground are seven lakes, all small bodies of water where you can drop in a canoe and spend a morning casting a lure. The most interesting lake is Little Presque Isle Lake, reached from the campground's boat ramp by heading south. At the south end of Moosehead Lake is a small marshy channel and somewhere in this channel you entered Wisconsin and become a cheddarhead. Presque Isle Lake is a body of water that was almost twice as big as Moosehead. There are a few cottages on the lake but most of them are along the south end and sit so far back in the trees that it's easy to miss them.

Season: The lightly used campground is open from mid-May to mid-October.

144

Henry Lake
Ottawa National Forest

Campground: Rustic
County: Gogebic
Sites: 11
Fee: $6
Nearest Community: Marenisco
Reservations: No
Information: Bessemer Ranger District ☎ (906) 667-0261

Henry Lake is a small campground in the Ottawa National Forest that makes for an ideal stop during a family camping adventure in the western Upper Peninsula. The lake is small enough where you can easily explore it in a canoe. There's a pier where children can cast for bluegills and have a good opportunity to catch them. And its remote location evokes a wilderness-sense of adventure when camping here.

Is that a bear on the other side of the lake?

If you do plan on camping at Henry Lake, pack along the mountain bikes. The campground lies in the middle of the Henry Lake & Pomeroy Lake Mountain Bike Complex where riders follow specially-posted gravel roads for easy outings.

Directions: The nearest town to Henry Lake is Marenisco, which is 26 miles west of Watersmeet along US-2. From Marenisco, head west on US-2 and then turn onto Old US-2, and follow it west four miles to Forest Road-8100. Turn south on FR-8100 to reach the campground in five miles.

Campground: Henry Lake is a small and pleasant campground with 11 sites well spread out in a heavily forested area. Five sites are located on a low rise above the lake and have a nice view of the water. Sites have tables and fire rings while within the campground are vault toilets and a hand pump for water.

Fishing: Henry Lake is only 43 acres in size but reaches depths of up to 30 feet. It supports a good fishery of largemouth bass, perch, bluegill and other panfish. The campground has an improved boat launch with additional parking for vehicles and trailers. Nearby is a large, T-shaped fishing pier where a 20-foot drop-off is within easy casting distance, even for children. Fish cribs have been placed both around the pier and elsewhere in the lake to improve the fishing. The nearest bait and tackle shops are in Marenisco.

Mountain Biking: The *Henry and Pomeroy Lake Mountain Bike Complex* is a vast system of forest roads in the lake-studded region of the Ottawa National Forest along the

North

- - - Mountain
Bike Route

2

FR-8190

FR-8170

FR-8100

Old US-2

Marenisco

State Line

Rail Trail

Heart
Lake

West Branch

Presque Isle River

Henry
Lake

Hawk
Lake

64

Mink
Lake

FR-8120

Eel
Lake

Moraine
Lake

HENRY LAKE MOUNTAIN BIKE COMPLEX

Michigan/Wisconsin border. The U.S. Forest Service posted the 86-mile network in 1994 in response to the increasing number of "where can we ride" inquires it was receiving from mountain bikers.

Part of the Mines and Pines Mountain Bike Trail System that spreads across western U.P. and into Wisconsin's Iron County, Henry and Pomeroy Lake was purposely set up for novice off-road cyclists and families. There are no twisty single tracks here or beaver dams to tiptoe across. All the routes are laid out on either gravel forest roads or the *State Line Rail-*

Trail, which resembles a two-track. You could ride most of the system on a road bike but it would be laborious at best. A hybrid is a better choice and a true mountain bike would provide the easiest trip of all.

The system is located south of the town of Marenisco and split by M-65. On the west half is the 22.8-mile Henry Lake portion; on the east the 63-mile network around Pomeroy Lake. The *State Line Rail-Trail* crosses M-64 to connect the two halves. The routes are well posted by a blue mountain biker symbol and easy to follow. The number of different loops you can ride in this complex is almost limitless. If passing through Watersmeet stop at the Sylvania Visitor Center for the Ottawa National Forest on US-2 and pick up a trail map.

Season: Henry Lake is open from mid-May to mid-October and is a lightly used facility.

145

Pomeroy Lake
Ottawa National Forest

Campground: Rustic
County: Gogebic　　**Nearest Community:** Marenisco
Sites: 17　　**Reservations:** No
Fee: $6
Information: Bessemer Ranger District ☎ (906) 667-0261

This is the other campground in the Henry & Pomeroy Lake Mountain Bike Complex, a lake-studded region of the Ottawa National Forest. Pomeroy Lake is not as heavily forested as its counterpart, Henry Lake, nor does it have a pier for shore anglers. But both the campground and especially the lake are larger and overall the fishing is better. Once again, bring a mountain bike to enjoy some scenic and interesting rides.

Directions: From Marenisco head east on US-2 and in four miles south on Forest Road 7300. FR-7300 reaches the national forest campground in 10 miles.

Campground: Pomeroy Lake has 17 sites that are spread out in a wooded area at the north end of the lake. Twelve sites are right on the lakeshore, the others a short walk away. Facilities include tables, fire rings and vault toilets.

Fishing: The campground also has an improved boat launch with additional parking for vehicles and trailers that is reached from a separate entrance from FR-7300. Pomeroy is 303-acre lakes with its deepest point only 15 feet. Most of the lake is less than 10 feet in depth. Pomeroy has a mixed bag for a fishery and includes walleye, northern pike, black crappie, largemouth bass, bluegill and yellow perch. At its southeast corner is a portage trail to Little Pomeroy Lake, a much smaller body of water that is fished for bass and bluegill.

Mountain Biking: The Henry & Pomeroy Mountain Bike Complex is split by M-65. The eastern half around Pomeroy Lake is a 63-mile network of marked gravel roads along with a section of the *State Line Rail-Trail* that in the summer resembles a two-track. The rail-trail makes for an interesting ride. From the campground it's a 4.5-mile ride north on FR-7300 to where the rail-trail crosses the forest road. Head east on State Line and in the next five miles you'll pass two isolated lakes and cross several creeks. State Line eventually skirts US-2; follow it to Langford Lake Road, which heads southwest back to Pomeroy Lake. Such a loop would be a 17-mile ride.

Season: Pomeroy Lake is a lightly used facility.

146

Lake Gogebic
State Park

Campground: Modern
County: Gogebic   **Nearest Community:** Marenisco
Sites: 127   **Reservations:** Yes
Fee: $12 and $14 plus vehicle entry fee
Information: State park office ☎ (906) 842-3341

Lake Gogebic State Park borders the largest inland lake in the Upper Peninsula and perhaps the most beautiful body of water anywhere in the state. But the 361-acre state park also lies on the edge of the rugged highlands that extend west into the heart of the Ottawa National Forest. These ridges and hills include a highpoint of 1,545 feet and are penetrated only by a two-mile trail.

M-64 conveniently separates the park's split personality. On the east side of the state highway is the 0.75 mile of Lake Gogebic shoreline and a well developed area catering to campers, swimmers, boaters and anglers. To the west is the park's rugged interior that intrigues hikers who want to view an impressive stand of old growth timber.

Directions: The state park is 25 miles east of Wakefield. Follow US-2 16 miles and then turn north (left) on M-64 for nine miles to the posted entrance. From M-28 turn south of M-64 for eight miles.

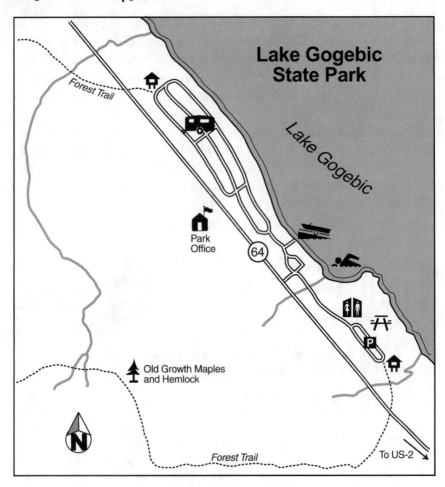

Lake Gogebic State Park

Campground: Lake Gogebic has 104 modern sites in its campground with a large portion of them situated right along the shoreline. The rest have a good view of the water, and all are in a semi-open area that is lightly shaded. There are also 22 semi-modern sites without electricity and a Rent-A-Tent. Facilities include tables, fire rings, heated restrooms with flush toilets and showers.

Day-Use Facilities: Lake Gogebic has a small, sandy beach bordered by a large grassy bank in its day-use area. Other facilities include a bathhouse, play area, parking for a 100 vehicles and an exceptionally pleasant picnic area situated on a small point with a nice view of the lakeshore to the north.

Fishing: The largest lake in the Upper Peninsula is also a noted one for walleye fishing. The 14-mile Lake Gogebic covers more than 20 square miles and is stocked annually with walleye. Although there are a variety of ways to fish for walleyes, many anglers prefer drifting or slowly trolling inflated nightcrawlers or leeches. Working rocky points and drop-offs with lead jigs tipped with minnows is another productive method. Lake Gogebic is also rated quite highly for its population of northern pike and perch. The park maintains an improved boat ramp near the day-use area. Just outside the park along M-65 there are numerous bait shops and resorts that rent boats and motors.

Hiking: Beginning at a marked trailhead in the back of the campground is the *Forest Trail*, a two-mile walk that ends at the parking lot for the day-use area. The trail crosses M-64 twice to wind through the park's wooded and rolling interior, passing a series of interpretive displays. The first mile of the trail can be wet at times as you pass a cedar swamp but the second half is a dry path through an impressive stand of old growth maple and hemlock.

Season: There are usually sites available in Lake Gogebic's scenic campground with the exception of Fourth of July weekend and the second week in August. You can reserve sites in advance through the Central Reservation Service at ☎ (800) 44-PARKS or online at *www.michigan.gov/dnr*.

147

Union Bay

Porcupine Mountains State Park

Campground: Modern
County: Ontonagon   **Nearest Community:** Silver City
Sites: 99   **Reservations:** Yes
Fee: $19 plus vehicle entry fee
Information: State park office ☎ (906) 885-5275

The Porcupine Mountains Wilderness is the largest state park in Michigan, stretching 58,335 acres across Ontonagon and Gogebic counties. The park is 25 miles long and 10 miles at its widest point. It contains 26 miles of Lake Superior shoreline, four lakes, including the impressive Lake of the Clouds, and numerous rivers, trout streams and waterfalls. This is impressive country to say the least.

Porcupine Mountains has five campgrounds accessible by road. At the west end is Presque Isle (see page 295). At the east end is Union Bay, the largest and most modern facility. In between these two campgrounds are three rustic facilities called outposts that offer a degree of privacy. A mile south of the visitor center on South Boundary Road is Union River Outpost with three sites. Another six miles to the west is Lost Creek Outpost

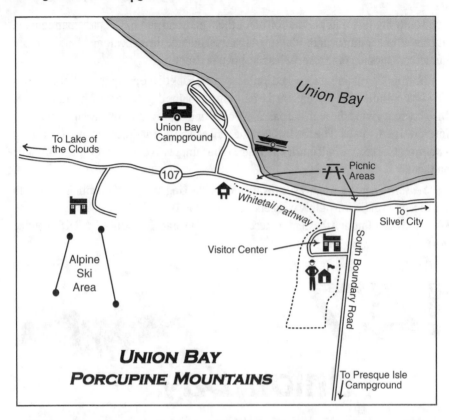

UNION BAY
PORCUPINE MOUNTAINS

Union Bay

Union Bay
Campground

To Lake of
the Clouds

107

Picnic
Areas

Whitetail Pathway

To
Silver City

Visitor Center

South Boundary Road

Alpine
Ski
Area

To Presque Isle
Campground

with three sites, and three miles farther still, White Pine Extension Outpost with seven drive-in sites.

At any of these campgrounds plan to set up and stay put for at least three days to enjoy the stunning scenery this park has to offer. Day hiking in the Porkies is excellent with destinations such as waterfalls, isolated lakes or sweeping views from the top of highpoints.

Directions: Union Bay Campground is near the park's east entrance. From M-64 in Ontonagon, head west on M-107 to reach the campground in 18 miles.

Campground: With 99 sites, Union Bay is the largest campground in the park. The sites are situated along a loop on a grassy shelf overlooking Lake Superior and the best swimming beach in the park. There are a few large trees in the campground but otherwise little shade. Facilities include tables, fire rings, electric hookups, modern restrooms with flush toilets and showers and a sanitation station for recreational vehicles. Nearby Whitetail Path departs M-107 and leads to the park's visitor's center, a mile walk through the woods.

Day-Use Facilities: There is a day-use area on each side of the park. On the east side of the park, a picnic area is adjacent to the Union Bay Campground and features tables and grills overlooking Lake Superior.

Interpretive Center: Porcupine Mountains has an impressive visitor center, located a half mile south of M-107 on South Boundary Road. Inside there are exhibits explaining the geological history of the mountains plus a three-dimensional relief map that every hiker should study before striking out. There is also a room devoted to the diverse wildlife in the park and a small theater where multi-slide presentations are repeated throughout the day. The center is the best source of maps and trail information for hikers and backpackers. It is open from May 15 to October 15 from 10 A.M. until 6 P.M.

Scenic Viewpoints: From the end of M-107, it's a short walk to perhaps Michigan's most famous panorama, Lake of the Clouds Overlook. The viewing point is set on the side of a vertical cliff, and from the high point of almost 1,300 feet, it's possible to see the picturesque lake set among forested ridges and much of the Porkies' rugged interior. Another spectacular viewing area is Summit Observation Tower. The deck and observation tower is constructed on Summit Peak, 1,958 feet, and reached with a half-mile walk from the end of Summit Peak Road. The view includes the center of the Porkies and a portion of Mirror Lake.

Hiking: The Porkies is best known as a destination for backpackers but not all hiking adventures in the park have to be overnight trips. On the perimeter, there are a number of short loops that make for scenic day hikes. Along M-107, west of Union Bay Campground, is the trailhead for the *Overlook Trail*, which is combined with a short portion of the Government Peak Trail to form a 3.5-mile loop to a number of scenic viewpoints above 1,200 feet.

The same trailhead is also the east end of the *Escarpment Trail*, a four-mile hike along a ridge that includes Cuyahoga and Cloud peaks and ends at the Lake of the Clouds Overlook on M-107. The views of Lake of the Clouds and the park's interior from this rocky ridge make this trail one of the most scenic in Michigan.

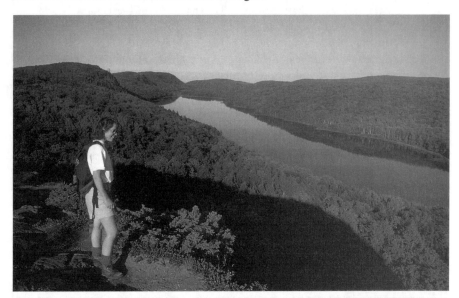

One of the most beautiful trails in Michigan if not the Midwest is the Escarpment Trail, not far from Union Bay Campground. The trail skirts a high rocky ridge above Lake of the Clouds.

THE CROWN JEWEL OF MICHIGAN TRAILS

The Escarpment is the crown jewel of trails not only in the Porkies but possibly in all of Michigan. The trail combines a high rocky bluff and alpine-like vistas with views of the park's rugged interior, Big Carp River Valley and, of course, the centerpiece of the park: Lake of Clouds. Unlike the tourists who simply drive to the overlook and look down, the Escarpment Trail provides you with view of the famous lake from several different angles, and if the day is clear, you can easily shoot a roll of film or more by the time you return to M-107.

The only drawback is that the Escarpment is a point-to-point trail. You begin here, you end up over there four miles from your vehicle. There is a spur reached halfway along the trail that can be used to access M-107 after two miles and, of course, you can always turn around and simply retrace your steps. However, it would be a shame to go that far to hike one of the most awe-inspiring trails in the Midwest and not finish it.

The easiest direction to follow the route is beginning from the Lake of the Clouds Overlook. Before departing remember to fill the water bottles. There is no drinking water at the overlook, and on a clear summer day the route across the Escarpment can be a hot one. You actually begin at the posted North Mirror Lake Trailhead. Within a half mile at a posted junction, North Mirror Lake Trail plummets toward Lake of the Clouds while the Escarpment officially begins with a climb through a mixed forest.

Quickly you arrive at the first overlook, staring down at middle of the lake. The trail resumes with a sharper climb and in a half mile you break out at a second vista. This vista is spectacular, as good or better than the overlook at the end of M-107 because you're at a much higher elevation (1,480 feet). Below you, 400 feet straight down, is Lake of the Clouds in royal blue. To the west you can see visitors who have just stepped out of their cars and to the east is the rest of the Escarpment and the Upper Carp River winding its way into the lake.

The trail continues along the open cliff where you enjoy the scenery almost every step of the way. You also pass the posted site of Carp Lake Mine. Carp Lake was the name for Lake of the Clouds when the mine was established in 1858. The operation lingered into the 1920s but reached its peak in 1865 when a company of more than 50 men used a small stamping mill to produce 13,000 pounds of copper from several shafts into the Escarpment. Near the trail is a fenced-off cistern where a spur leads down the slope to the twin boilers of the stamping mill that can still be seen today.

You depart the mine site by immediately ascending toward Cuyahoga Peak, climbing more than 200 feet to the highpoint of the day of 1,600 feet. In less than a half mile from the junction, you break out to another panoramic scene of the Upper Carp River where the trail skirts the edge of the Escarpment.

Along South Boundary Road, two miles south of M-107, is *Union Mine Trail*. This mile-long loop features the ruins of the old Union Copper Mine that are explained in an interpretive brochure available at the Visitor Center

Fishing: The park also has an improved boat launch at Union Pier Campground for anglers who want to troll Lake Superior for lake trout in June and July as well as steelhead, salmon and brown trout at other times of the year.

Season: The restrooms and other facilities in Union Bay are open from mid-May to the third week in October. The campground fills daily for two weeks from late July through mid-August and is full five out of seven nights during the rest of the summer. Sites are easy to obtain before mid-June and beginning in September. To reserve a site call the Central Reservation System at ☎ (800) 44-PARKS.

148

Presque Isle

Porcupine Mountains State Park

Campground: Semi-modern
County: Gogebic **Nearest Community:** Wakefield
Sites: 88 **Reservations:** Yes
Fee: $15 plus vehicle entry fee
Information: State park office ☎ (906) 885-5275

The Presque Isle River in the Porcupine Mountains Wilderness State Park is one of the most spectacular spots in Michigan. In its final mile before emptying into Lake Superior, the Presque Isle descends more than 100 feet and in doing so has carved a rugged and steep-sided gorge that is filled with impressive waterfalls and wild whitewater.

On the bluffs above this scenic waterway is the park's Presque Isle Campground. The semi-modern facility provides access to both the scenic end of this river and Lake Superior. It also allows you to hike the trails in the west end of the park without having to carry a backpack.

Directions: Porcupine Mountains Wilderness State Park is 17 miles west of Ontonagon via M-64 and M-107. Once in the park, head south on South Boundary Road and follow it until it ends at County Road 519. Head north on CR 519 to reach the campground. Presque Isle can also be reached from US-2, where the campground is 16 miles from Wakefield at end of County Road 519.

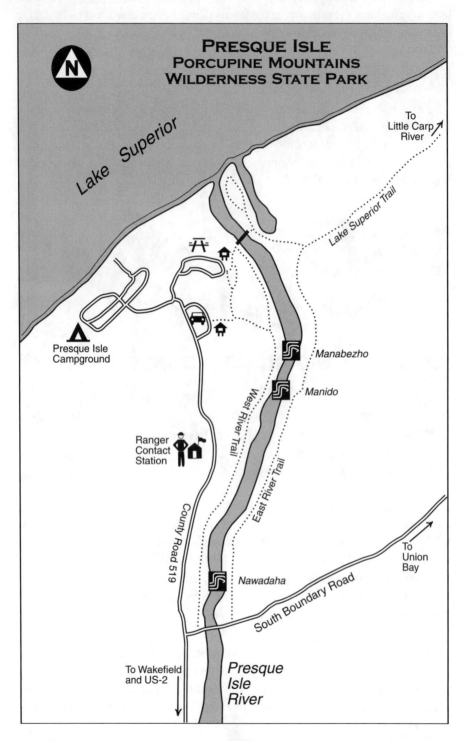

PRESQUE ISLE
PORCUPINE MOUNTAINS
WILDERNESS STATE PARK

N

Lake Superior

To Little Carp River

Lake Superior Trail

Presque Isle Campground

Manabezho

Manido

West River Trail

East River Trail

Ranger Contact Station

County Road 519

Nawadaha

To Union Bay

South Boundary Road

To Wakefield and US-2

Presque Isle River

The roaring whitewater of the Presque Isle River in the spring as seen from the West River Trail.

Campground: Presque Isle has 88 semi-modern sites on several loops with restrooms and showers but no electricity for recreational vehicles. The campground is located in a lightly wooded area with a handful of sites on a bluff overlooking Lake Superior and all of them an easy stroll from the overlooks at the end of the Presque Isle River.

Day-Use Facilities: There is a picnic area with tables, grills and separate parking on the east side of CR-519 near the campground. From the picnic area you can access the stairs and boardwalks to the waterfalls in the Presque Isle Gorge.

Hiking: The *Presque Isle River Trail*, also referred to as the East and West River Trails, is a two-mile loop that climbs in and out of the gorge and passes three waterfalls. Pick up the trail in the Presque Isle Day-Use Area, where you immediately descend to an impressive swing bridge. What appears on maps as a peninsula on the other side of the bridge is actually an island in the mouth of the river with a dry channel on one side.

You can follow a spur on the island to view the rugged shoreline of Lake Superior or cross the waterless channel to the east bank. Here you follow the *East River Trail* south to the South Boundary Road Bridge and then return north along the *West River Trail*. Along the way the trail on the west bank becomes an extensive boardwalk that puts you right above Manido Falls and then Manabezho. You're so close you can feel their cooling mist on a hot afternoon.

The East River Trail also passes a junction to *Lake Superior Trail*, at a length of 16 miles the longest foot route in the park. Lake Superior Trail departs from the Presque Isle River and follows the shoreline before emerging at M-107.

Fishing: Porcupine Mountains State Park is best known for its steelhead and salmon runs in the spring and fall. Presque Isle River attracts the most attention with wading anglers either surf fishing or working the mouth of the river, as Manabezho Falls blocks farther runs upstream.

Season: Demand on the campground varies from year to year, but the busiest period is Monday and Tuesday with the weekends being considerably slower. Presque Isle often fills up from mid-July to the end of August, and reservations are advisable during this period. Sites are booked in advance through the state park's Central Reservation System (☎(800) 44-PARKS) or online at *www.michigan.gov/dnr*.

149

Black River Harbor
Ottawa National Forest

Campground: Semi-modern
County: Gogebic   **Nearest Community:** Bessemer
Sites: 40   **Reservations:** Yes
Fee: $10
Information: Bessemer Ranger District ☎ (906) 667-0261

County Road 513 is a trip in itself. Also known as Black River Road, it heads north from Bessemer, passes the towering Copper Peak Ski Flying Hill and then the trailheads to five stunning waterfalls. The road finally ends at Black River Harbor, a Ottawa National Forest recreation area on Lake Superior where you could easily spend the rest of the week camping.

One of only two harbors located in a national forest, Black River Harbor offers recreational opportunities to not only boaters and campers but also hikers, agate hunters, anglers and people who simply like to spend an afternoon listening to the roar of a waterfall. This is a popular place to camp during the summer, a breathtakingly beautiful one in late September when the surrounding hardwood forests ignite in fall colors.

The Potawatomi Falls, one of five spectacular waterfalls accessed from Black River, Road on its way to Black River Harbor Campground on the shores of Lake Superior.

THE VIEW FROM COPPER PEAK

From Bessemer, Black River Drive heads north past steep rocky bluffs, ski hills waiting for winter's first snow and finally the highest point of all, Cooper Hill Peak, 10 miles north of town. It's impossible to miss the peak, there's a ski ramp at the top, so you might as well pull in.

Built by the Gogebic Range Ski Association in 1970, the 469-foot slide towers 241 feet above the summit of Copper Peak. The structure is so immense they needed 300 tons of steel grids to support the ramp. Call it the Eiffel Tower of the U.P., the ramp is only one of six ski flying peaks in the world and the only one in the Western Hemisphere.

For all that steel, the hill is used by a lot more by leaf peepers in the fall, who have no intention of leaving the ramp, than by skiers looking for a world record in the winter.

A small fee puts you in the chairlift for a ride 810 feet to the summit where you step inside an elevator and continue your journey up another 188 feet. Once you step out of the elevator, you can still walk up a little higher. And you want to. The view on a clear autumn day is spectacular. You can see parts of three states—Michigan, Wisconsin and Minnesota—as well as Canada and the endless blue horizon of Lake Superior.

Colors traditionally peak from the last week of September to early October. Copper Peak is open for non-skiers from Memorial Day into early October. The fee to the top for adults is $8. For a fall color check call the Ottawa National Forest office in Bessemer at ☎ (906) 667-0261. For information about Copper Peak call ☎ (906) 932-3500.

Directions: From Bessemer, head west on US-2 and then turn north on Powderhorn Road, which is marked by the Big Powderhorn Mountain skier statue. Powderhorn Road merges into CR 513 (Black River Road). It's 15 miles from US-2 to the harbor at the north end of CR 513.

Campground: Black River Harbor has 40 well-secluded sites in an area forested in hardwoods and pines. Although there are no hookups for recreational vehicles, both the campground road and the sites are paved and there are flush toilets and a sanitation station. None of the sites are on Lake Superior but short trails lead to sweeping views of the Great Lake or descend to the beach. Facilities include tables, fire rings, restrooms and a pressure water system. There are no showers.

Day-Use Facilities: Also on the west side of the river next to the campground is a picnic area surrounded by impressive pines and hemlocks and featuring tables, grills, play equipment for children and a unique stone pavilion. The Lake Superior shoreline on either side of the river's mouth is a broad sandy beach. The west side beach is reached from a trail in the campground while a suspension bridge over the Black River provides access to the beach east of the river. The water is usually too cold for most people to swim in but the beaches are excellent for beachcombing or agate hunting.

Fishing: The recreation area has an improved boat launch on the Black River with additional parking for vehicles and rigs as well as docks inside the breakwalls on Lake Superior. A concessionaire sells fuel, sewage pumping services and limited supplies. On the Great Lake, anglers troll for lake trout in June and July as well as brown trout, salmon and steelhead in the spring and fall. Shore fishermen will also cast off the docks and breakwalls to catch brown trout and coho salmon at various times of the year.

Hiking: The *North Country Trail* passes through the recreation area and can be picked up at the day-use area parking lot. To the south the NCT is a stunning stretch of trail that skirts the Black River to pass five waterfalls before arriving at Copper Peak Ski Flying Hill. It's a one-way hike of five miles from Black River Harbor to Copper Peak. To the east the NCT crosses the suspension bridge over the Black River and heads south to Rainbow Falls before swinging east for the Porcupine Mountains.

Waterfalls: Five waterfalls can be accessed from CR 513 (Black River Road). The closest to the campground is Rainbow Falls, a 40-foot-long cascade that—when the sunlight is right—creates a rainbow with its mist. You can follow the North Country Trail from the day-use area parking lot and reach the falls after a 0.75-mile hike.

Most people reach the other falls by driving to posted trailheads along CR 513 and then descending a half-mile of trails and stairways into Black River Canyon to the cascades. Not far from the Copper Peak, you pass the parking lot of the first waterfall, Great Conglomerate Falls, and the others quickly follow one by one along the road: Potawatomi, Gorge, Sandstone and finally Rainbow Falls. All are well worth the extra effort spent, but especially Potawatomi and Gorge, which are practically next to each other. Potawatomi is a thin, 130-foot wide veil flowing over a rock embankment while just downriver is Gorge Falls, a narrow, 24-foot drop of water between two granite walls of the canyon.

Season: Black River Harbor is open from mid-May to mid-October and will occasionally fill in July and August. You can reserve a site in advance through the National Recreational Reservation Service at ☎ (877) 444-6777 or through its web site at *www.reserveusa.com.*

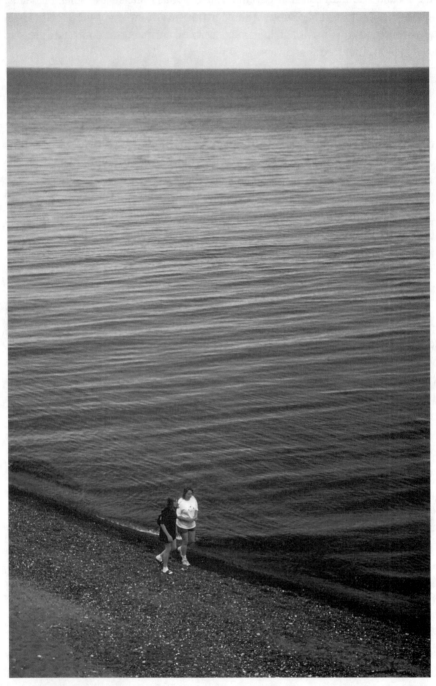

Campers stroll along the Lake Superior shoreline at Little Girl's Point Campground, which is a Gogebic County park.

150

Little Girl's Point
Gogebic County Park

Campground: Modern
County: Gogebic   **Nearest Community:** Ironwood
Sites: 30   **Reservations:** Yes
Fee: $12
Information: Park office ☎ (906) 932-1913

This campground may be as far west as a person can drive in Michigan, but the Gogebic County Park is well worth all the hours you have to spend in the car to reach it. There are very few campgrounds like this one anywhere in the state.

Perched on bluffs above Lake Superior, Little Girl's Point is a well-maintained park with an edge-of-the-world view. To the northeast you gaze on the rolling silhouettes of the Porcupine Mountains and to the southwest the Apostle Islands. At night the suns melts into the endless blue horizon of Lake Superior.

Directions: Little Girl's Point is located 17 miles north of Ironwood on County Road 505. From US-2 in Ironwood head north out on Hemlock and then Vanderhagen Road, which becomes CR-505.

Campground: Little Girl's Point has 30 sites with four of them overlooking Lake Superior. The rest are set back from the bluff. Facilities in the campgrounds include tables, electric hookups and vault toilets. In the day-use area of the park there are flush toilets. Camping fees are $12 for a site with an electric hookup or a tent site. Either one is a bargain.

Day-Use Facilities: The park has a picnic area with tables, grills, pavilions, a classic stone bathhouse and that million-dollar view. A trail also leads from the picnic area down the steep bluff to Lake Superior. The shoreline here is a sandy beach and during the summer brave souls can be seen swimming in the frigid Great Lake.

Fishing: West of the campground, a road leads down to an improved boat launch on Lake Superior. Anglers arrive at the park to troll for lake trout in June and July and steelhead, salmon and brown trout in the spring and fall.

Season: The campground is open from May through September and occasionally this facility will be filled on the weekends. You can reserve sites in advance by calling The Gogebic County Forest and Parks Division at ☎ (906) 667-0411 during the winter or the park office at ☎ (906) 932-1913 after May.

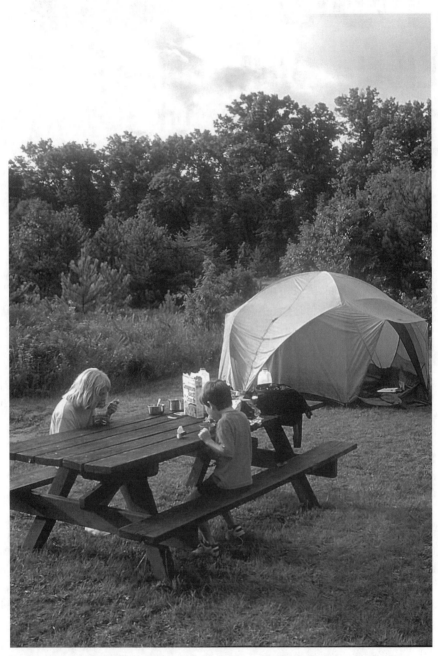

Young campers enjoy the outdoors at a rustic campground in the Upper Peninsula.

Facilities Index

Modern Campgrounds

Rustic Campgrounds

WESTERN UPPER PENINSULA

Campgrounds with Boat Launches

WESTERN UPPER PENINSULA

Handicapped-Accessible Campgrounds

Campgrounds with Rental Cabins, Tents, and Tipis

Alphabetical Listing of Campgrounds

About The Author

Jim DuFresne is an outdoor writer based in Clarkston, Mich. and author of more than a dozen wilderness\travel guidebooks. His books cover areas from Alaska and New Zealand to Michigan's own Isle Royale National Park. He is also a staff writer for Booth Newspapers, where he covers both recreational outdoors and travel.

DuFresne is a journalism graduate from Michigan State University and the former outdoors and sports editor of the Juneau Empire, where in 1980 he became the first Alaskan sportswriter to ever win a national award from Associated Press.

Among DuFresne's other titles are *Porcupine Mountains Wilderness State Park* (Pegg Legg Publications), *Isle Royale National Park: Foot Trails & Water Routes* (Mountaineer Books), *Glacier Bay National Park: A Guide To The Glaciers And Beyond* (Mountaineer Books), *50 Hikes In Michigan* (Backcountry Publications), *Tramping In New Zealand*, *Hiking In Alaska* and *Alaska* (Lonely Planet).